GATEWAY TO WINE

AN INTRODUCTION TO THE WINES OF THE WORLD

By

The Editors of *Wine Tidings*

Illustrated by

Gael Plant

Other books in the Gateway to Wine series:

- Gateway to Wine and Health
- Corkscrews in the Kitchen: A Gateway to Wine and Food

Canadian Cataloguing in Publication Data

Main entry under title:
Gateway to wine

1. Wine and wine making – Addresses, essays, lectures.

TP548.G37 1981 641.2'2 C82-007748-8

Published by
KYLIX MEDIA INC.
MONTREAL CANADA

Hardcover Edition, 1981 ISBN 0-919571-00-X

First Paperback Edition, 1981 ISBN 0-919571-01-8

Second Printing 1983
Third Printing 1984
Revised 1985
Second Printing Revised Edition 1986

Contents

Foreword

One day in 1974 a group of us was sitting around commiserating on the paucity of information about wine as it concerns Canadians. True, American and English magazines were available, which merely made us envious of the consumer's freedom of wine selection elsewhere. True, too, there were many informative books; but these were aimed at an English or American audience and usually were available only by special order. In spite of great enthusiasm in the quest for knowledge about wine, there seemed to be a paltry amount of information available. We speculated that there must be thousands of other Canadians just like us, thirsting to know about wine from a Canadian standpoint.

The outcome of this meeting was a wine newsletter. Later it grew to become a periodical. Now it has blossomed into a magazine. From the start the aim was to inform, to exist on revenue from readers' subscriptions rather than that from advertisements, and to call our own tune. While the editorial quality, content, and style has varied over the intervening years, many articles have stood the test of time and are imminently readable today.

Gateway to Wine has harvested the best offerings of *Wine Tidings* and gathered them together into a single volume. It seeks not only to satisfy the needs of the neophyte and experienced wine drinker who craves further knowledge, but also to offer current, more technical information for the real expert. Throughout, there is the common link - the love of wine and the pleasures associated with it.

The basics of wine knowledge are all there, in a two-column format with specific technical highlights, such as grape varieties, shown in the margins. It is a great primer as well as a useful reference source for the more knowledgeable reader who seeks verification of a specific point. Special chapters are followed by relevant essays from *Wine Tidings*. These illustrate particular aspects of the preceeding chapter and are readily identifiable by the larger type and single column layout.

For those who search for wine knowledge, particularly in the context of Canada, we present this volume. Whether you are a newcomer to wine or an *amateur de vin* we think you will find it entertaining, informative, and useful.

John Sambrook

Introduction and Acknowledgements

One does not have to be associated with the world of wine for very long to realise that information and basic knowledge are continually circulating and re-circulating in a variety of forms. Rarely is very much truly original material produced. Inevitably, therefore, we have been influenced in the production of this book by the true pioneers in the contemporary journalistic wine scene. If you are familiar with these classics, their inspiration upon us will be apparent to you. We are happy not to re-invent the wheel and feel that our book is all the better for their influences.

Hugh Johnson's *World Atlas of Wine* was constantly referred to, as was Alex Lichine's *Encylopedia of Wines;* upon this basis, frequent reference was made to Pamela Vandyke Price's *The Taste of Wine*. An invaluable work was George Masson's *Wine from Ontario Grapes* as were the following special interest books; Len Evans, *Australia and New Zealand - the Complete Book of Wine*; Heinrich Meinhard, *The Wines of Germany*; Vinicio Ortolani, *Wines of Italy*; Jan Read, *Guide to the Wines of Spain and Portugal*; and Clifton Fadiman and Sam Aaron, *The Joys of Wine*.

The trade commissions of the wine producing countries are an invaluable source of information and produce pamphlets, statistics, photographs and maps on demand. Particularly helpful were Armondo Godinho of the Portuguese Trade Commission, José Perez Sanchez of the Spanish Embassy, Alain Laferrière, Sopexa, Canada, Dr. J. Sorrentino, Italian

Trade Commission, John Garran of the Australian Trade Commission and the Ontario Wine Institute.

The unsung heroes of the wine trade in Canada are the wine agents, who spend their time dealing with provincial liquor boards and cajoling restaurants to improve the selection of wines on their lists. Two great supporters of our efforts are Russ Ledger of Featherstone and Company Limited and Dan O'Brien of Corby Distilleries Limited, who made their "Place Corby" in Montréal available for us to compose our cover picture.

A "love" project of this nature leans heavily on friends for advice and sometimes material. Wilfrid de Freitas, a book lover, provided many conceptual ideas in the early stages as did Gillian Gayton and David Lank, who has produced enough special interest books to be well aware of most of the pitfalls. Gerry King, our *Wine Tidings* graphics consultant, had good words for us whenever we needed them and we leaned on loyal friends Frank Prazak, Sheila Swerling-Puritt and Bill Thomas to produce specific pieces of text. Leo Ryan was an early contributor helping editorially. Kennon Cooke joined the project late and invigorated our flagging efforts with her contagious enthusiasm. Specific essayists selected for inclusion in the book are John Baldwin, Eleanor Boyle, Kenneth Christie, Gillian Gayton, John Kalbfleish, Paul Marks, Ian Mottershead, Judith Posner, Leo Ryan and Margaret Swaine. All have been great supporters over the years, and were most helpful in editing and updating their material for inclusion.

Early in the project we made the difficult decision to illustrate the book with drawings rather than photographs. This required countless hours of work by Gael Plant, who provided all the illustrations, as well as the maps.

Finally all the talk and words had to be put into genuine hard copy, laid out, and produced. Doug Cassidy of Estrie Graphics provided the early printing advice and Pierre des Marais Inc. of Montréal then provided their expertise by actually printing the book. To reach the printing stage Katie Nicholls and Debra d'Entremont typeset and re-typeset at the cues of proof-reader Mary Sambrook. Debra also provided invaluable back-up to the spark behind the whole project. Coordinator was Judy Rochester, whose incredible vitality and competence can always be relied upon to produce.

Gateway to Wine is the result of bringing together the varied skills listed above. In the end a book is the work of many people and I am happy to express my warm appreciation of their efforts.

John Sambrook

Historical Highlights

Canada is in the unenviable position of having a system of alcoholic beverage distribution and sale by monopoly control of the provincial governments. To appreciate how this situation has evolved, one should look at the history of wine in North America and backward to its beginning in Asia Minor at about 5000 BC.

In Europe

Early civilizations quickly perceived that not only was wine relatively easy to make and pleasurable to drink, it also seemed to be a source of nutrition and have medicinal and disinfectant properties. With this impressive line-up of assets it also acquired a magical and religious symbolism which made it a prized asset and measure of wealth. It is no surprise therefore to see that cultivation of the vine spread quickly to Mesopotamia, Babylon and Egypt.

The Phoenicians took vines with them in their explorations of the Mediterranean and Greece became the centre of winemaking as a natural extension of the Greek Empirical power. The problem of keeping wine had not been solved at this time. Wine was stored in large earthenware jars and covered with a layer of olive oil. Tree resins were added as the wine lost its freshness to make it more palatable.

Although Greece was the centre of the wine world, knowledgeable Greeks were already talking about Enotria - the land of wine across the sea. This land - Italy - only came into its own with the growth of the Roman Empire so that by 600 BC wealthy Romans were operating large scale vineyards, and had developed the means of storage by using amphorae with the tops sealed in plaster of Paris. Wine could now be kept for up to 100 years, far longer than the single year when olive oil was used as the sealant.

The Romans had a sophisticated urban lifestyle and advanced road network, yet needed a means of transporting wine, as amphorae were too bulky and heavy for the job. Wine merchants had their own in-house small amphorae and transported wine from the vineyards in skins. While this means of transport was adequate for local supply, it was useless for supplying the far flung legions of Roman soldiers who demanded their daily ration. Inevitably, wherever a Roman fort was built, vines were planted nearby. In this manner vineyards spread throughout Gaul (France) via the river network and in Iberia, Tarragona became the nucleus of winemaking; vineyards were also started in the Balkans, Germany and Britain.

Even with these local supplies the Roman soldiers' voracious thirst could only be assuaged by Italian wine and the transport of the cumbersome amphorae became a way of life for many. Each year the vintage was named after the Consul in power and as the wines were highly variable in quality, some named vintages became highly prized. Most famous was the 121 BC Falernum named after Lucius Opimius which was quickly recognized by the cognoscente of the day as being the best in living memory. It was thus never released to the retail market but instead was reserved in the private cellars of the privileged few for their own consumption. In 21 BC Trimalcio an emancipated slave, who word has it had made a fortune on the Roman real estate market, held a particularly Bacchanalian party where at an appropriate moment he called for silence, compared the ever improving Opimian Falernum (now 100 years old) to the ever degenerating human body and called for the opening of his last amphorae while his body at least could still appreciate it. His command to those around were the famous words "Tangomanus Fachiamus" which in loose translation means "let's make whoopee." The continued successful growth of wine throughout Europe stimulated such a fall in prices that in 92 AD Domition decreed that no new vineyards would be established in Italy and 50 per cent would be destroyed in the rest of Europe. The effect of this decree appears to have been for the long term good, as the only vineyards that actually ceased production were those of marginal or poor quality. By the time Probus repealed this decree in 280 AD the great vineyards of Bordeaux, Burgundy and the Rhône were firmly established.

Before its collapse in 300 AD the Roman Empire had developed the wooden cask in France and the cork in Iberia, but with the coming of the Dark Ages wine development ceased. Cork disappeared, many vineyards fell into disuse and the few remaining skills were continued only in the monasteries. One of them near Tours in the Loire Valley of France, was the home of St. Martin who in 350 AD is credited with recognizing and documenting the value of pruning vines for improved quality. His donkeys ate some of the grape clusters and he noticed that the grapes remaining grew to be bigger and more luscious. This monastery continued to be a leader in French viticulture and it was there in 770 AD that Alcium, a Yorkshireman and wine writer, retired after educating Charlemagne in the appreciation of wine and winemaking.

Charlemagne used this knowledge to develop the vineyards of Schloss Johannisberg in Germany.

From 1100 AD onwards, southwest France was under the control of the English and under their guidance the vineyards of Bordeaux were revitalized and developed. Bordeaux became a pivotal winetrading town, as it was on the famous pilgrims' route - the road to St. James of Compostella. All manner of persons used this route and many chose to settle around Bordeaux as they were not allowed to live inside the walls of the old city. Wine purchased or made by these outsiders could only be exported after the "clairet" of the insiders had been sold. How times change - nowadays it is the outsiders of the Quai des Chartrons who have inherited the premier position and are now known as the noblesse de Bouchan. Wine from Bordeaux is still known as Claret.

In North America

When Leif Ericson arrived in Massachusetts in 1000 AD, he found a land full of wild vines and described the area as Vineland the Good. Unfortunately what he found was the vitis labrusca, a hardy climate and disease resistant vine, the grapes of which make a wine of high acidity and curious flavour. No one could foresee what a critical role this vine would play in the 1880's to save the great vineyards of the world from complete failure.

It was the Spanish who began viticulture in North America in the 16th Century when Cortez had vine cuttings sent to him from Spain. These early winemakers were usually missionaries and soldiers and they quickly met the great enemy of the European vitis vinifera, the phylloxera vastatrix. This aphis feeds off the roots of the vine and kills it within three years. The missionaries noticed that the indigenous labrusca was resistant to the phylloxera and successfully grafted vinifera stocks onto labrusca roots. This technique was "rediscovered" in the 1880s in Europe thus saving the European vineyards.

A series of mission houses were built along the coast of California as far north as Sonoma. Jesuit Father Ugarte was the leader of this pioneering activity in the 1690s and for the next 100 years a single grape called the Mission was used to make a wine used primarily for Mass.

Concurrently with the developments in California, the English were colonizing the eastern states and from 1600 onwards planted vinifera vines from New York to Virginia. All their efforts proved disastrous, as those vines that survived the intensely cold winters and the oidium (powdery mildew) of the hot humid summers succumbed to the phylloxera. The colonists finally gave up by 1700 and when settling New York state concentrated on producing wine from labrusca. The most successful was a light carbonated red wine with sugar added, which is still a very popular beverage.

The Mission was the staple wine grape on the west coast until the 1850s, when Count Agoston Haraszthy, a Hungarian adventurer living in California, persuaded the state government to underwrite a trip to Europe for him to acquire cuttings of all the noble European grape varieties. He established vineyards at Buena Vista in Sonoma Valley and although the cuttings grew successfully, Haraszthy was not paid for his efforts by the government and went on a voyage of exploration to Nicaragua where he died accidently under mysterious circumstances. His legacy was the new vines, spread throughout California and included a mysterious grape called the Zinfandel. For over one hundred years this grape appeared to have no direct connection with any other grape variety. Some authorities thought it came from Hungary or was a natural hybrid which sprung from cross pollination of Haraszthy's early cuttings. It is now generally agreed that the original grape comes from southwest Italy where it produces a particularly undistinguished wine. The combination of California climate and soil seems to particularly suit this grape however, and Zinfandel is produced in various attractive forms, depending on the area of production.

With the coming of the "great experiment" (Prohibition) after World War I the California wine industry stagnated with only a small quantity of mass wine being produced. Most vineyards converted to the production of orchards and some table grapes. With the repeal of Prohibition in 1934 the California wine industry started again. Since World War II, aided by advanced technology and an array of graduates from the University of California at Davis, and an abundant capital investment, California now produces 70 per cent of the wine consumed in the United States.

A Treatise on Canadian Liquor Laws

by Eleanor Boyle

Eleanor Boyle is a Vancouver born journalist with extensive experience in newspapers and television. Currently a financial reporter with "The Toronto Star," she has also worked as a columnist and on-air television interviewer.

The fascinating and pervasive social phenomenon called drinking has troubled legislators for centuries. Today wine lovers are convinced they're overtaxed and subject to anachronistic liquor control laws; on the other side of the fence governments just can't forget those wild days of pre-Prohibition Canada. While public officials charged with controlling alcohol use and abuse are slowly liberalizing many relevant laws, revisionists are fighting what has to be a drawn-out battle in a nation weaned on the alcoholic binge.

Governments are, and always have been, schizophrenic in their involvement with booze - committed to keeping drinking and related community problems to a minimum while maximizing the number of dollars they gain from the trade. It's this particular schizophrenia that is the chief reason for the dilemmas inherent in government control.

On one side it seems clear that certain liquor laws need desperately to be liberalized to promote saner and more intelligent drinking attitudes. On the other side it also seems clear that the public sector does have some rightful place in the bars of the nation protecting citizens, and society, from what is ultimately a dangerous drug.

Today's wine drinker tends to favour 'liberalized' liquor laws, which for this purpose shall mean any which make alcoholic beverages more accessible. We shall also use terms such as 'liquor laws' and 'alcohol beverage control laws' interchangeably. Wine is included, since most laws cover all alcoholic beverages, though that has changed somewhat as many governments push what they call drinks of moderation.

But are the views of today's wine drinker the majority view?

Certainly there are the Bill Temples of the world - the octogenarian crusader who has kept West Toronto dry for years. "Booze enslaves, corrupts, destroys the moral fibre of a community," he says. Certainly there are prohibitionists. Most wine lovers, however, consider them not only misguided, but few in number.

The question of which is majority opinion is almost impossible to answer. Much has been studied, little concluded. But there is some truth in the words of one recent official of the Liquor Control Board of Ontario (LCBO). "People don't like change." And another bureaucrat: "You're probably talking to an elite group when you hear people say liquor laws are outmoded. In rural areas there's a very conservative element. I think the laws reflect people's wishes."

There's little doubt most Canadians welcome some degree of alcohol control. Whether they'd opt to retain specific current laws is another matter.

One law that drives Ontarians in the wine industry to despair is the one stipulating that restaurants, including wine bars, must sell the same dollar value in food that they sell in alcohol. For the proprietor of one wine bar in Ottawa, that meant when wine prices went up (frequently) she had to increase her food prices far more than she liked. The consumer suffered, as did she. Summoned to liquor control hearings on at least three intimidating occasions, she was finally reprimanded and forced to close her premises at 10 p.m., then to shut down altogether.

It is difficult to understand the lack of empathy from a public sector purporting to encourage alternatives to traditional, hard-drinking bars. The Ontario government is considering modifying that law.

The 1 a.m. closing in a number of provinces is another point of contention. "Our drinking laws are archaic," says one wine expert. "Why does a wine cellar have to close at one o'clock?" Would society really be enroute to ruin if bars chose their own closing times, like private enterprise restaurants?

Wine "bars", too, have been outlawed in Ontario. That Ottawa entrepreneur called her establishment a wine bar when she opened in the mid-'70s, but was told the terminology was prohibited.

As well, laws regarding the advertising of booze are complex and a continual frustration to the ad industry. Lists detailing regulations from every province in the scattered federation show a formidable network of dos and don'ts depending on the advertising medium and the strength of the alcohol involved.

British Columbia has a notorious reputation for conservative liquor laws, some of which is justified. It was only in the late '70s there that pubs and bars could allow patrons to stand up with drinks in hand. Many B.C. pubs, particularly those in hotels, look more like cattle barns - vast seas of grimy tables with little to break the monotony but occasional strippers of widely varying talents who now adorn some premises. But this latter is something new, one of the concessions being made by some provincial governments to the theory that drinkers won't drink so much if you give them something else to do.

Whether strippers provide the sort of entertainment that encourages moderation is a question that doesn't appear to have been addressed.

But any trend toward change must first contend with an argument the roots of which lie in Prohibition-era problems. Should drinking establishments be as grim and oppressive as possible so the guilty will toss back a few and leave, or should they incorporate elements of everyday enjoyments so drinkers learn to incorporate moderate alcohol use into their lives and stop the binge?

Those many Canadians who pranced out and got royally smashed when they came of age often feel in retrospect they did so precisely because it was forbidden fruit. Less novelty would probably have resulted in less desire. But governments are charged with caring for the public health, and many doctors say liberalization of liquor laws tends to lead not to more intelligent drinking but to more problems and increased alcoholism.

In the whirl of conflicting views, however, provinces are indeed effecting some change. Even B.C. now allows private grape growers to set up their own little stands, advertise their wine and sell direct to the consumer. No government. No middleman.

But how did Canadian laws evolve? Much of our current legislation can be traced directly to the Prohibition era, although laws have been imposed upon drinkers for hundreds of years. Politicians have historically tried to duck the issue, knowing there were votes to be lost no matter what positions they took on such contentious moral questions as those involving alcohol. But the issue would not disappear.

In Britain, temperance organizations have existed since the 17th century and the very licensing of taverns in North America occurred at least as early as 1710, when drinking was such an integral part of daily life. Pubs played such a pivotal role in community affairs that "the upper classes believed that they should be well regulated, orderly and respectable, that only men and women of good character should operate them, and this requirement could best be met through the device of licensing." That quote is from a fascinating book called *The Alcoholic Republic* (W.J. Rorabaugh, Oxford University Press, 1979) which chronicles an amazing period of American history in the 1700s and 1800s when alcohol, particularly the hard stuff, was drunk morning, noon and night by persons of both sexes, all social classes and just about every age.

Indeed, although anti-drinkers would have us believe we imbibe a lot today, our standards don't approach those of that era. "Americans between 1790 and 1830 drank more alcoholic beverages per capita than ever before or since," says the book. The enormous changes in society at that time, and resultant anxieties - which, interestingly, we face in different forms today - were major catalysts for the historic binge. At one typical upper class party thrown by a New York governor about 1790, 120 guests downed 135 bottles of Madeira, 36 bottles of port, 60 bottles of English beer, and 30 large cups of rum punch.

The Prohibition period was a real turning point in the history of Canadian drinking. It symbolized the historical Canadian attitude toward alcohol as a wicked purveyor of social and personal misfortune, and the gradual change of that attitude and acceptance of the then revolutionary concept of moderate drinking. The fact is that alcohol had become an enormous social problem by the turn of the 20th century, and the eventual province-by-province establishment of prohibition was perhaps inevitable if the experiment itself was not entirely successful. And it had widespread support. Prohibition was not the dream of a handful of teetotalers. At the start of the First World War, only Prince Edward Island had a total prohibition law, but the drive to abolish intemperance spread, and by the end of the war only Québec among the provinces stood outside the temperance act system. The several years following were wild ones in which authorities learned that complete prohibition was an impossibility. Bootlegging was rife, as were other means by which normally law-abiding citizens could get their snort.By 1919 prohibitionary laws had begun to relax, and in the early 1920s provinces began to set up the liquor control boards most people felt were the best compromise.

A look at pre-Prohibition Canada makes it pretty clear how some of our current laws were rationalized. In 1880, New Westminster, B.C. had one bar for every 13 residents, and Regina loaded its drunks into wheelbarrows, according to one good study called *Canadian Alcohol Policies* (George Geraghty/ Roger McMeans, University of B.C. Faculty of Law, 1975). And though temperance-movement claims that one drink was a step on the road to ruin were obviously distorted, there's no doubt North Americans were then drinking intemperately enough to slow the progress of nation-building and destroying more than one family unit.

Most of that heavy drinking occurred in bars - noisy,

stand-up, 'make the next one a double' spots - which etched an indelible concept in the minds of Canadian legislators of the bar as a source of evil and drunkenness. It's probably the reason 'bar' as a word is frowned upon in Canadian law; it's certainly the reason pubs have been designed to be unattractive and uninviting; it's the reason live entertainment has for years been banned in the drinking environment.

Every one of us has at one time wondered why 20th century North America doesn't have 'English-style pubs,' comfortable, inviting places to meet your friends. One theory has it that although Britain suffered the same alcohol problems as did Canada at the turn of the century, Britain didn't suffer another phenomenon: vital fundamentalism in the form of tough pioneers who saw much of life in absolute terms. "If liquor presented a threat to decency, then it was evil and had to be proscribed; if the saloons were the centres of the liquor trade, nothing good could be said for them and they had to be banished," say Geraghty and McMeans in their book.

But there's a funny thing about liquor control laws. Study after study comes up with statements like this one from the U.S. National Institute of Alcohol and Alcoholism: "Alcoholic beverage control laws generally don't seem to have much effect on drinking behaviour." No wonder booze has sparked imaginations for so long, this magic substance that pervades human lifestyles no matter what the law or time.

So some of our laws are phony, in a sense, cover-ups to make the conservative portion of the public feel its government cares about alcohol problems. If all of these studies are correct, and regulations on alcohol consumption don't actually cut consumption, then laws are safe refuges for government, since they don't cut revenue from the liquor trade.

Admittedly, elected officials charged with handling liquor are in a tough spot, trying to maximize profit while minimizing alcohol abuse. It's obvious then, why our wine costs so much.

The general trend in Canada toward more liberal liquor laws does involve tradeoffs, and past evidence shows that increased per capita alcoholism may be one. Today North Americans value their personal freedoms enough to accept that tradeoff, and would rather take more civil rights in exchange for the consequences.

But hedonism isn't the prevailing rationale for relaxed liquor laws. Liberals contend that alcohol problems will decrease once society removes the 'forbidden fruit' labels and accepts the idea that drinking should be done in pleasant, social surroundings rather than the saloons so conducive to drunken brawls. Ironically, one outgrowth of Prohibition was at-home social drinking, a civilizing influence which introduced moderate drinking to Canadians and made Prohibition itself unnecessary.

It is also said that alcohol use can't entirely be judged on past statistics. Today alcohol "is being used for entirely different reasons than in the past," say Geraghty and McMeans. North Americans today live their lives under tension unknown to members of simpler societies; alcohol lets us release tension.

Okay. Wine lovers know they want to drink, and have come to terms with their hobby; they drink moderately to heavily yet are confident they're not alcoholics. Under what system, then, should they imbibe?

There are pros and cons to government control of the alcohol beverage industry. For those who argue that more retail sales should be turned over to private enterprise, arguments against seem largely spurious. As one official of the Liquor Control Board of Ontario has said for years: "The little Joe's Wine Store is not going to happen. It's a romantic notion." Corner stores, traditionalists say, can't handle the expensive import procedures. But as revisionists are proving, corner stores dealing in wine can do so just as well as those dealing in any other commodity. They buy products from local importers or distributors through a standard free enterprise network. No one ever expected Joe to be on the phone to Italy every week personally ordering two cases of some Barbaresco.

Liquor stores have always claimed to offer 'convenience' too, whereby buyers know precisely what they'll find. But homogeneity and lack of surprise aren't what most wine shoppers seek.

Ontario's liquor board has long claimed to offer more choice than "anywhere else in the world," although travellers disagree, saying choice spots such as Martin's Wine Cellar in New Orleans stock far more. Yes, selections offered by government stores are sufficient for the majority, but not for a few select drinkers. And that's the point.

Observers who speak in favour of total public sector domination of the industry often hint at all manner of trouble should a system not be government regulated. Particularly, they say, quality control would be difficult to maintain, since hordes of fraudsters are waiting to ship Canadians plonk under the label of some great château should government control loosen its grip. But this is crazy. Quality control is handled quite nicely in the free enterprise food business.

The rationale given for government control is largely economic; galloping government social programs and necessary public sector intervention in all walks of life require dollars, and the liquor trade supplies them. Too, supporters point to the social responsibility of a government system, which often discourages rash purchases, and indebtedness, by demanding cash, for example.

But on the revenue question, detractors counter that profits prop up the bureaucratic machine itself, which exists to collect those profits. Herein lies the popular conception that private enterprise is simply more efficient about it all. Independent stores, they also say, would offer plenty of choice. As one business person says: "Mom and Pop wouldn't have the same selection as the government stores ...Mom and Pop are too smart for that."

Whether provincial governments retain their grip on the retail end of the business, they fully intend to continue legislating alcohol use. One means of legislation is price control, and some original and interesting thoughts on the topic come from Dr. Eric Single of Toronto's Addiction Research Foundation. Single says price control would be a far more effective means of curbing alcohol problems than would some of the

other legislative methods employed. Firstly, Single says, the 'drink of moderation' campaigns waged in recent years by governments to promote wine and beer rather than spirits don't necessarily result in less, or less dangerous, drinking. "If you try to liberalize by changing drinking habits, the effect is an additive one. If people drink wine with dinner, they keep having their cocktail beforehand. People continue their old drinking patterns. All you do is add to total drinking."

He suggests alcohol beverage prices be linked to the consumer price index because the cost of alcoholic beverages has declined in real terms in the last 25 years. "While the price of milk is double today what it was in 1971, a bottle of Scotch is only 50 per cent more." Of course, the cost to consumers of some wines has more than doubled in that time, so would decrease under the proposed scheme.

Single has another interesting observation. Liquor boards, he says, use price increases to stimulate sales, not cut them. "Every six or eight weeks prices go up, and everybody goes out and stocks up." And consumers are spurred into panic buying because the media hypes up the increases, quoting price rises of $15 a bottle on "obscure French wines that nobody buys."

The insolubility of the dilemma faced by governments is obvious from the emotions sparked by the topic and from the widely varying liquor laws within North America. Down south, "dry" Kansas enshrined that philosophy in its 1880 constitution, stating: "The open saloon shall be and is hereby forever prohibited." If you live in Kansas and want a drink in 1980, you have to join a private club to get one. Meanwhile in Québec, bars stay open Sundays and beer and wine are sold in grocery stores.

Most moderate drinkers tend to forget the hazards, and profess to be unable to understand the schizophrenia inherent in liquor legislation. But alcohol is a deadly poison when wrongly used, and its abuses are a serious problem for society. One report says more than half the drivers and pedestrians killed on Ontario roads in a recent 12 month period were under the influence of alcohol; U.S. figures put the annual cost to

American society from alcoholism ''somewhere between $25 billion and $40 billion, in terms of lost labour productivity, health and medical costs, highway carnage, criminal procedures, treatment and welfare.''

But the author of that statement isn't prohibitionist; the quote is from John Koffend's ''The Case for Alcohol,'' from *Atlantic Monthly* magazine of December '79. Despite problems associated with alcohol, Koffend says, evidence is mounting that moderate drinking may confer health benefits that are simply not shared by abstainers, heavy drinkers, or those who have quit.

The battle of both fact and opinion wages on. The sheer emotion in the issue may forever prohibit uniformity of alcohol beverage laws.

to "the peace, order, and good government" of Canada

Grape Varieties

Throughout the world there are four categories of grape, *Vitis Vinifera* (with three sub groups), *North American Vitis* (with three sub groups), *North American Hybrids* and *French Hybrids*. They have in common the definition of their fruit being a berry of varying colour which is made up of mainly water; 80 per cent in the pulp, skin and stalk, and 40 per cent in the pips. When crushed, the skin, stalk and pips provide tannin. In addition the skin also gives colour and sometimes bouquet. Yeast adheres to the skin and feeds on the sugar in the pulp when the grape is crushed (fermentation). The pulp also contains tartaric, malic and citric acids which preserve the nitrogenous matter - minerals, pectins and pectores. After fermentation these constituents, combine with alcohol - the by-product of the yeast feeding in the sugar to form wine, the distinctive smells and tastes being the homogeneous melding of these constituent parts. The smells and tastes vary according to the category and variety of the grape and some are much more attractive to mankind in the form of wine than others.

Man's technical abilities in the areas of crossbreeding and controlled vinification have resulted in the development of wines of specific style and character, particularly in the *vitis vinifera* category.

VITIS VINIFERA

This category is made up of three distinctive groups, the most important being *occidentalis*, a grape of small size and bearing which is vulnerable to inclement weather and disease, but when carefully tended in the right soil and micro-climatic conditions produces very high quality wine. These are referred to as the *noble* varieties and include Cabernet, Pinot, Gamay, Riesling, Chardonnay, and Chenin Blanc.

Pontica grows prolifically in Mediterranean climates, the ensuing wine being large in quantity and unremarkable in quality. The vines need little attention and produce the staple wine of the people from Georgia in Russia to Spain.

Orientalis is the third of the *vinifera* category. The grapes are large, often seedless, and the resultant wine mediocre at best.

NORTH AMERICAN VITIS

The three groups that make up this category are indigenous grape varieties. *Vitis Labrusca* is the best known and originally grew in the forests between the Alleghany Mountains and the east coast. In its natural state it bears very little fruit, but when cultivated it produces large quantities of juice which has an aroma variously described as foxy, mousy or musky. Indeed the group as a whole has long been known as the Northern Fox grape. The juice is low in sugar and acidity but the variety has been used as the basis of most North American hybrids. The Concord is the most common variety in this group.

Riparia is indigenous to Canada but it found growing wild from northern Québec to the Gulf of Mexico. Found usually on river banks this type is very hardy but the grapes are high in acidity and low in sugar. However the aroma is virtually free of foxiness. It does not lend itself to hybridization but has been used extensively as a root stock upon which *vinifera* is grafted.

Cordifolia is also Canadian and is often confused with *riparia*, as it too grows along river banks. However it is a small bearer and does not readily accept grafting. It therefore has no importance in viticulture.

NORTH AMERICAN HYBRIDS

Usually a cross of *labrusca* and a *vinifera*, these ensuing varieties are hardy, require little care and produce large quantities of fruit. The best known varieties are Catawba, Delaware Isabella Agawam, Niagara Elvira and Dutchess.

In an effort to reduce the foxiness of the above varieties, they are continually being recrossed with *vinifera* stock, but only the Dutchess has developed with little of this aroma. When grown in limestone soil the foxiness is accentuated.

FRENCH HYBRIDS

Although *vinifera* produces superb wines in selected locations, it does not warrant the labour intensity required in marginal areas, as the wine produced is usually of small yield and ordinary quality. Consequently, from the turn of the century, the French industry has been experimenting with hybrids designed to have the quality of *vinifera* and the quantity and hardiness of *North American vitis*. They have concentrated on carefully developed varieties of aromaless *riparia* bred with *vinifera*. Early success in these experiments do not appear to have lasted as, since the 1930s, several new varieties have been triumphantly introduced only to have quietly disappeared over the years.

Pioneers in North America are the New York State Agricultural Station in Geneva, N.Y., the University of California at Davis, and the Horticultural Research Institute of Ontario at Vineland. In the past few years the following hybrids have been successfully developed to a commercial level; Seibel, Baco, Seyve-Villard. Although the wines made from these varieties are not comparable to the *noble vinifera* varieties, they are significantly better than the North American hybrids and have the advantage of being much more resistant to mildew, frost and phylloxera than *vinifera*. Most of the vineyards of Ontario and British Columbia are switching to these varieties as economic conditions warrant.

The Role Of North American Vitis In Modern Winemaking

Until the late 1870s the resistant properties of *North American vitis* were not fully appreciated, although the search for a cure to *oidium* (downy mildew) led directly to the infestation of the phylloxera epidemic. British horticulturalists were researching a cure for oidium in the 1840s and they and their French counterparts imported *labrusca* stock to aid their experiments. The cure introduced in the 1850s was sulphur powder which stops oidium when sprayed on the leaves.

Unrecognized by the oidium researchers, the imported *labrusca* stock had an aphis, *phylloxera vastitrix*, living in the roots. This aphis has a complex life cycle - the wingless female lives on vine roots planted in anything but very sandy soil.

First indications of a new disease appeared in France in the early 1860s and within 10 years most of the vineyards of France were threatened. The Spaniards in Mexico in the mid 16th century had overcome the problem by grafting *vinifera* to *labrusca* root stocks, but although this was suggested by scientists in 1869, the European wine farmers were reluctant to adopt the technique. Instead wild schemes were introduced in an effort to kill the aphis. Vineyards were flooded or up-rooted and left fallow for years. Concentrated arsenic was sprayed over the ground in some vineyards. It failed to kill the phylloxera but did enter the water table and had a deleterious effect on the health of farmers and livestock.

Finally in the 1880s, with no other recourse except to see the disappearance of *vinifera*, the winegrowers adapted grafting as a technique and root stocks were grown in nurseries from *riparia* and *labrusca*, then replanted into the vineyards with *vinifera* varieties grafted to them. The life of the grafted vine is about 40 years compared to 65 with natural roots but most oenophiles feel that the quality of the wine has not suffered.

Grape Varieties Commonly Found In Wines Available In Canada

VITIS VINIFERA - OCCIDENTALIS
The Noble Grape Varieties:

Aligote. A white grape found in northern France. It grows well with little care and is usually planted in vineyards where it is impracticable to grow Chardonnay. The wines lack personality and are early maturing.

Cabernet Franc. Found throughout the world, it is a black grape and is best blended with Cabernet Sauvignon. In most parts of the world it is the grape variety in any bottle labelled "Cabernet."

Cabernet Sauvignon. Generally considered to be the supreme black grape, the wine is very assertive, hard, austere and astringent. It requires considerable bottle age to soften and is usually blended with fruitier softer wines like the Merlot.

Carignan. A black grape with an intense nose, it grows well in hot arid climates and is the main constituent in the V.D.Q.S. wines of southern France.

Chardonnay. Sometimes erroneously called Pinot Chardonnay, this white grape makes the fullest most complex white wines in the world. Usually full-bodied and dry it is at its best in Burgundy and California. The flavour is reminiscent of fresh butter with a long lingering aftertaste.

Chenin Blanc. This white grape is cultivated throughout the world in a variety of climates and the wine can be excellent whether vinified bone dry or slightly sweet. It is always flowery and fruity with a subtle aftertaste.

Cinsaut. A black grape which thrives in mediterranean climates making a robust full red wine.

Gamay. A black grape which thrives in temperate climates on non-chalky or sandy soils. The wine has a marked fruitiness with an attractive fragrance and bright red/purple colour. It lacks tannin and is best drunk young.

Gewürztraminer. This spicy development of the Traminer is found in temperate climates and makes a white wine of full fra-

grance and body sufficient to stand up to flavourful though delicate foods.

Grenache. A black grape at its best in mediterranean climates, it is usually blended with other fruity wines. It is assertive and hard. When lightly vinified and removed from its skins it makes a particularly appealing rosé.

Merlot. A black grape which thrives in temperate climates, it gives a wine of close-textured fragrance and soft full-bodied fruitiness. Traditionally blended with Cabernet Sauvignon it is being increasingly marketed as a varietal in its own right.

Müller-Thurgau. A white grape evolved from the crossbreeding of Riesling and Sylvaner, it is ideally suited to cool temperate climates, as it ripens early and gives a light wine with a perfumed bouquet.

Muscadet. A white grape evolved from the Melon de Bourgogne it is uniquely grown at the mouth of the Loire in France and gives a wine of fresh mouth-watering fruitiness.

Nebbiolo. A black grape grown extensively in Italy, it makes a wine that has high tannin and acidity which takes many years to soften and mature. It is at its best when grown in Piedmont.

Petite Syrah. Descended from the Syrah, this black grape has developed its own characteristics and produces a soft medium-bodied early maturing red wine.

Pinot Blanc. There are many different varieties of Pinot, both red and white. This white grape is blended into Champagne and, with Chardonnay, into some burgundy. Occasionally it is bottled alone, particularly in Italy and California.

Pinot Noir. A great black grape, it is used exclusively in the great wines of Burgundy and is also used to blend in Champagne. The wine has a full fruity bouquet and has a distinctive velvety fruit taste, although these characteristics vary enormously, dependent on the micro-climate and soil type. The grape does not do well in a mediterranean climate.

Riesling.A white grape which many argue surpasses the Chardonnay in absolute quality. There are several subspecies of this variety. The best is the Rheinreisling, followed by the Welschriesling, which is the most common and found around the world. Wines labelled "Riesling" from anywhere but Germany are usually made from Welschriesling. The wine has a delicate fruity smell whether it is dry or sweet.

Sangiovese. A black grape extensively cultivated in Italy it is the primary grape variety used in the making of Chianti.

Sauvignon Blanc. A white grape which thrives in temperate climates, it makes a wine of distinctive bouquet with varying flavours depending on climatic and soil factors.

Semillon. A white grape used in the making of blended, dry or sweet wines. It has a high level of malic acidity which gives a wine of considerable roundness and fragrance.

Sylvaner. A white grape from temperate climes it makes a wine that is light, crisp and fresh which should be drunk young.

Syrah. A black grape of ancient history which is usually associated today with the northern Rhône where it gives finesse when blended with less elegant wines. It is also bottled alone as Côte Rôtie or Hermitage.

Trebbiano. A white grape which makes very successful white wines in many parts of Italy. The same variety is grown under the name of Ugni Blanc in Cognac and southern France to make the wine for distilling into brandy.

Viognier. A white grape grown in small quantities in the Côtes du Rhône.

Zinfandel. A red/black grape now identified with California, although originally it probably came from southwestern Italy. It takes on different characteristics dependent on the soil, micro-climate and vinification technique. The wine is usually open textured and agreeable.

North American Hybrids:

Concord. A black grape making a low quality unbalanced wine typical of most *labrusca* varieties. It has an intense foxy aroma, low alcohol and low acidity.

Delaware. A white grape generally considered to be the best American hybrid. The wine has a flowery, fruity bouquet with only a hint of foxiness. It is particularly suited to sparkling wines.

Dutchess. A white grape which makes a dry white of delicate sylvaner-like flavour with virtually no foxiness when grown on clay soil.

French Hybrids:

Baco Noir. A black grape making a dark full-bodied rather nebulous wine which ages well. Ideally used for blending where colour and body are required.

Chelois. A black grape making a deep coloured wine reminiscent of Pinot Noir.

De Chaunac. A black grape making a bright red, fruity, balanced wine that is easy to drink.

Foch. A black grape which ripens very early. The wine resembles Pinot Noir in texture.

Seyval Blanc. A white grape that has developed into the best white hybrid. The wine has a good bouquet, and has a delicate flavour resembling a Muscadet.

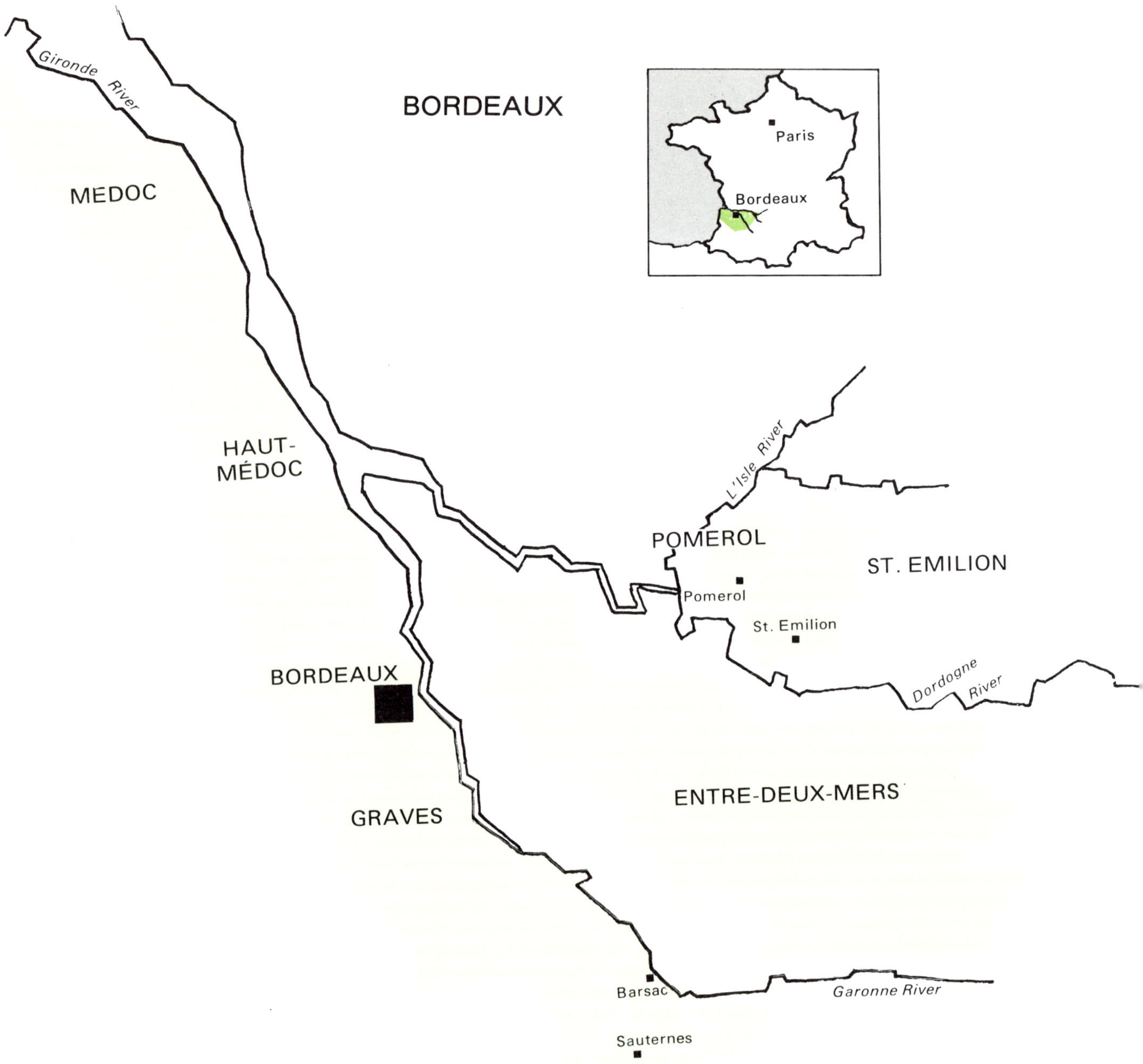
BORDEAUX
Gironde River
MEDOC
HAUT-
MÉDOC
BORDEAUX
GRAVES
L'Isle River
POMEROL
ST. EMILION
Pomerol
St. Emilion
Dordogne River
ENTRE-DEUX-MERS
Barsac
Garonne River
Sauternes
Paris
Bordeaux

France

A happy combination of history, soil and climate make France, still and always, the queen of wine-making countries, the ultimate arbiter of excellence. Although it produces only 25 per cent of the world's wine (Italy, for example, makes more), the great variety of French wines include the best of each type. The top quality reds of Bordeaux and Burgundy, the dry whites of Burgundy, and the sparkling wine of Champagne are, generally held to be the finest in the world. The only field in which there is competition is among sweet white wines, for those of Sauternes-Barsac can be equalled by the German sweet wines. (It should not be forgotten, however, that most of the wine produced in France is not of high quality: it is what is called *vin ordinaire*, and this is what the average Frenchman habitually drinks.)

Before describing the wines of France in detail, it is important to explain the magic term *appellation contrôlée*. It means "controlled name," and indicates that the wine in a bottle so labelled is guaranteed to come from the area specified on the label. Less than 15 per cent of French wines are entitled to this term, and they are, of course, the best, legally protected in this manner from inferior imitations. In addition to the words *appellation contrôlée* (A.C.), the label will indicate a region (Bourgogne, Bordeaux), a district of that region (Côte de Nuits, Médoc), a particular village (St. Julien, Vosne-Romanée), or even a vineyard within that village (Château Ferrière, Romanée Conti). The more precise the delimited area, the finer will be the wine. That is why it is helpful to be familiar with the names within the well-known regions. Price is also, alas!, an indication of quality, although not invariably.

BORDEAUX

In the world, France: in France, Bordeaux. Other regions make great wine, but nowhere else produces so much of it. The *département* of the Gironde, at the confluence of the rivers Garonne and Dordogne where they meet to run to the Atlantic, contains about 287,000 acres of vineyards which in a good year can produce 132 million gallons of wine. Although much of this is white Bordeaux it is best known for its red wine, which is often called claret. (This name dates from the twelfth century, when barrels of light red wine, called *clairet,* were shipped to England.)

Main white grape varieties of Bordeaux
Merlot Blanc
Muscadelle
Sauvignon
Sémillon

Main black grape varieties of Bordeaux
Cabernet Sauvignon
Cabernet Franc
Carmenère
Malbec
Merlot Noir
Petit Verdot

There are many wine districts in Bordeaux. The four which produce the best red wine are the Médoc, Graves, St. Emilion, and Pomerol. The only sweet white district is Sauternes-Barsac.

The Médoc

In 1855 a list was made of the 60 greatest wines of the Médoc, where paradoxically, the thin, poor soil makes some of the world's best wines. The list classified the 60 wines according to merit, in groups of one to five. These groups are known respectively as the first, second etc. growths, or *crus.*

Only one wine from outside the region, a red Graves, Château Haut-Brion, was included among the *premiers crus*, or first growths. Nevertheless, the Médoc contains 300 other châteaux which produce excellent wine, and it is well worth one's while to seek out these lesser vineyards, since the price of the classified growths is now prohibitive.

Graves

The best red wines of Graves include 13 which rank almost as high as those of the Médoc. These clarets are perhaps a little difficult to appreciate at first. They are dry and delicate, full of tannin when young, and take many years to mature.

St. Emilion and Pomerol

The red wines of these two districts mature sooner than those of the Médoc and Graves, and have a rounder, softer taste, more like Burgundies. Richer soil and a greater proportion of the Merlot grape is responsible for their fruitier taste. The wines from these districts were classified in 1955, and the finest of them are equivalent to the best Médocs. However, the two regions produce far less than does the Médoc.

Before discussing the white Bordeaux, the importance of the vintage, or harvest year, should be explained. Oddly enough, the best wines in the world are always made where the soil is poor and the climate temperate, and frequently unpredictable. Too much hot sunshine makes grapes produce sweet or rough wine. Particularly in Bordeaux, the weather of the vintage year is of paramount importance. Rain or frost during the flowering or fruiting season can make all the difference between one year's wine and another's. This is the reason for all those vintage charts, which are worth checking from time to time. However, since weather varies over only a few miles, one can still find good wines from a "bad" year and vice-versa.

More than half of the wine made around Bordeaux is white, produced in three main districts; *Sauternes-Barsac, Graves,* and *Entre-Deux-Mers*. The finest of these, and one of the mystic names among wines, is Château d'Yquem (pronounced "Dee-*Kem*"). It is a golden wine like liquid honey. Although great with dessert, anyone lucky enough to obtain some would be wise to drink it by itself, well chilled. The reason for the exquisite sweetness of this and other wines from the region is that the grapes are left to ripen until they shrivel, so that they are full of sugar. Sometimes in magic years they develop *botrytis cinerea,* the "noble rot," a sort of mildew, which remarkably enough makes the finest wine of all. (The best German wines are made by the same method.)

All the wines from Sauternes and Barsac are sweet, as are many from Graves, although the latter region also produces some fine dry whites. Entre-Deux-Mers wines are usually inexpensive, and most are dry enough to drink with fish. And finally, just outside the Gironde, the town of Montbazillac on the Dordogne produces a sweet golden dessert wine at a reasonable price.

To sum up, the beginner who wishes to learn about the wines of Bordeaux should start by trying an *appellation contrôlée* labelled simply Bordeaux, then one from a particular area, say an A.C. Médoc, and finally one from a commune of that area, say St. Estèphe. The improvement in quality from good to better will be apparent, and the wine-lover will be starting to learn the typical taste of good claret.

BURGUNDY

This is the second greatest wine-making region of France, producing fine red wines equal to the best of Bordeaux, although different in character and fewer in number. Burgundy also makes the greatest dry white wines in the world. Within the old duchy of Burgundy there are five main wine-growing districts, the most important being the Côte d'Or, the heart of Burgundy proper, which produces the very best reds and whites, although in small quantities. The others are Beaujolais, the Mâconnais, the Chalonnais and Chablis.

The Côte d'Or

The legendary "golden slope," which runs more or less north-south between Chagny and Dijon, is sub-divided into two sections, the Côte de Nuits and the Côte de Beaune.

The Côte de Nuits make the great reds of Burgundy, including the legendary Romanée Conti, possibly the world's greatest red wine, which comes from a vineyard of only four acres. All of the eight villages on the Côte de Nuits produce truly great wines, the best being bottled under the vineyard name, with a large amount under the commune name. A bottle labelled Gevrey-Chambertin or Chambolle-Musigny will be fairly expensive, but will give all the pleasure of fine Burgundy; one labelled Le Chambertin will be an unforgettable experience.

South of the Côte de Nuits lies the Côte de Beaune, which produces fine red wines with a softer taste that mature earlier than their northern counterparts. The best and most famous of these are from the towns of Beaune, Pommard (not to be confused with Pomerol, a claret), and Volnay. But it is the great white burgundies that are the glory of the Côte de Beaune: Le Montrachet (pronounced Monrash-*ay*) from Puligny-Montrachet, Corton Charlemagne from Aloxe-Corton, and Meursault-Charmes from Meursault. For the average pocketbook, an A.C. Meursault will adequately demonstrate the qualities of white burgundy.

Beaujolais

The southernmost part of Burgundy is the region whose name is almost synonymous with red wine. Beaujolais produces a great deal of light, fruity wine (up to 15 million gallons a year) which is drunk before it

Main black grape varieties of Burgundy and the Mâconnais

Gamay
Pinot Noir

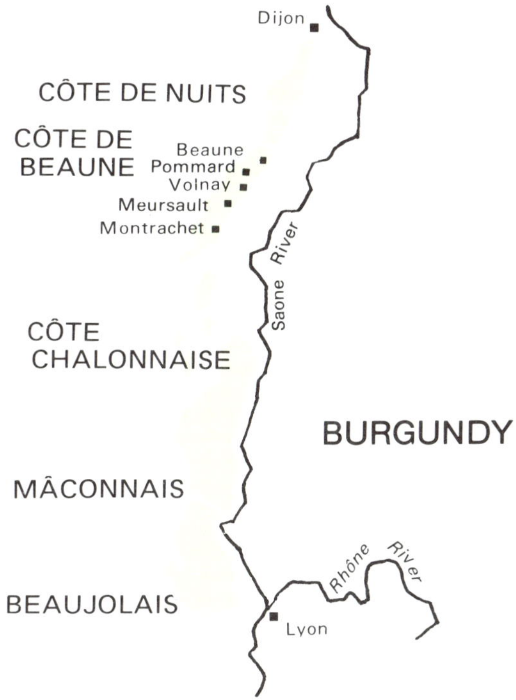

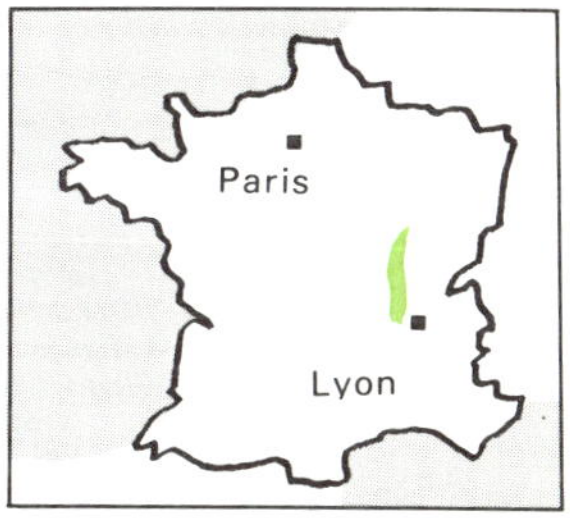

Main white grape varieties of Burgundy, the Mâconnais and Chablis
Aligoté
Chardonnay
Pinot Blanc

Main grape varieties of the Loire
Aligoté
Blanc Fumé
Cabernet
Cabernet Franc
Chasselas
Chenin Blanc
Gamay
Grolleau
Muscadet

Main grape varieties of Champagne
Pinot Chardonnay
Pinot Noir
Pinot Meunier

Main grape varieties of the Côtes-du-Rhone
Carignan
Gamay
Grenache
Marsanne
Rousanne
Syrah
Terret Noir
Viognier

years old. *Beaujolais nouveau*, the new wine made in September and consumed at Christmas, has become something of a fad in Europe and North America, and is certainly worth trying for its delicacy and charm. The very best Beaujolais, Moulin-à-Vent or Morgon, can improve for up to five years in bottle.

The Mâconnais and Chalonnais

The area between Beaujolais and Burgundy proper produces very sound red and white wines, of which the best are red Mercurey from the Côte Chalonnaise and white Pouilly Fuissé from the Mâconnais. A bottle labelled A.C. Mâcon, red or white (the latter is of slightly higher quality), is usually a good buy.

Chablis

The white wine from the vineyards around this little town, northwest of Burgundy proper, is one of the world's great white wines, very dry and crisp with a lot of body. Although the name has become as synonymous with white wine as Beaujolais is with red, the real article is in fact produced in very limited quantities and costs a great deal. To have any idea of the quality of true Chablis, one must spend a fair amount and buy a *premier crû*. Few wines have been so imitated, adulterated or abused.

CHAMPAGNE

True French Champagne, now protected by law against imitations, is made in the Marne valley east of Paris, and is the most difficult of wines to make, for its sparkle, its *raison d'être*, is the result of natural fermentation and not of artificially added carbon dioxide. Its high price is due to the innumerable man-hours of skilled labour necessary to capture that sparkle in a bottle. Sugar is added in various degrees to make the wine *brut* (very dry), *sec* (dry), *demi-sec* (rather sweet) or *doux* (very sweet). Champagne is the only wine, they say, which can be drunk throughout a meal.

THE LOIRE

The valley of this great, 600 mile long river produces a variety of pleasant wines, mostly whites, although the sweetish rosé d'Anjou is also from this region. Muscadet, Sancerre and Pouilly Fumé are the most distinguished of the Loire wines, which should

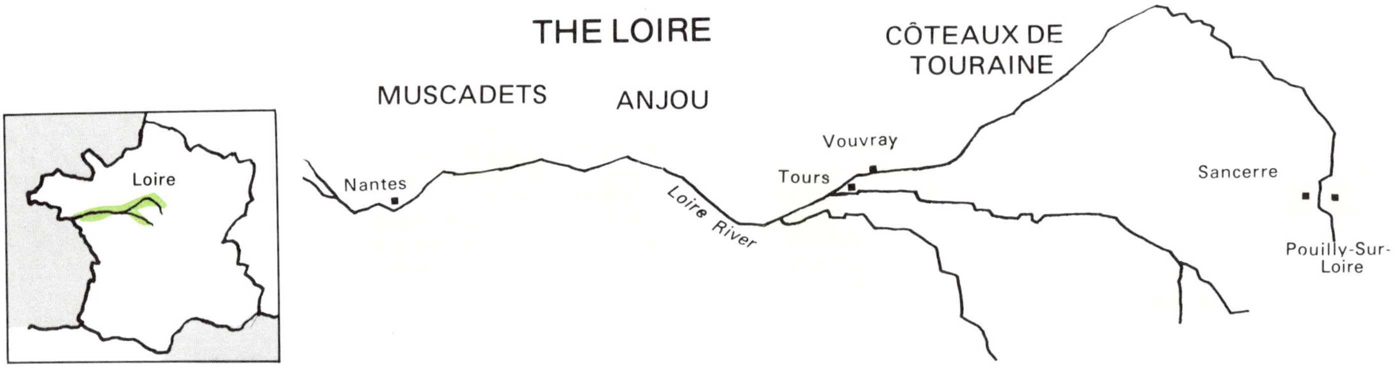

all be drunk young, within three years of the vintage.

Muscadet, a good substitute for Chablis, is a dry, light white wine which accompanies shellfish admirably. The best comes from the district of Sèvre-et-Maine, is labelled accordingly, and is not expensive. Sancerre, from the little town of this name, is made from Sauvignon, the same grape as the dry whites of Bordeaux. Although it is a dry white wine, it has a full flavour and excellent nose. It is a good companion to white meats or fish.

Pouilly-Fumé is another excellent dry white wine from Pouilly-sur-Loire near Sancerre. Not to be confused with Pouilly Fuissé from Burgundy, it is similiar to Sancerre.

The town of Vouvray, near Blois, makes still and sparkling whites, the latter said to have been Balzac's favourite wine. It is a very pleasant and reasonably priced "Bubbly," and the Château Moncontour label is widely available. Other lesser-known Loire whites include the Saumur (slightly sparkling but crisp), the Anjou Blanc and the whites of Quincy and Reuilly. Chinon and Bourgueil produce pleasant light reds.

THE COTES DU RHONE

The excellent, rather heavy red wines of the Rhône valley are increasingly sought after as the price of claret and burgundy soars. About 20 million gallons are produced annually, and an A.C. Côtes du Rhône a strongly alcoholic, full flavoured red, usually represents a reliable buy. The best Rhône reds, Châteauneauf-du-Pape, Hermitage, Côte Rôtie, Gigondas and Cornas, have a lot of character and are well worth trying. Tavel and Lirac, from the same area, are among the finest of rosés, and Château Grillet and Condrieu produce fine flowery whites.

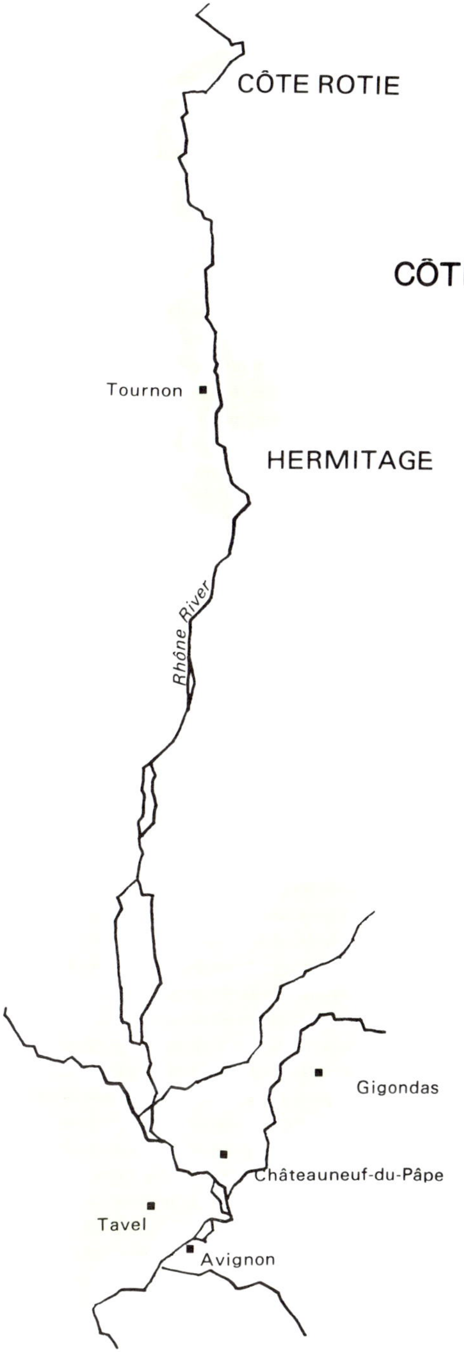

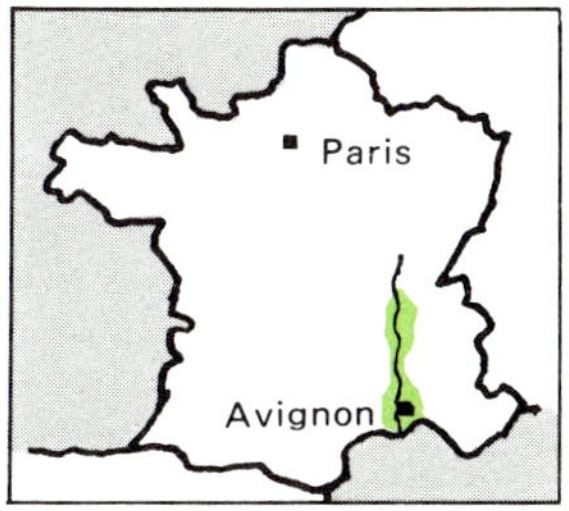

ALSACE

Main grape varieties of Alsace
Muscat
Riesling
Sylvaner
Traminer
Gewürztraminer

The white wines of Alsace, which are rather German in character, are increasingly popular abroad. They are generally dry and full flavoured and are usually identified on the label by the grape variety used, not by the place of origin. The Muscat, delicate and flowery, and the Gewürztraminer, dry and spicey, are perhaps the best. But both the Riesling and the Sylvaner, which are close to their German counterparts, are very good, and accompany most light meals very well.

Alsatian wines should be drunk young, although the Gewürztraminer and Muscat from fine vintages may be kept a little longer.

THE JURA

This region of France, bordering Switzerland (also called the Franche-Comté), produces several admirable wines which are quite unique. The *vin jaune,* or yellow wine, of which the best is from Château Chalon, is dry, perfumed and heady, almost like sherry. There are a number of excellent rosés, including the *vin gris* (Grey wine) and *pelure d'oignon* (onion skin), a bubbly called *vin fou*, and some straightforward whites from Arbois.

LANGUEDOC-ROUSSILLON

Last in quality but largest in quantity, the reds from this area, which is west of the Rhône valley, have traditionally provided the *vin ordinaire* of France. Over 500 million gallons are produced annually. Many wines entitled to the V.D.Q.S. denomination (*vins délimités de qualité supérieure*) such as Côteaux du Languedoc, Minervois, St. Chinian and Corbières, can be quite pleasant.

From just outside Languedoc proper comes the red wine of Cahors, an old A.C. designation. This is a fine red wine when sufficiently aged to lose its edge of tannin.

PROVENCE

East of the Rhône, the Provençal rosés are the best value. Côtes de Provence, Côteaux du Tricastin, and Côtes de Ventoux, produce powerful red wines which have sufficiently improved in quality in recent years to have been upgraded from V.D.Q.S. to A.C., joining the existing A.C.s of Bandol and Palette.

The Noble House of de Figeac

by Ian Mottershead

Ian Mottershead, investment counsellor and oenologist, is a member of the Vancouver chapter of the Commandeur de Bordeaux and was twice winner of the Opimian Society's Winetaster of the Year contest.

If one travels about forty kilometres east from Bordeaux across the rivers Garonne and Dordogne, one arrives in the old city port of Libourne. A small country road, also eastward, takes one that few remaining kilometres to St. Emilion.

The district is divided into two main areas: the "côtes," on an escarpment of chalk and clay around the village of St. Emilion; and the "graves," a plateau of gravel and sand between the village of St. Emilion and the district of Pomerol to the north of Libourne.

Most of the top châteaux of St. Emilion are on the "côtes." The two major exceptions are Château Cheval Blanc and the adjoining Château Figeac, which are in the "graves" area, virtually in Pomerol. The significance of this location is great.

The greatest vineyards in the Bordeaux area are virtually all on the so-called "siliceous" soil of gravel and sand. Relative to the St. Emilions of the "côtes," Cheval Blanc and Figeac tend to be richer, fruitier and more flavoured.

The second significance of the location is that the area of Pomerol and Graves-St. Emilion is in the shape of a saucer with a slightly undulating bottom. In the winter, the vines in the lowest areas of the saucer can be badly damaged by frost. The most famous example of this was a February night in 1956 when the temperature reached a low of -24 degrees centigrade. Virtually no wine was produced at Figeac in that year. Many dead vines had to be replaced, and almost ten years later vines were still mysteriously dying as a result of the same frost.

Historically there were five noble houses in the St. Emilion area, but the de Figeac seigneurie was probably the largest. The current vineyard and estate of Figeac was, in the 18th and 19th centuries, the heart of a much larger estate which included all of the present day vineyard of Château Cheval Blanc, together with many other vineyards that were split off and subdivided. For example, Château La Tour-Figeac was split off in about 1879 and was subsequently divided into two parts, both apparently called Château La Tour-du-Pin-Figeac. Many other châteaux in the area include Figeac in their name. Some are undoubtedly part of the original estate. Others may have simply ''adopted'' the name of the best known nearby château.

The wines of Château Figeac acquired a great reputation in the last century. For a period they were considered superior to the wines of Château Cheval Blanc, and outside of France at least, they were apparently better known than the wines of Château Ausone.

Around 1870, Château Figeac was purchased by the Manoncourt family and it has remained in the family to this day. During part of the last 100 years, Figeac's fortunes slipped a little. For a considerable length of time, absentee ownership was a problem. The grandfather of the present owner was a resident of Paris, where he was a senior municipal official. He treated Château Figeac as a holiday residence only. A second major problem resulted from frost damage in 1956 to which reference has already been made.

The current proprietaire, M. Thierry Manoncourt has been largely responsible for development of the high reputation that the wines of Château Figeac enjoy today. This gentleman is well known for his knowledge of architecture, geology and history as well as oenology, M. Manoncourt has put considerable energy into promoting the wine of St. Emilion in general and Figeac in particular. For example, for more than a decade he was a Premier Jurat in the well known Jurade de St. Emilion.

The Château was, according to one authority, burnt down on two occasions. The current edifice was principally built towards the end of the 18th century and is one of the largest in the area. The approach to the Château is via an avenue on both sides of which is a park which adds considerably to the appearance of the estate. M. Manoncourt and his wife Marie-France, live in one wing of the building, the remainder being used solely for guests.

The working part of the Château is a mixture of old and new. The vat house includes 10 wooden vats which were installed in the last century and are now only used for excess wine that may be produced. Alongside the old vat house is a new one containing 10 vats of stainless steel which were installed relatively recently.

The cellars of Château Figeac are also of recent construction. They are built of light coloured stone, and the overall impression is that one is in Mexico or California rather than the Gironde. Figeac's storage facilities are probably now the largest and most modern in St. Emilion.

One of the most impressive sights at Figeac in the new chai are the row upon row of new wooden casks. Each vintage is aged in 100 per cent new casks. No other château in St. Emilion does this and in fact, virtually the only châteaux in the whole of Bordeaux that do this are the Premiers Crus, such as Mouton Rothschild and Latour. The expense alone would prohibit most châteaux from using 100 per cent new wood.

Wine produced at Figeac is notably different from the wine produced at other châteaux in the district. Partly, this is the result of location on gravelly soil. But the encépagement is an equally important factor. The vineyard is currently planted with about one-third Cabernet Sauvignon, one-third Bouchet (the local name for Cabernet Franc), and one-third Merlot. The encépagement used to include five per cent of Pressac (the local name for the Malbec grape). The removal of the Pressac vines resulted from an interesting investigation.

In at least one year (and possibly two - 1953 and 1964), M. Manoncourt made wine 100 per cent from each of the grape types, as well as the normal blend. (Château de Pez in St. Estèphe tried the same thing in 1970). To most tasters, the blend was the best. The 100 per cent Cabernet Sauvignon wine was impressive, although lacking a certain subtlety. Wine made only from the Bouchet and Merlot was also pleasant. In contrast, wine made from the Pressac was extremely disappointing, with the result that M. Manoncourt decided that it had no place in his vineyard.

The high proportion of Cabernet Sauvignon in Figeac's encépagement is unusual for St. Emilion. In many châteaux in this district no Cabernet Sauvignon is used at all. The dominant grape elsewhere in the district is virtually always the Merlot. Even at Château Cheval Blanc, adjoining Figeac, the encépagement includes no Cabernet Sauvignon. (Cheval Blanc uses approximately one-third Merlot, two-thirds Bouchet, and a tiny amount of Pressac). Perhaps as a result of a high proportion of Cabernet Sauvignon, Château Figeac wines tend to take somewhat longer to mature compared to most St. Emilion and their longevity is similarly great.

Château Figeac currently has about 95 acres of vines. Production averages about 12,000 cases but in big years such as 1970, as many as 19,000 cases may be produced. This production is one of the largest in the whole district of St. Emilion. A second wine is sometimes produced and is given the name Château de Grangeneuf.

For a variety of reasons, the well-known Classification of 1855 included only the wines of the Médoc (plus one Graves) and the Sauternes. The French Institut National des Appellations d'Origine officially classified the wines of St. Emilion in the summer of 1955. The vineyards were divided into just two groups: 12 Premiers Grands Crus, and about 70 Grands Crus. The vineyards were listed in alphabetical order so none was accorded special status, the exception being Châteaux Ausone and Cheval Blanc which were listed at the beginning of the list of Premiers Grands Crus.

Château Figeac is officially classified as one of the Premiers Grands Crus St. Emilions, but Figeac's reputation is now at least equal to that of Ausone (one can say the same of Château La Gaffelière), and in some years Figeac produces a better wine than Cheval Blanc. Figeac is, in fact, regarded as the equivalent of a deuxième cru Médoc.

Wines of the Médoc

by Paul Marks

Paul Marks, musician and oenophile, spent several years in Canada on the staff of McGill University. He is a freelance wine writer living in New York State.

France's largest *département* or political division is the Gironde, covering much of the southwestern corner of the country. Within this division lies its largest demarcated wine producing region, named after Bordeaux, the second city of France and a major commercial port since the early Middle Ages. The eastern part of this huge area is mainly undulating plateau, some 100 to 130 metres above sea level and broken up by deep valleys. By contrast, the plateau on the western section is almost flat, with a gentle slope toward the estuary. While the strip of land along the Gironde which produces the best wines is relatively sheltered by the Atlantic seaboard forests, the weather here remains fickle and, for the most part, poor. Consequently the Médoc is relatively underdeveloped apart from its large-scale wine production. The old French saying about the necessity for vines to suffer is nowhere reflected better than in this region.

The soil of the Médoc is the basis for its division into two parts. Originally, the entire eastern section of Bordeaux was called Graves because of its gravelly-pebbly outcroppings. These pebbles appear in the soil of vineyards producing the Médoc's greatest reds, and in soils that, dominated by other substances, produce lesser wines. Since the late 17th century, however, when agriculture became the main business of Bordeaux, the name Graves has been reserved for that area south of the city of Bordeaux. The name Médoc applies to the land north of the first of a series of drainage canals called the Jalle (meaning small stream or gulley) de Blanquefort, that divide several of the most important communes.

A further division of nomenclature splits the Médoc itself into two parts, the southern three quarters known as the Haut-Médoc (also called the Médoc Maritime). This division was in use long before the famous 1855 classification of the 61 best selling wines of the Médoc (plus Haut-Brion from Graves). It was officially confirmed by the A.C. laws begun in the 1930s and completed during the 1950s. The 1855 classification of the very best wines of the Médoc was done at the request of the French government of Napolean III, in order to show off the greatest wines of France's most prestigious region at the international exposition in Paris. The job was handed over to the Bordeaux Chamber of Commerce, which then relegated the duty to the body of the city's *négociants.*

In recent years there have been a number of attempts to update the 1855 classification - as in many respects, pricing and quality have been out of date for years. Some of the original châteaux are no longer even in existence and others have sold much of their best land to neighbouring vineyards. Yet the work of those mid-19th century *négociants* has stood up remarkably well. The fact is that opponents of the classification who attack it from within the Bordeaux trade, never advocate a complete abolition of classifications, but support a more republican restructuring of the vinous caste system.

The vines used throughout the Médoc are planted on grafted rootstocks. This became a necessity when the dreaded *phylloxera vastratrix* first showed itself in France in 1860. The Médoc, Graves and the Sauternes were attacked very late, mainly because their soil mixtures contain a high level of sand, which is not conducive to the propagation of the louse. The vines are usually grafted onto hybrids or rootstocks of *vitis labrusca*, the native North American vine. But, this is not a static procedure and rootstocks are constantly being cloned and hybridized to suit new vineyard expansion.

Almost a third of the Médoc vineyard area is planted with Merlot. This grape is the most tender, the earliest to mature, and the most fragile where weather is concerned. The resultant wine is blended with Cabernet Sauvignon and the

Cabernet Franc which together constitute a full two-thirds of the grapes grown in the Médoc. The Cabernet Franc makes a lighter, more unctuous wine, while the Cabernet Sauvignon produces the best, finest and greatest wines of this illustrious region. Each château has its own combination of blends of the above, which sometimes includes Malbec. Where increased colour is required, they add about three to eight per cent of the Petit Verdot, an alcoholic wine from dark skinned, red-juiced grapes.

The vintage in the Médoc normally takes place between September 10th and 30th. Harvesting is usually done by imported hands from Spain and Portugal, as well as by vacationing students from other countries and other parts of France, although there is some experimentation with mechanical harvesting. The French already have a modern aphorism: "The machine is blind, but the growers not." The dates of harvesting, however, depend on the varietals, which reach maturity (balance of sugar and acid) at different times. Malbec, Merlot, Cabernet Sauvignon, Cabernet Franc, and Petit Verdot mature in that order and are harvested accordingly. It can be easily deduced that those vines are susceptible to frost damage in that order as well.

The old method of vinification left the wine on the skins for at least three weeks or a month, in an open vat. Men were to punch down the *chapeau* of skins three or four times a day. A variety of more modern methods has come into use, and a great many winemakers vinify for only one or two weeks, some as little as a few days. The wine is placed in closed, temperature controlled vats, with either *overflow* to moisten the cap of skins, or a wire mesh to keep the skins submerged. The wine, once in barrel, is topped twice a week to prevent *ouillage* (the empty space at the barrel head, caused by evaporation), and racked every three months during the first year of aging.

St. Estèphe is the largest and most northerly of the Médoc's four most important communes. St. Estèphe wines are too often characterized as exaggerating bigness, colour, alcoholic strength and tannin. They are frequently considered to be too hard in their youth, and require many years of aging to mature to a greatness. The truth, however, is that the best wines do not exaggerate anything.

Until about 100 years ago, the wines of St. Estèphe, with the exception of the Château Calon-Ségur, were considered to be the poor cousins of the Médoc. In fact, St. Estèphe is a comparatively new commune. Château Montrose, for instance, one of the most popular of the classified growths of St. Estèphe, was not hacked out of the pine and scrub until the early 19th century. The commune has become almost one continuous vineyard.

The styles of wine coming from St. Estèphe vary. There are the blander, somewhat sweet, pale wines produced by the co-operatives which are ready to drink immediately. The châteaux wines are different, being generous, astringent, grainy, rich wines with a full and lingering aftertaste.

The wine most frequently said to epitomize St. Estèphe is Château Calon-Ségur, the oldest wine made in this commune. Aside from its classified châteaux, St. Estèphe has the largest supply of good *bourgeois* and *bourgeois supérieur* growths of any commune.

The commune of Pauillac runs south to St. Lambert into the vineyard appellation area of St. Julien. The vineyards stretch west and north of the town of Pauillac itself. Some southern vineyards like Château Latour are in fact, transitional to those of St. Julien.

The best bottles of wine from Pauillac characterize all that makes the wines of the Médoc so special: richness of nose, flavour and colour, a special cedar-cigar-box quality of aroma and bouquet, a texture both firm and polished, and an intense varietal quality of the Cabernet Sauvignon. These wines have a full-throated, yet somehow austere fruitiness, with a long, complex finish and aftertaste. Added to all this are the unique, individual personalities of each wine.

Château Latour stands alone as a standard for all of Bordeaux, let alone for the Médoc. This wine most completely exemplifies the characteristics that were listed above as the most individual and unique in Pauillac.

Latour emphasizes all the harmoniousness of style and the range of possibilities from great Médocs. As one moves from one's novitiate in wines, to an awareness of the classic virtue in great Médocs, one is likely to react with veneration and esteem even at the mere mention of this name. The château regularly makes wine of above average quality even in the poorest vintage years. In 1950 was a *light* year, but, to quote Steven Schneider "... it is hard to think of another château whose 1950 one would hesitate to open today for fear that it might improve still more with a few years."

Yet, France's great monument is in English hands, for Latour belongs to Viscount Cowdray and the merchants, Harvey's of Bristol. Château Mouton-Rothschild, also produces superb wine tending to be even more "individual" than Latour, but that is part of the character of a Pauillac. To set the record straight, since so much nonsense is written about Mouton and sheep and who knows what, the word is a corruption of the Medieval word *motte*, another one of those words for a hill.

St. Julien stands at the heart of the Médoc and perhaps, for this reason, makes more fine wines than does any other commune. As a whole, its wines demand the highest prices and, like the wines of St. Emilion, those of St. Julien are more often requested than those from any other commune. St. Julien contains some of the best vineyards in all of Bordeaux - thus, in all of the world.

There are the subtle, invidious, silky and perfumed delights of Beychevelle, and Leoville-Poyferré, and the classic pleasures of Gruaud-Larose, Ducru Beaucaillou, and Léoville-Las-Cases. Then the wines made at Branaire are plusher, those from Château Talbot more mouth-filling, and those from Léoville and Langoa-Barton harder, in the style of Pauillac. However, as in all the communes, no single style is the exclusive monopoly of any château.

One of the most popular features of the wines of St. Julien is their appeal to beginners in claret. With strength, harmony, good acidity, tannin and glycerine, these wines have plenty of fruit, which may give an impression of sweetness that generally appeals to the inexperienced palate. Even in poor vintages, more fruit is evident here.

The commune of Margaux (the only one which contains a great château bearing its name) also makes wine of several types, but all seem to be based on the quality of finesse. The one weakness in Margaux stems from the way its appellation borders were laid out: the appellation of Haut-Médoc was reduced to carve out the Margaux appellation. This caused Margaux to be weakened by reduction, and Haut-Médoc to be weakened by the addition of too many peripheral communes struggling to maintain the standards of Château Margaux.

A Pilgrimage to Château d'Yquem

by Leo Ryan

Leo Ryan is a Montréal journalist who spent sixteen years in France as special correspondent for the "Globe and Mail" and other English language papers.

In Bordeaux, goes an old adage, the sun never sets. When it disappears in the horizon, the bottle of wine gracing most household tables in this part of southwestern France keeps the sun shining through the dark hours and into the next day. Such lyrical musings certainly apply to the magnificent, golden yellow Sauternes of Château d'Yquem, universally regarded by oenophiles as the finest sweet wine in existence. Indeed one does not simply drink a Château d'Yquem, one "experiences" it - basking in its incomparable unctuousness, rich perfume, and elegant strength filled with nuances; the very quintessence of the grape.

To make a pilgrimage to the gourmet's historic site, you must proceed to the strictly delimited Sauternes area that begins about 20 miles southeast of Bordeaux on the left bank of the Garonne. It's a pleasant drive through tranquil countryside, half an hour or so from the city that was once a proud ornament of England's empire.

Built on the grounds of an ancient, 12th century fortress, the Château d'Yquem sits gracefully atop a slope overlooking a domain that is stunning in beauty and harmony. In the Middle Ages, it belonged to an English family with the name of Eichem. The castle was called the Château d'Eichem before being frenchified into the Château d'Yquem.

Since 1786, the château has been owned by the family of the Marquis de Lur-Saluces. In recent years, the Comte Alexandre de Lur-Saluces, an elderly, distinguished-looking aristocrat, has opened up the courtyard of his château to the public every month of May for a music festival organized by the city of Bordeaux.

All told, there are five communes in the district which may carry the Sauternes Appellation Contrôlée: the town of Sauternes itself, Barsac, Bommes, Priegnac and Fargues. In the 1855 classification of the Sauternes vineyards, Yquem was placed in a category by itself - First Great Growth - that it has held ever since.

The special character of Sauternes wines stems from four factors: the soil in which the vines are grown, the grape varietals from which the wine is made, the way in which the grapes ripen, and the method of harvesting them. In addition, one should mention an exceptionally mild and stable climate. Although the Sauternes region is barely 35 miles from the Atlantic, only the beneficial effects of this proximity to the ocean are felt, thanks to the protective screen constituted by the Landes forest, which stops the salty winds. Come the autumn, the interaction of the mists rising from the Garonne and Ciron Rivers and the warm sun create the ideal conditions for the production of Sauternes.

The soil of Sauternes, except for that of Barsac which is somewhat more calciferous, is a combination of clay and sandy gravel. Tart Sémillon, which accounts for about four-fifths of the wine, and fruity Sauvignon Blanc grapes are used almost exclusively. A very small amount of Muscadelle is sometimes added to lend more balance.

But, more than the soil and the grape type, it is the manner and picking time that make Sauternes, and Château d'Yquem in particular, so unique among French wines.

Starting in October, the pickers go into the vineyards to clip, one at a time, only those clusters of grapes that have been attacked by the dusty mould *botrytis cinerea.* This fungus transforms the grapes from the state of complete ripeness to one of *pourriture noble*, or "noble rot." The intricate method of harvesting may be repeated, weather permitting, as many as

eight or nine times up till late November.

The origin of *botrytis cinerea* is, of course, the stuff of legends. In the Middle Ages, by one account, it was the custom for feudal proprietors of a vineyard to set a date for the vendange, the annual harvest. Prior to this important event, it appears that one of the big proprietors, while hunting for game, came across a lovely damsel, set about to conquer her, and did not return until well after the grapes should normally have been picked. Despite the fears of the angry vignerons, the vintage was not ruined. After the master ordered the shrivelled grapes harvested anyway, the result, to everyone's surprise, was a delicious wine. (Incidentally, a similar tale of dalliance is told about the origin of Roquefort cheese, which turned out to be a splendid companion to Sauternes.)

Then you have another legend, related by the owners of Château d'Yquem. According to this version the Marquis de Lur-Saluces returned in the autumn of 1847 from a trip to Russia to find that most of the grapes were entirely contaminated. They were harvested nevertheless and the quality of wine was soon hailed around the world.

What is certain is that the wine of Château d'Yquem continues to be the fruit of extraordinary late harvesting and of awesome gambles with the weather. A too rainy autumn, an early winter, a sudden hailstorm can destroy the most promising harvest, or render it sub-standard. In fact, in some years the vintages were just written off.

Out of the domain's 173 hectares (420 acres), 120 may bear the A.C. label, but only 102 are actually planted in vineyards. The latter are themselves divided into vineyards in production and those under regeneration. Consequently, barely 85 hectares (210 acres) of manicured vines are utilized for producing wine.

As early as January, pruning, the first task in the vegitative cycle, is carried out in an especially restrictive fashion. Great attention is paid to the respective flowering and maturing characteristics of the Sémillon and the Sauvignon grapes. The sole fertilizer employed at Yquem is organic and contains leaf-mould.

On a permanent basis, about 57 people work at the Yquem domain. This doesn't count the extra field workers hired for the harvest. Final production is very limited - the equivalent of nine hectolitres a hectare from vineyards which would yield 50 to 60 hectolitres if developed by classic methods. Each bottle is, therefore on average the product of six to seven vine stocks. That's one glass per stock per year!

Selection is very severe when it comes to actual bottling three years after the harvest. In the interval, twice a week each barrel is filled, as necessary, so that the precious, golden liquid never comes in contact with air. And every three months, the wine is transferred to another barrel, so that it remains perfectly clear and healthy. Never have all the barrels from the same harvest been deemed worthy of the Château d'Yquem label.

Such a rare and understandably expensive wine cannot be distributed like any ordinary wine. You cannot buy it directly from the proprietor. Comte de Lur-Saluces prefers to leave sales totally in the hands of prestigious Bordeaux wine merchants.

Some 82,500 bottles on average are sold annually to enthusiasts in several countries including Canada. Certain old vintages are sought after as collectors' items and are worth their weight in gold. Like gold too, Château d'Yquem has its attractions as an investment, providing one can resist the temptation of succumbing to the pleasures of a true nectar of the gods.

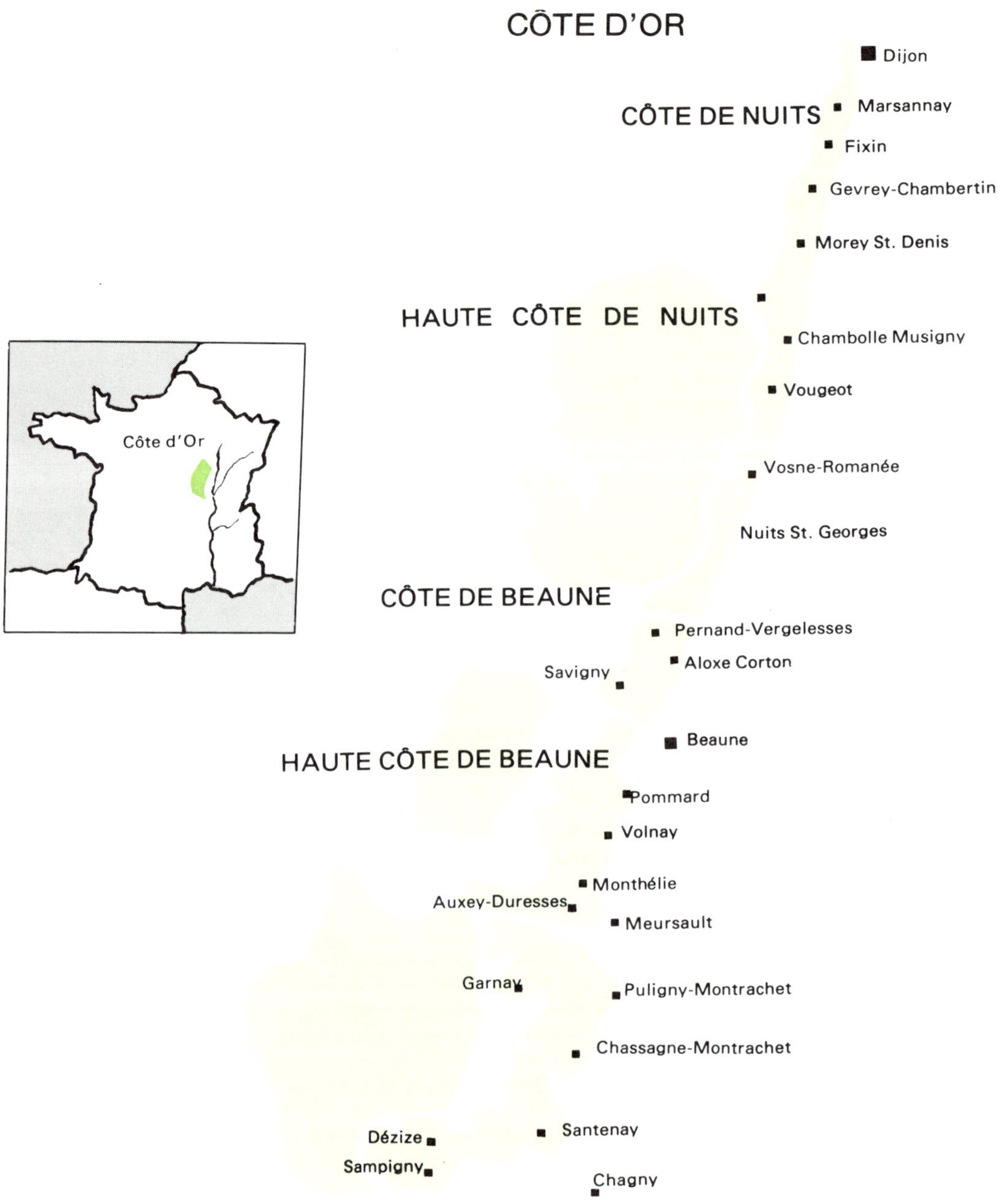
CÔTE D'OR
Dijon
CÔTE DE NUITS
Marsannay
Fixin
Gevrey-Chambertin
Morey St. Denis
HAUTE CÔTE DE NUITS
Chambolle Musigny
Vougeot
Côte d'Or
Vosne-Romanée
Nuits St. Georges
CÔTE DE BEAUNE
Pernand-Vergelesses
Aloxe Corton
Savigny
Beaune
HAUTE CÔTE DE BEAUNE
Pommard
Volnay
Monthélie
Auxey-Duresses
Meursault
Garnay
Puligny-Montrachet
Chassagne-Montrachet
Dézize
Santenay
Sampigny
Chagny

The Premiers Grands Crus of Burgundy

by Paul Marks

A very small part of the total production of Burgundy, some of the greatest wines of the world, are the Premiers Grand Crus (First Great Growths) of the Côte d'Or. They are neatly divided, with all the greatest reds coming from the Côte de Nuits, and the whites, possibly the greatest white table wines, from the Côte de Beaune.

These best wines of the Côte d'Or are more immediately obvious than those of the wines of their rivals from the Médoc. This is not a difference of quality between the two giants, but of tone of style, the tenor of sublimity.

The only grapes allowed for A.C. wines of higher than regional level, are the Pinot family grapes for the reds: Pinot Noir (Pinot Noiren), Pinot Buerot and Pinot Liebault (only a first-rate expert in these matters can even pretend to differentiate among the members of this family), and the Chardonnay grape for the white wines.

The better vineyard areas make wine which may find its way into bottles with the following Appellation d'Origine Contrôlée (A.O.C.) labels. I have to add here, that to find exact statements as to what the levels of the Appellation Contrôlée are, and how their labels should read, is to all intents and purposes a matter for the ending of great friendships and the founding of greater vendettas. The terms of the 1860 classification are used interchangeably with those of the 1936-37 A.O.C. laws, even though many of the Têtes de Cuvées (First Great

Growths) were declassified one notch in the latter legislation.

The first important commune of the Côte de Nuits, is Fixin, some five miles south of Dijon. There are no Grands Crus in Fixin, although the 1860 classification listed two, Clos de la Perrière and Clos des Châpitre. The 1936 classification demoted them to Premiers Crus.

Eight miles south of Dijon lies the commune of Gevrey, which in 1847 added the name of its greatest vineyard, Chambertin, to its own: for the simple, pragmatic reason of confusing buyers. The village itself offers little more than the ruins of the castle of the Abbots of Cluny as historical interest.

The other Premier Grand Cru of Gevrey, is the older, Clos de Beze. In 630 the Duke of Lower Burgundy, Almagaire, founded the Abbey of Beze near Dijon. One of the holdings of the Abbey, of 15 hectares, was in Gevrey. It was planted by the monks and tended until the 13th century, when it moved into the hands of another order. Neither the wine of Chambertin nor of Clos de Beze were considered exceptional until the 18th century, when a M. Joubert, secretary of the King's legal council, obtained both Chambertin and Clos de Beze, and made both famous. Until the effects of recent publicity, Clos de Beze had in fact been considered the superior vineyard. Not much wine is made in any one year in Clos de Beze, with an average of 510 hectolitres, some 6,000 cases.

The vineyard Chambertin is considered the Grand Seigneur of Burgundy. Its greatness is linked to Napoleon, who took its wines with him on all his campaigns - although the reputation of both the wine and Napoleon might be diluted if the fact that the little corporal watered his wines were better known. The vineyard lies on the midsection of its slope, south of the village, adjoining Clos de Beze, next to the Route des Grands Crus. The vineyard gets its name from a wily peasant, Bertin, who knew a good thing when he saw it, planting his field next to Clos de Beze using the same vine stocks as the monks.

The two vineyards, in fact, share their wine today. Clos de Beze may hyphenate itself with Chambertin: Chambertin-Clos de Beze, with the Chambertin A.C., but no wine of Chambertin may be sold as simply Clos de Beze. The two vineyards together amount to about 70 acres owned by some two dozen growers with the usual variations in style. Chambertin itself, some 37 acres, produces about 7,000 gallons per year on the average, including the Clos de Beze wine sold as Chambertin. There is never enough.

The Chambertin I have tasted has been characteristic of "desired image" for this wine - big, sturdy, of a very deep colour, with a pronounced and very long aftertaste. The aroma and bouquet could be the biggest of the Côte de Nuits. The word "overpowering" is often used in classic descriptions of Chambertin, but it more often refers to the power of the impression of the wine, not alcoholic strength - though alcohol is never lacking in a fine Chambertin. It is a wine that seems to develop well adding more austerity and firmness as it ages.

The next commune down the road is Morey, two-and-a-half miles from Gevrey. It hyphenated its name with the vineyard of St. Denis only as recently as 1927, though St. Denis is no longer considered the vineyard it once was. In 1860 several vineyards were considered as Têtes de Cuvée, but only that section of Bonnes Mares, 4.6. hectares out of 37.8 which lies in Morey, is listed as a Premier Grand Cru. Since most of Bonnes Mares lies in Chambolle, it is best to move on. The wines of Morey have not been well known on their own, much of the wine having been sold as Gevrey or Chambolle.

Chambolle, one-and-a-quarter miles south of Morey, hyphenated itself with its greatest vineyard, Les Musigny, in 1875. Chambolle's two Premiers Grands Crus surround the village. They are Bonnes Mares in the north, Les Musigny in the south, next to the commune of Flagey. Bonnes Mares is always sold as its own A.C., neither Morey nor Chambolle ever appearing on the label. There are a number of growers, but the wine is not really well known, being overshadowed by the other greats of Burgundy, though it is certainly their equal. The wine is lighter than most other Moreys, much more like Les Musigny in elegance and finesse. Yet, I have tasted a Bonnes Mares

(1959) the equal of the big wines of Vosne (Richebourg) of the same year. Bonnes Mares usually has more tannin than most burgundies and will keep very well. Bonnes Mares as a name is a mystery, but is probably a corruption of either Maires, one of the goddesses of the harvest, or *marer*, to plough.

Les Musigny, first mentioned in chronicles as early as 1110, is generally referred to as the most feminine, the most delicate of the wines of the Côte de Nuits. The vineyard lies along a small dirt road, on culturally priceless land, across from brush and rubble! The vineyard is, like Caesar's Gaul, divided into three parts. The section of Musigny in Chambolle is cut in two by another dirt road, into Grand and Petit Musigny (referring merely to their size). The vineyard continues right over the border into Flagey, where it is called La Combe d'Orveau, though the wine is sold as Musigny. On its slope, Petit Musigny overlooks the Château de Vougeot with its own vineyards on a plateau below.

The Pinot Noir is blended by some of the growers and shippers with some Chardonnay, which certainly enhances the desired image. The law allows up to 15 per cent of white grapes to be blended with the red. Les Musigny is generally at its peak earlier than other burgundies, but the best can continue to develop for a considerable time. The 16 acres of Les Musigny generally produce some 3,600 cases per year. The very small quantities of white Musigny made each year is even more expensive than the red!

The next village, only half a mile from Chambolle, next to Route National 74, is the smallest of the Côte de Nuits, but probably the most well known - especially since the institution of Les Chevaliers du Tastevin, and the international publicity given to meals presented at the château. The village was originally called Gilly, then Gilley-les-Vougeot (after the stream, Vouge). Now the village is known simply as, Vougeot.

The land of the vineyard was worked by the monks of Citeaux in the early 12th century, though it took centuries before the famous vineyard reached its modern 50 hectares (124 acres). The château was built by Dom Jean Loiser, 48th

Abbot of Citeaux, in 1551. The vineyard was owned by the monks until the revolution, when it was parcelled off as a "national asset." The vineyard is now owned by about 65 growers, some of whom own no more than a row or two of vines. The most famous story about the vineyard is told by Stendhal. A Colonel Bissen, on his way to join the Army of the Rhine, stopped at the vineyard's wall and presented arms to bugles and drums. The same story is told about the Duke of Aumale.

The wine of Clos de Vougeot is almost a swing back to the power of Chambertin, retaining much of the silken elegance of Chambolle wines. Like the greatest burgundies, there is an intensity and directness of colour, nose, flavour and aftertaste that stays with one for a very long time. The great problem is that there are 65 different Clos de Vougeot wines, some obviously coming closer to the desired image than others.

The next village, Flagey, attached the name of one of its great vineyards, Les Eschezeaux, in 1886. Despite the hyphenated name, the village itself is not a legal A.O.C. place name for wine. The two best vineyards go to market as Le Grand Eschezeaux and Eschezeaux, Grands Crus of Vosne-Romanée.

The last commune of the Côte de Nuits to contain Premiers Grands Crus is Vosne-Romanée. What immediately comes to mind about this village is the oft repeated statement, "there is no common wine of Vosne." The commune is two miles from Vougeot, with all the best vineyards on the other side of the village from the Route National.

The greatest of the Vosne vineyards produce a miniscule amount of wine on a comparatively microscopic, but enormously valuable, amount of agricultural land. Both Romanée and Romanée-Conti are so rare and costly that they put the most expensive Médocs to shame. Drinking one of these must always be the event of a lifetime - and if more than one bottle is available one must feel a favourite of the gods.

La Romanée is the smallest - just over two acres. It is divided from Romanée-Conti by a footpath. Supposedly La Romanée lacks some of the elegance and finesse, of Romanée-

Conti, but ordinary mortals need not worry ourselves about such differences. If one accepts the reports of differences, one might concede a greater robustness to La Romanée. Romanée-Conti came into the possession of the Prince of Conti in 1760 after a battle for ownership with Madame Pompadour. The reputation of the wine has since been connected with the Conti name.

Romanée-Conti was the last of the vineyards of the Côte d'Or to refuse to bow to the phylloxera, using direct bearers until the Second World War when the last vines gave up the ghost because of the shortage of carbon disulphide to fight the louse. Since 1945 the vines have been grafted onto Rupestis stocks. After 1945 the quantity of wine produced rose rather sharply, but the wines still retain the same reputation.

La Tâche (The Task) is made on about three and a half acres, plus the output of Les Gaudichots and La Grand Rue vineyards. In the last 10 to 15 years, La Tâche has been considered better than the Romanées.

Richebourg is the giant among the Premiers Grands Crus of Vosne. It has 19.8 acres and only Romanée-St-Vivant is larger. Richebourg is not a monopoly, but is owned by eight growers with only four of any size: Louis Gros, Romanée-Conti, Charles Noellat and Bichot. The vineyard produces a wine of rich sumptuousness, with all the attributes of Romanée-Conti, and must be lingered over as long as possible.

The vineyard of Montrachet, an extraordinary patch of land producing the most celebrated and expensive dry white wine of France, is divided between the two adjoining communes of Puligny and Chassagne, with just over half of the vineyard in Puligny. The two villages are about ten miles south of Pernand-Vergelesses, in the Côte de Beaune. They are the centre of a series of the greatest white table wines of the world, from vineyards that again hyphenate themselves with Montrachet, such as Chevalier-Montrachet, Bâtard-Montrachet, etc. The two villages added the name Montrachet to theirs in 1879.

Of course, only the Chardonnay grape is used in Montrachet, whose name is said to come from the Latin Mons Rachicensis, which become Mont-Rachet, "Bald Hill." The barren hilltop behind the stony vineyard is in fact nearly bald of growth. Nevertheless, like the great vineyards of the Côte de Nuits, Montrachet is among the most valuable agricultural land in France. With its small yield, the growers and shippers of Montrachet profit from probably the highest monetary ratio of land to production for any plot in the world.

Though the wine is rivalled in some instances by its hyphenated versions immediately adjoining, the Montrachet is wholly remarkable. Pale gold in colour, with some hints of green, it is high in alcohol, with tremendous bouquet, flavour, and breed. Montrachet is a dry wine, but there is a powerful apple-like buttery lusciousness, giving a foundation of softness to the wine. This is especially true in the better years.

The most famous quote about Montrachet comes from Alexander Dumas, père, who felt that one should only drink this wine bareheaded, on one's knees. Perhaps less romantic, but still evocative is that Montrachet is "not so much a wine as an experience." In fact, this is equally applicable to all the great wines of the Côte d'Or.

* * *

After the greatest of the wines of the Côte d'Or, those wines that theoretically cannot lay claim to the supreme pinnacle of Burgundy, both reds and whites, in fact do often either challenge the Chambertins, Musignys and Montrachets for first place, or in many years take over first place. So it is only fair, as well as just, that notice be taken of the Grands Crus (*not* Premiers Grands Crus) and Premiers Crus. These wines are the basis, the foundation, the touchstones of Burgundy's greatness and reputation, for they are more readily available and more widely distributed. These greats and near greats offer the full range of subtlety and nuance representative of the best of Burgundy.

All the communes of the Côte de Nuits and the Côte de Beaune offer wines of this level. They are made from the same grapes as the Premiers Grands Crus, the Pinot family for the reds, Chardonnay for the whites. The Grands Crus and the Premiers Crus, as with all the wines of Burgundy, are more in the way of a creation of their maker than, say, the wines of Bordeaux might be - each grower making his row or acre of grapes into wine. Though all these wines are ostensibly single vineyard wines, the goal of the honest shipper is to make the best wine possible consistent with his house style - which does not preclude subtle blends of vineyards.

The wines of Burgundy, in the hands of a fine grower-négociant, can be among the finest wines possible. Despite the disparities of style, the limitations of the plots owned by most growers has helped to retain some touch of the enthusiasm and idealism, as well as care and integrity, that seem to go along with smallness.

The Flavour of the Mâconnais

by Paul Marks

Following the river Saône south from the towns of Chalon-sur-Saône, Rully, Mercurey, Givry and Montagny, one quickly arrives at the town of Mâcon, the largest after Chalon. This lies in the first truly southern valley in Burgundy, where the people speak and move more slowly, and wear their berets like shields to protect them from the southern sun. The town is also in the centre of a wide stretch of country that gourmets speak of in hushed tones. It is the country of Charollais cattle, the chickens and blue cheese of Bresse, and the fish and frogs from the Saône.

After the rolling ground in the Chalonnais, the hills here have enough height to bear with dignity the name of Côtes; it is a rough broken area, both mountainous and convoluted. The Mâconnais is a good place for archeology, with layers of rock formation and the 6,000 year old fossils which have been found near the village of Solutré, and where many Roman artifacts have been collected.

The appellation of Mâcon, which can apply to both the white (Mâcon Blanc) and the large amount of red (Mâcon Rouge), is the generic of the region, without any other qualification. The grapes for the white wines are Pinot Blanc and Chardonnay. The reds are made from the Gamay Noir *à jus blanc,* Pinot Noir, and Pinot Gris, including about 15 per cent Gamay *coloré,* with a Gamay Teinturier that is a grape with red juice, which grows in big fat clusters. These large, heavybunched grapes are the same "disloyal plant" which Philip the Bold banned from Burgundy in the 15th century. It is in fact still banned from Burgundy proper, since only the red wines made from the Pinot Noir in the Mâcon may go to market as Bourgogne Rouge. The white wines can be sold as Bourgogne Blanc with either of its grapes. Indeed, since the Mâconnais borders immediately on the Beaujolais (and in fact overlaps its appellation with that region slightly) the commune of La-Chapelle-de Guinchay may, in fact, sell its red wines as Beaujolais Rouge.

Mâcon Supérieur, an appellation for reds, whites and rosés, and Mâcon-Villages, which is reserved for white wines only, will be a little higher in price and alcohol. Yet, since the wine is still one of the more reasonably priced in France, one will feel the alcohol more than the cost. The red wines, whether Mâcon or Mâcon Supérieur, are not really outstanding. The whites, however, are another story. The production area is large enough, so one can easily come across the work of a master blender. Mâcon-Villages can be as good as the best commune appellation wines in the area.

There is one more appellation which should be mentioned, Mâcon-Pinot-Chardonnay, at the same level as the lowest appellation. It is a double misnomer: there is no Chardonnay in the wine, and the Pinot is in any case not a member of the Chardonnay family. This is one of the few instances in France of a varietal labelled wine outside of Alsace. It is done mainly to assure us that the wine is not made from the Aligoté grape, and at the same time is useful to compete in the world market with the California labels.

The area is older and has a longer history of respected wines than the Beaujolais; it does no disservice to the latter to have some Mâconnais wines use its name. The Mâcon region has been famous since the 17th century. The history of the wine outside of its local area begins with a story about Claude Brosse, who would have done very well in today's market. A huge and obviously brave fellow, he loaded up two barrels of the best of the Mâconnais, and went off to Paris, along 400 kilometres of mud and robbers. He arrived in the capital in about one month. Louis XIV eventually ''noticed'' Charles - his size and aggressive business sense made that inevitable - and his wines. When the king tasted Brosse's wines from the Mâcon, the winemaker was given an immediate order for the royal cellars, and the wines of the Mâconnais began to be famous in France.

The soil of the region is mainly chalk (where its neighbour Beaujolais is mostly granite), although the soil in which the best vines of Mâcon are grown is limestone and slate, formed at least 150 million years ago.

Mâcon Blanc is the ''all-purpose'' white wine of greater Burgundy, not as severe as Chablis, harder than Meursault, not as delicate in colour as either, but firm and strong. It is not acidic enough to be a true companion to shellfish but it does accompany fish, chicken or veal as well as does any regional white wine. And it is thirst-quenching.

During the 1970s, however, one white wine from the Mâconnais reached the fame and price level of a Chablis or a Meursault. This is Pouilly-Fuissé, and though at times it does reach the standard of the better (not the best) whites of the Côte d'Or, it somehow attained a prestige and price in the United States out of all proportion to its quality.

Pouilly-Fuissé is made from the Chardonnay grape, with a permitted production of 400 gallons per acre. The best is sold with a vineyard appellation as well as one of five village names; Fuissé, Pouilly, Solutré, Vergisson, and Chaintré.

The rolling green countryside is dotted with seemingly thrown-together farmhouses. The chaotic pattern of green vines is broken by fallow or pasture land. The viticulture methods, because of the warmer climate, are different from those of the rest of Burgundy. The Chardonnay is allowed to grow higher, and to ripen about two weeks longer.

The wine is mainly made by small peasant farmers, with some two to five acres, who sell their wine to shippers for blending with that of their neighbours. The eight to ten *pièces* are kept until the négociant arrives, often unsolicited. Yet there are also estates, such as the Château de Fuissé, with its 15th century manor in the midst of some 70 acres. The best wine of Pouilly-Fuissé, which is bottled under a château label, may in reality consist of several different parts of the same vineyard, each bottled separately.

Pouilly-Fuissé at its best is a delicate and fresh wine, light and very dry, with a *gout de terroir* and a light bouquet. The colour is a light gold, with tinges of green. However, too often it is hardly better than a Mâcon-Villages. It could be instructive to compare, say, Drouhin's Laforêt, a Mâcon-Villages, with any Pouilly-Fuissé at twice the price.

There are two other villages that carry their own name on the label, Loché and Vinzelles. They make the same kind of wine, and can prefix the name Pouilly to their own. It is well known that a Pouilly Loché or a Pouilly-Vinzelles can offer the same fine quality as Pouilly-Fuissé.

In 1971 a new appellation was created for a group of villages on the outskirts of Pouilly, spilling over into Beaujolais to Saint-Amour. This Mâcon appellation is Saint-Véran, but don't be confused to learn that one of the villages making Saint-Véran is Saint-Vérand! The slightly green, delicately coloured, clean, fresh wine with it's fine acid/sugar balance is often confused with a white Mâconnais or a Beaujolais. However, Saint-Véran comes from an appellation area with Chardonnay and Pinot Blanc as the grape varieties but granite will give a significantly different character to the wine.

With some homework, and a "pleasantly pudgy" wallet, one can drink some very fine white wines from the Mâcon. With slimmer means, and a sharp eye, wines like Mâcon-Villages and Saint-Véran can provide fine every-other-day drinking.

Meeting the Burgundian Vintners

by Gillian Gayton

Gillian Gayton, linguist and gourmet, is wine columnist for the "Montreal Gazette" and former editor of "Wine Tidings."

A fortnight's holiday on the Côte d'Or in late spring, among the roses, lilies and vines in flower, left us with few memories more vivid than that of a drive along a little gravel road, one golden afternoon, in the company of Jean Germain of Meursault, grower, shipper and palate extraordinary. From Meursault to Chassagne-Montrachet, a mere four kilometres, we passed through the little green plots of vines from which come the world's greatest white wines, Meursault Goutte d'Or, Genevrières, Charmes, Perrières, then on to Puligny-Montrachet les Caillerets and the great trumpeting names of Montrachet. Note the red earth, the situation, not too high and not too low. The great Genevrières are those from below, on the left of the track. Of the Meursault Charmes the greatest are those acres next to Puligny Referts. The finest wines of Puligny come from the 16½ acres of Les Combettes, and of those the far end contains the best.

We stopped at M. Germain's own plot of vines, three quarters of an acre, "une jolie parcelle. Elle est belle, ma vigne," he said, pointing out with some pride how his grapes, because of earlier ploughing between the rows, were more advanced than his neighbours'. Standing there in the late afternoon sunshine, the faint perfume of vine blossom around me and the vines with their noble titles stretching away on either side of me, we saw Burgundy at last as a real and living place, not a fabulous name.

Of the vintners we met in the Côte d'Or we choose to speak first of M. Germain, for he represented all facets of the wine trade. Proprietor, vintner and shipper, he seemed to balance traditional skills and modern science perfectly despite the fact that he was not born to the business. As a young man of 17, a Burgundy farmer's son, he came to Meursault in 1951 and soon acquired his first small *parcelle*. Hard work and a keen intelligence, aided by a fine palate, made him one of the most successful and respected of the propriétaires/négociants of the Côte. His total acreage of vines was 25 *ouvrées*, (about 2½ acres) making him an average small grower. Like many others, M. Germain owned small plots in several areas. The wines produced by these little properties, however, brought him recognition and honours, including medals from the Confrérie des Chevaliers du Tastevin at Clos Vougeot and a first prize gold medal at the Paris exhibition in 1960 for his Meursault les Tillets.

Nevertheless, although he has taken great pride and pleasure in his vines, and in making his own white wines from Meursault and Puligny-Montrachet Pinot Blanc grapes, the greater part of M. Germain's business became that of négociant, or shipper. Together with a *courtier* or broker of wines, he established a company called L'Elevage et le Conditionnenement des Vins Fins. The business included choosing, fostering, maturing, and selling the wines of small growers who make their own wine but have neither the capacity nor the capital to store it until it is drinkable, nor the equipment to bottle it. Over 80 per cent of burgundy passes through the hands of shippers like M. Germain, most of it made by small independent proprietors whose reputation for integrity is of paramount importance. Growers who entrust their wine, of which they are justly proud, to the négociants, are glad to know that it will not be adulterated, improperly mixed with other vintages or otherwise abused, but stored and cossetted with the same care and attention they themselves would give. I cannot resist here quoting from M. Delagrange, a grower from Chassagne-Montrachet whom we will meet at greater length later on; "Wines are like children, one must know how to bring them up."

Considerable knowledge is required of a successful shipper, especially if he is a négociant-éleveur who matures the wine. First he must choose and buy the wine, preferably in the

June following the vintage, although tasting can be done in December and in a boom year the young "must" has been bought before November. This is where M. Germain's remarkable palate comes in, for the discernment to recognize and choose the best of the young wines is not given to everyone. Then he must store it, bottling it at the right time after racking and fining it. Apart from a fine palate and a thorough knowledge of the business, the final requirement for a shipper is a good cellar. "C'est la bonne cave qui fait le bon vin. Faut connaître sa cave."

Out in the vineyard I learned about pruning, planting, tying up, sulphuring, sulphating, pinching back and was bombarded by information. Most growers need plant only once in a lifetime, as a vine in good soil will be productive for 35 years or more. The vine requires 22 centimetres of earth, and when it washes away down the slopes it must be carried back up, so precious is it. There are 90 cms. between plants and one metre plus five cms. between rows, to allow for the tractor. One should sulphate against disease between five and nine times a year. Each plant should, after judicious pruning, be left with four shoots, two having branches, on each of which will hang one bunch of grapes.

Interesting to us, were his opinions on yield per acre and on the new improved grapes. On the Côte d'Or the French government allows a maximum yield of 35 hectolitres of wine to a hectare of vineyard. In exceptional years it permits 40 to 50 hectolitres. The government's aim is, of course, to protect quality by ensuring that growers are not reimbursed according to quantity alone. However, most growers can and do, without prejudice to their wine, obtain yields of 45 to 60 hectolitres per hectare, 65 in exceptional years. The result is that only two-thirds of their wine is allowed to be sold under its vineyard or commune name, and the rest, which is of equal quality, must be sold at a much lower price under the generic name of Bourgogne Blanc or Bourgogne Rouge. This is a permanent grievance with many growers who feel that in good years all the wine should be classified, and that less should be permitted

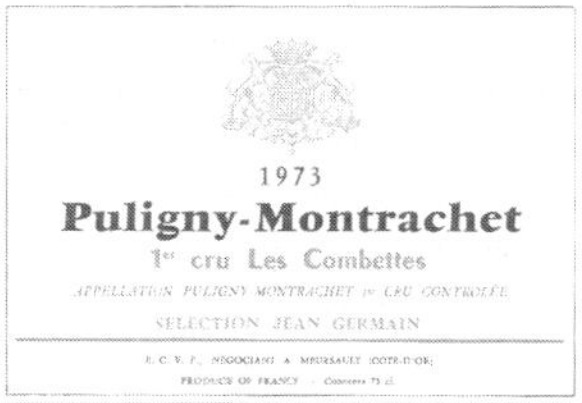

from mediocre or bad years.

However, on the other side of the coin, the new grapes are too big and watery, and make too much wine of diminished quality. In the old days, when spraying against oidium was done with a mixture of copper and chalk, the plant suffered somewhat and grew less, producing as a result fewer and smaller but stronger, more concentrated grapes of thick, dense pulp. These made for less wine but of a much higher quality than today, although being high in tannin it was hard at first and took longer to age.

From the hot sunny fields we moved into the cool dark cellar and here, in between tastings, I learned about the technique of winemaking and the differences between wines. More facts. New barrels must always have brand new wine put into them, year old wine is too old. The taste of the young oak (always French oak) never fails to make good wine. New dry cellars are good for new wine, old cellars for old. A new wine won't use up its sugar in an old damp cellar. Fining or clarifying the wine is very important, and vintages vary in their need for it. Rainy years make "fat" wine, full of impurities. Fining, *le collage,* fatigues some wines, and they may take up to two years to recover.

For us, the tasting is the thing, and the fascination was in hearing M. Germain expound on the differences. Vintages, years, *les millésimes,* are, he said, easy, but it is harder to recognize the *goût du terroir*, the taste of the particular vineyard. For example, the 30 hectares of Meursault Charmes were divided into four quarters, all of which taste different, at least to people with his palate.

Another day M. Germain took me to Chassagne-Montrachet, along that memorable road I have already described, to meet M. Delagrange. A big cool house full of lovingly polished old furniture, brass and copper. Below, a stone cobbled yard with rose bushes and hydrangeas in bloom, a very old cellar full of hundreds of barrels. M. Delagrange, was a vintner, son and grandson of vintners. One of three brothers, sons of a small vigneron in Volnay, he went to Chassagne in 1924 to work for M. Bachelet. In 1934 he married M. Bachelet's daughter and their honeymoon was spent turning the old hand press which requires four people - it was harvest time. Since the age of 14 he worked in the vineyards, later with his wife alongside him - "Ce n'était pas l'école, c'était la vigne." To bed at 11, up at five. It used to take an hour and a half to groom, feed and harness the big Ardennais horses, and, to feed them, part of the land had to be given up to hay and oats.

In the late 1960's, he stopped using horses, and admitted that he missed them. However, M. Delagrange was not sentimental about the old days. Fifty years ago the work was grindingly hard. "It's a joke, how little we have to do now," Mme. Delagrange agreed. For what they used to do "faut l'avoir dans la peau," she said. Her mother too, was a vintner, and carried on during the 1914-18 war, working the fields alone without the menfolk.

Although changes brought the leisure to enjoy their family, even to travel, M. Delagrange kept old, thorough methods of vinification, fining with egg whites, *le batonnage* or the mixing in of the lees. He was proud of his "belle domaine."

⚜

What Montrachet is to white Burgundy, Romanée is to red. The *grand crus*, Romanée-Conti, la Tâche, le Richebourg, are to most of us as familiar by name as they are likely to remain strangers to our palates, for they are among the world's rarest and most expensive wines. But there are no ordinary wines in Vosne-Romanée, and some of the first growths of that commune, les Malconsorts, les Suchots, would in any other area be classed as *grand crus*.

"Take off thy shoes from off thy feet, for the place whereon thou standest is holy ground." Like all the villages of the Côte d'Or, Vosne-Romanée seemed very small and quiet. Dogs were alseep in the street, the inevitable cabbage roses of Burgundy lay along the walls, and the houses had no numbers. "M. Gérard Mugneret?" "But of course. Turn left at the church, it's the third house down." We turned into the cobbled

yard of a very old house, more farm house than villa. Through the half-open doors of a great barn we glimpsed the huge presses and realized that this must be the *cuverie* or pressing room. A small boy was rolling happily around in the dust beside an old hand pump. M. Mugneret came out to greet us and introduced the child, his grandson. Would we like to see the *cuverie* and the *cave*? We would indeed, this being our first opportunity to see how the whole process takes place, from lorry-loads of fat black grapes to a glass of good burgundy.

The huge barn we had already noticed contained the stemmer-crusher, a machine that crushes the grapes to release their juice and throws off the stalks after separating them from the skins and juice. (The crushing operation should burst the grapes without damaging the pips and stalks, in order to avoid releasing too much tannin into the must.) Then the crushed vintage runs down through tubes in holes in the barn floor into the *cuverie* below, where it is collected in great *cuvés* or vats. Some of these are the old oak ones which hold 30 hectolitres but M. Mugneret was gradually replacing them with cement ones of 50 hectolitre capacity, because the wooden ones occasionally impart an undesirable taste to the young wine. It stays in the vat with the skins and pips for four to six days and is then drawn off and separated from the *marc.* The latter is pressed once only in the pressoir ("it works like a washing machine" said M. Mugneret - I think he meant a mangle) and the must thus obtained is added to the free-run juice. The press wine represents ten to twenty per cent of the free-run wine.

Now the fermentation begins. It should take place between 22° and 30° C., and lasts from twelve to fifteen days. In the first few days when the must is still mixed with the skins, a floating cap of the latter forms and reforms continually on the surface, pushed up by the release of carbon dioxide. Most people mix this in again by pumping, to stimulate the fermentation and distribute the colour given by the skins. In the Mugneret household, however, they still adhered to the old method. What is that? "On plonge tout nu dedans." I thought of the idyllic scene in Fellini's "8½" where the naked children frolic in the wine vats, and sighed with envy.

From the *cuvés*, after no longer than 14 days, the must is transferred to the casks in the cellar itself. These casks (*pièces* is the Burgundian term), each holding 228 litres, were made of French oak by a cooper only 30 kilometres away. A barrel will last 30 years. As with white burgundies, a new barrel must have only new wine put in it. "You put it in its cradle and bring them up together," said M. Mugneret. The wine usually stays in cask for about two years and is then bottled. During this maturing period little needs to be done to the wine. The casks are topped up from time to time, as evaporation or cooling down and absorption by the wood causes air pockets in which harmful ferments can develop. The wine is also fined and racked several times, to precipitate the lees and separate the clear wine from it. According to M. Mugneret, 60 per cent of the quality of a wine is due simply to the grapes, and 40 per cent to the care and skill of the vintner. The cellar is of course immensely important. "La cave c'est notre petit capital," said M. Mugneret, who noted that he kept a constant temperature, never above 15° C., usually between 10° and 12°. All the houses in Vosne-Romanée have their own cellars, unlike those of Puligny-Montrachet, where the vintners are obliged to use cellars in other nearby villages.

The last process of all is the bottling, which takes place after two years of maturing in cask, when the wine has cast off its lees and become limpid, sound and free of fermentation. To my mind, the "bourguignonne," with its long sloping shoulders and dull leaf green colour, is far more aesthetically satisfying than the slim, bright green Bordeaux bottle. It is in fact a more old-fashioned shape, as a visit to the Musée de Vins in Beaune will attest.

We came up from the cellar into the sunshine and sat on the warm stone steps, and I asked M. Mugneret to point out to me on the map where his 15 acres of Vosne-Romanée and Nuits St. Georges are located. The Mugneret properties are, from south to north, les Chaignots and les Bondots from Nuits, and la Croix Blanche, les Jacquines, la Colombière, les Suchots, les

Ormes, les Chalandins and les Echézeaux of Vosne-Romanée. Many of these were acquired by his father, who died during the war in his late seventies. M. Mugneret disappeared into the house, and re-appeared smiling, with a bottle of his les Suchots 1973 which I had tasted and rhapsodised over down in the cellar. As he escorted us to the gate, I looked back at the grandson and asked M. Mugneret if he hoped the child would follow in his footsteps as a Burgundian vintner. "Oui," he says, "c'est un bon métier. On en voit les résultats."

Wines of the Côtes du Rhône

by Paul Marks

The Rhône River provided the prime route from the Mediterranean northward for some 2,500 years, first for the Phoenecian Greeks, founders of Massilia (Marseille), then for the Romans. The vine waited some 600 years before moving northward from the plains between Massilia and Narbonne. It only reached Lyon about one A.D., generally moving up the Rhône with traders and settlers who carried back iron, amber, and furs from the beer-drinking Celts. It made a slight detour at Lyon, - though a fortunate and delicious one, - up the Saône to Burgundy. Greek wine amphorae have been found in the upper Saône Valley and the Jura.

Of course, classical sources give us rather extreme views of Massilian wines and the Italians may have gagged on the wines of Marseille. But the Celtic and Germanic tribes seemed to think it a fine status symbol, a way of keeping ahead of their less educated neighbours who still drank their awful beer. The "smoked" wine of Martial probably had some superficial resemblance to the "estufa" wines of Madeira, but that was not the only modern touch. The winemakers of Narbonne put together a spiced wine very much like today's vermouth.

The fact is that northward to Lyon lies one vast archeological dig of Greek and Roman artifacts. Ampuis was founded by the same colonists who built Marseille. Martial, Ovid, Pliny and Plutarch all mention the wines of Cornas. Columella and Martial write about the wine made of the Picata grape (Vinum

Picatum) at Vienne.

The Côtes du Rhône is the oldest first-rate wine area of France and Laudun can probably lay claim to being the oldest continually-producing wine town in France.

By the 14th century all the major wine producing areas on the Rhône had been established including Avignon and its long succession of Popes, who are said to have introduced white wine to the region, in order to celebrate Mass.

The major wines of the Côtes du Rhône range from the medium dark to very dark (even black) among the reds, with big, full-flavoured, fruity bodies. The reds need an average of one to three years in bottle, minimum, although again on the average they should be drunk with pleasure at an older five to six years (Côte Rôtie, Hermitage and traditional Châteauneuf-du-Pape need much longer.) The white table wines usually have a full gold colour, and need at least two years in the bottle. They are, however, among the longest-lived white table wines. The rosés range from a medium pink to a coral colour and are dry, fresh and fruity. They should be drunk before their third year.

There are two quite distinctive sections to the Côtes du Rhône appellation region. South of Hermitage lies the world of Provence, which has inspired many writers to wax romantically poetic. The southern Rhône is the only major A.C. region in France that has a Mediterranean climate. But this is only part of it, for the ears and nose tell it all. The scent of Provence is that of wild herbs, thyme, lavender, rosemary, and laurel, and some say that perfume is in the wine.

The northern section of the Côtes du Rhône runs from Vienne to Valence, the two most important vineyards being Côte Rôtie and Hermitage.

Côte Rôtie, the "Roasted Slope," is made in the communes of Ampuis and Tupin-et-Semons. There are some 54 *quartiers* (climats) which produce grapes from Côte Rotie, but vineyard names rarely if ever appear on any label. The only words other than the wine's name are "Blonde et Brune." The legend is that the vines of two hillsides, one with darker soil

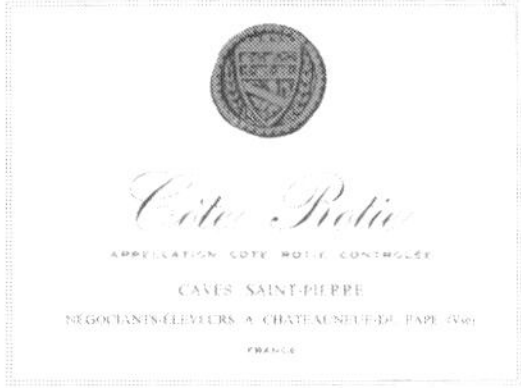

than the other, were left to two daughters of a ruler of the area, one blonde, one brunette. The wines produced from the grapes of each hillside are said to represent the personalities of the daughters, one beautiful and extrovert, but fickle and flighty (the blonde, of course), the other more reserved but with hidden qualities, and dependable. Occasionally one may find a label with only Brune or Blonde, but almost always Côte Rôtie is a blend of the wines of the small terraced plots, some only 20 by 20 feet.

The two grapes allowed are the Syrah and the white Viognier, which may be blended up to 20 per cent with the Syrah. The wine is a big one, of deep colour and body. With sufficient age the colour becomes garnet. The aroma and bouquet have been associated with raspberries, violets and truffles, and it is surely a complex wine, of a supremely velvety texture. It is safe to say (even with fear of contradiction) that Côte Rôtie is the finest wine of the Côtes du Rhône.

The harvest of the 60 hectares usually begins in mid September and lasts until late October, producing about 2,000 hectolitres. The wine is fermented in open cement, wood or enamel vats for 8 to 15 (mostly 10 to 12) days, with the skins and stems. The Syrah and the Viognier are fermented together. The wine is aged in small oak or chestnut casks for two to five years. The wine can continue to improve for more than 30 years in bottle, producing lots of deposit.

Condrieu, which is just beyond the next bend in the river, is a small A.C. vineyard area where two dozen owners work some 17 acres of Viognier grape vines. The white wine is strong (a minimum of 11°), with a distinctive *goût de terroir*. The wine is best young but, like other Rhône whites, is relatively long-lived. Château Grillet, made in Verin and St. Michel-sous-Condrieu, is not in fact a château, but the name of a four acre A.C. in France. This wine is comparable to a Pouilly-Fuissé, but more austere and dryer, a harder, bigger, more vigorous wine than a Meursault. It has the glamour of any commodity which is scarce and which we somehow feel we must have, generally living up to its reputation, despite its exotic fame.

Hermitage is the other great red wine of the northern Rhône, perhaps the greatest of them all. It is made at Tain L'Hermitage, across the river from Tournon. The name refers to a hilltop retreat, part of another legend. This time you can take your choice of three stories. You may care to believe that St. Patrick of Ireland passed through Hermitage, whereupon the angels planted vines for him. Or, you can choose the more colourful legend, which has it that the 12th century Provençal crusader (against the Albigensian heresy), Henri Gaspard de Sterimberg, was the hermit in question. As he was praying at the chapel of St. Christopher on the steep hill above the river, a vision appeared and told him to stay. He appealed to Queen Blanche of Castile, the secular ruler, and to the Abbey of St-André-le-bas, the owners of the chapel. They allowed him to stay and retreat from the world. A twist in the story has Sterimberg bringing the Syrah vine with him from either Syracuse or Persia, two places he had never seen. The spot may be good for hermits, but only for those who like to roast, freeze and be blown about by the Mistral.

The vineyard works its way 300 metres up above Tain, with owner's and shippers' signs rearing above the vines, some visible eighteen miles away. Hollywood has nothing on Hermitage. There are other crops on the hill too: apricots, even wheat fields. The Hermitage A.C. is the southernmost of the *great* wines of France (if one omits Châteauneuf). Yet there are still rains and storms, and the dry, cold Mistral, although the weather is mainly warm, not hot, with many days of bright sun shining on the southerly exposed vines.

The vineyards are divided into what are here called *Mas* (climats), 18 of them among 60 owners. However, it is very rare to find an unblended *mas* wine. The soil is mainly granite with rocks and pebbles; the lower section of the hill is loess and limestone, where the Marsanne and Roussane grapes are grown for Hermitage Blanc. The soil is poor and well drained, the *richest* for fine wine. The upper slopes require mostly manual labour, the soil being carried back on men's backs after heavy rains. The granite must be blasted in some places before planting.

Eighty per cent of the vines planted are the Syrah, here a clone called the Petite Syrah. The harvest lasts from mid-September to early October. The A.C. allows 40 hectolitres per hectare of the harvest for the Syrah. Although the law allows the use of up to 15 per cent of white grapes, this practice is less common than in Côte Rôtie. More often Hermitage is 100 per cent Syrah. A few producers still ferment with the skins and stems for two to three weeks.

The colour of the wine is deep, the wine throwing a heavy port-like sediment. The aroma and bouquet are, at their best, very intense, spicy and full of raspberries and truffles. The roughness of youth is ameliorated to a robust but smooth wine with age, the colour turning appropriately to the brownish side. Hermitage certainly needs six to eight years in bottle, with 15 to 20 years doing the wine of a good vintage no harm.

About two thirds of the wine made is red. The rest is white, a full, long-lived wine, best from six years in bottle, three to four years minimum. Hermitage Blanc is one of the whites of France that has as much body as a red.

Crozes-Hermitage hardly seems to merit the Hermitage that is part of its name. This wine is made from grapes grown at the top of the hill and over on the other side. The wine can be very good and a considerably cheaper substitute for Hermitage, but the name implies a possible greatness that can never be achieved.

Just south of Tain-Tournon and Saint-Joseph, the latter a relatively recent appellation (as of 1956) making a perfumed fine red from the Syrah, and fruity whites of the Marsanne and Roussane, is Cornas, a Celtic word for "burnt earth." This is the first area that seems to be and looks southern. Figs and almonds compete with the grapes for space. Along with Côte Rôtie and Hermitage, Cornas is the oldest vineyard of the Rhône. The A.C. can be described as "Syrah in granite" on steep slopes facing south at a 45° angle. The A.C. only allows 100 per cent Syrah red wine. The white, grown on chalk soil, can only be called A.C. Côtes du Rhône.

Since 1949, because of expense and the difficulty of cultivation, half the vineyards have been abandoned, though since inflation a few have been reclaimed. The usual production is about 1,000 hectolitres from 75 hectares, about half allowed by the A.C. The must is fermented on the skins and stems for approximately 10 days, the cap punched down twice daily. The wine absorbs lots of colour from the dense skins.

The literary image of Cornas is that it resembles Hermitage. Perhaps it does, visually, but that is hardly true of the taste. With age, however, the wine becomes soft, velvety, and filled with fruit.

The largest concentration of vineyards in the entire Côtes du Rhône is at Châteauneuf-du-Pape, and five villages make the wine of the A.C: Châteauneuf-du-Pape, Curhuézon, Orange, Bédarrides and Sorgues. The soil is chalk and clay, covered with what in the area are called "pebbles" but are in fact large stones. The vines are planted further apart than in any other A.C. vineyard in France, five to six feet between rows. The vines have the highest minimum alcohol requirement of any A.C. wines of the country, 12.5° (along with Gigondas and Côtes du Rhône-Villages). Low bushes and cyprus trees are planted along the ends of the rows to protect the vines from the Mistral.

After the first World War Châteauneuf-du-Pape was in poor shape, with a bad reputation for adulteration with foreign wines. In 1923 the Baron LeRoy Boiseaumarie, a lawyer, devised a plan for quality control. This was based, not on geography, but on soil, grape cultivation, alcohol, and acidity. LeRoy wisely won his case for legalized quality control through litigation in the courts of Orange, rather than by governmental decree. In 1936, when Senator Capus prepared the new national A.C. laws to pass through the national assembly, and the INAO was established, it was all modelled after the Baron's work. The appellation laws for Châteauneuf-du-Pape are strict, even limiting the amount and time of irrigation (none is allowed after August 15th.) In fact, since rain is irregular, watering is done four out of every five years.

Thirteen grapes may go into the blend that is Châteauneuf-du-Pape, but few makers use all of these. Grenache is in fact on the decline and the wines now tend to be fruitier because of the higher percentage of Syrah, Cinsault, Mourvèdre and Muscardin.

White Châteauneuf-du-Pape is made from the white Grenache, Picpoul, Bouboulenc, Roussane and Terret blanc. However, Châteauneuf-du-Pape turns only two per cent of its grapes into the white, dry and strong wine.

The traditional red Châteauneuf-du-Pape is another big Rhône, deep coloured, robust and tannic, needing seven to eight years in the bottle for maturity, living well for another ten to twenty years. The newer style is less alcoholic, fresher, fruitier, softer, more quickly mature and more quickly dead. The new softness does not fit with the 12.5° to 13° alcohol.

North of Châteauneuf-du-Pape are the vineyards of Gigondas, a good wine resembling Châteauneuf-du-Pape made from Grenache, Mourvèdre and Syrah.

Across the river lie Tavel and Lirac, producing what are called the best rosés of France. The commune of Laudun makes both reds and rosés. Tavel in particular is dry and nervy, with a nose of wild strawberries. It reaches as much as 15° alcohol, although 13° is more usual.

In the north (except for generic Côtes du Rhône) the winemaker can combine only three or four available varieties, while in the south any combination of 20 grape varieties is permitted. Except for the fortified wines, all southern A.C.'s can use any combination of at least nine of the 20 (Châteauneuf-du-Pape, 13, Lirac, 11, Tavel, 9.) The south uses different methods of vinification as well, both the traditional and a semi-carbonic macération. Côte Rôtie, Hermitage and their neighbours use only long-standing traditional methods. The must is fermented with skins and stems, and aged long in wood.

As for the barrels in which the wine is aged, there seems to be a rather flexible attitude. Perhaps "casual" would be a better word. Oak (chêne), and chestnut of Russian, Yugoslavian, and American provenance, are used freely, and the growers even admit to using French Nevers oak.

Generally in France the more specific the name, the better the wine. This is not always so in the Côtes du Rhône, because alcoholic strength is probably a more vital consideration in quality than anywhere else in the country. For example, the Côtes du Rhone A.C. minimum is 11°, Côtes du Rhone plus the département name need only reach 9.5°, while Côtes du Rhône plus a commune name must reach 12.5°. The regional Côtes du Rhône is allowed 50 hectolitres per hectare, but no chaptalization permitted. Côte Rôtie and Hermitage are allowed to chaptalize, but their natural alcoholic minimum is set at 10°. Should the latter two be declassified to a regional A.C. they must get up to 11°!, otherwise they become *vin ordinaire.*

Until the 1970's, Rhône wines remained a very viable and economically feasible substitute for Burgundy. Now that the French have discovered their own fine wines, there can only be an increased demand (which unfortunately can lead to a further dilution of traditional quality), and higher prices for wines that have been in the shadow of Burgundy and Bordeaux for much too long.

Gael Plant

Italy

The Italians make more wine than anybody else in the world, more than two billion gallons a year. As the largest producer, Italy also boasts of more types and varieties of wine than any other nation. To arrive at a quality control system for this large production, the Italian government in 1963 established the *Denominazione di Origine Controllata,* which can be used by consumers as a guide to quality purchases.

D.O.C.: defines specific grape types from a specific area and aged as precisely outlined by the law.

D.O.C.G.: a guarantee for wines of outstanding quality has been awarded to a few carefully regulated wines from top quality zones.

Many of Italy's very good wines however, are only eligible for the *Vino di Tavola* or 'table wine' appellation.

The Romans called Italy ''Enotria Tellus,'' the land of grapes, for the vine thrives almost everywhere in this predominantly hilly country, but the most distinguished wines come from the north.

PIEDMONT

This is by far the most important of the northwestern regions being the source of Barolo, Barbaresco, Dolcetto, and Grignolino, which are generally regarded as Italy's champions against the world's great red wines.

The most famous of these is Barolo, a DOCG made from the Nebbiolo grape, a big wine of great perfume and flavour, which can stand considerable aging. Barbaresco, its younger brother, made of grapes grown lower on the slopes, is also a DOCG.

Slightly lighter and fruitier are the Barberas made from the grape variety of the same name. The best of these wines have their district of production attached to their names (Barbera d'Asti, Barbera d'Alba, etc.) and should reach at least 13% alcohol.

The bulk of Piedmont wine is red but small quantities of whites and rosés are also made. The famous Asti-Spumanti is a sweet sparkling white from the Moscato grape.

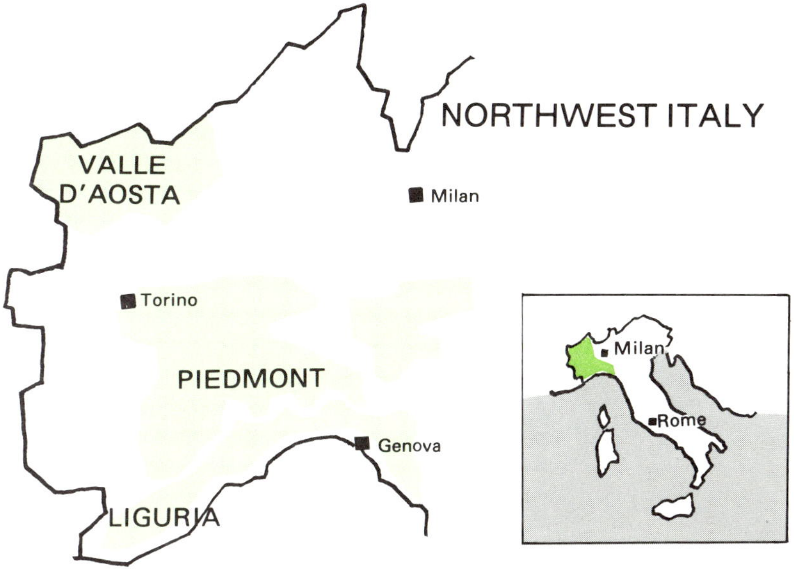

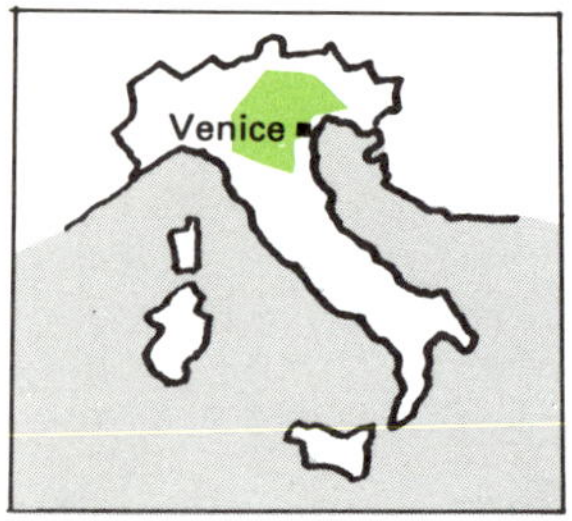

THE VENETO

This lovely region, which lies between Lake Garda and the Po River, extending eastwards towards Venice, produces three great Veronese wines, Valpolicella, Bardolino and Soave. Valpolicella is a light but sturdy, fresh dry red wine with a slightly bitter aftertaste. Bardolino, from the same grapes grown in lighter soils, is a soft, velvety red. Soave, Italy's most famous white wine, comes from a small hill district east of Verona. It is dry, pale and slightly fruity, an ideal accompaniment to seafood and white meats.

TRENTINO-ALTO ADIGE

From the Alto Adige or upper part of the valley leading towards the Austrian border, come very elegant white wines similar to those of Alsace.

The vineyards of Trentino in the south are in beautiful narrow valleys and on steep hillsides, with the vines frequently planted on narrow terraces. The vines are unusually attractive, being for the most part trained on pergolas in the Lens Moser style.

The bulk of the wines of Trentino are of a high standard with the dominant grapes being the familiar Cabernet, Merlot, Riesling, White Pinot and Gewürztraminer that produce the great wines of France and Germany

TUSCANY

A half day's drive south from Piedmont towards Rome lie the beautiful hills of Tuscany, another important region of the north half of the country, and home of Chianti.

In 1984 the Chianti wines were upgraded to the DOCG classification. The predominant grape is Sangiovese (50 to 80%), plus 10 to 30% Canaiolo and sometimes 5% Colorino. The blend is also required to include a minimum of 5%, maximum 10% of white grapes, Trebbiano and Malvasia. Chianti Classicos require only 2 to 5% white grapes, allowing for wines of even deeper colour and fuller body.

A "Riserva" must age at least three years but the ideal drinking age is approximately the same as that for a claret, 10 to 15 years. This is particularly true of wines from favoured hillsides and vineyards.

Tuscany produces other wines than Chianti, the most famous of which are undoubtedly the Brunello di Montalcino and Vino Nobile di Montepulciano, both wines of DOCG classification.

EMILIA-ROMAGNA

This area around Bologna, famous for its rich cooking, makes four wines of importance. Lambrusco is a strange dry semi-sparkling red wine from the grape of the same name. Its fresh taste and prickle in the mouth have made it a prime favourite in North America. The Sangiovese grape, the main variety used to make Chianti, produces in the Romagna hills a full-bodied well-balanced red wine which ages well. Trebbiano di Romagna is a dry, elegant white wine from the grape of the same name, and Albana di Romagna a light, fresh white.

OTHER NORTHERN REGIONS

Still in northern Italy are many smaller regions producing fine wines. In the north-west corner of the country is Valle d'Aosta with only two DOC wines. Slightly larger is Friuli-Venezia Guilia with six DOCs, the Colli Orientali del Friuli blending as many as twelve different grape types. Liguria, a narrow strip along the Italian Riviera produces three DOCs including Cinqueterre.

In the very centre of the country is Umbria, best known for the great white wines of Orvieto. Orvieto is made both dry (a flinty, crisp, wine) and semi-sweet or *abbocato*, and it is the latter version, sweetish but delicate and clean tasting, that is the better known.

LATIUM

Moving to the southern half of the country and on the west coast in the hills surrounding Rome are made numerous wines called generically Castelli Romani, from the Roman castles. Colli Albani and Colli Lanuvini are straw-coloured, fruity whites that should be drunk young. The most famous of the Castelli Romani wines is Frascati, in both *secco* and *abbocato* styles. Both are strong and fragrant, with a pronounced flavour of grapeskins.

The other important wine of Latium is the romantically named Est!Est!Est!, a dry, light, white with a bitter finish. One Canadian wine writer feels that its name is the only remarkable thing about it. A certain German bishop Johann Fugger, on his way to Rome in 1110 for the coronation of the Emperor Henry V, sent his majordomo Martin ahead of him to write on the door of

Main white grape varieties of Italy

Moscato
Riesling
Pinot Bianco
Trebbiano
Malvasia
Greco di Torre
Verdello

Main red grape varieties of Italy

Nebbiolo
Barbera
Grignolino
Freisa
Pinot Nero
Lambrusco
Sangiovese
Aleatico
Brachetto

Other red grape varieties of Italy
Dolcetto
Cabernet
Merlot
Teroldego
Canaiolo
Montepulciano
Aglianico
Connonau
Corvina
Rondinella
Negrara
Rossignola
Schiava
Bonarda
Brugnola
Sassella
Pignolo
Toscano
Forcellina
Pindarella
Negara

Other white grape varieties of Italy
Prosecco
Tocai
Gewürztraminer
Verduzzo
Albana
Verdicchio
Torbato
Fiano
Procanico
Garganea
Biancame

any inn where the wine was good the word "Est!" ([Here] it is!). On arriving in Montefiascone, a small hilltop town overlooking Lake Bolsena, 60 miles north of Rome, Martin, overcome with enthusiasm, wrote on the tavern door "Est!Est!Est!" Whether the good bishop went on to the coronation or remained to drink, we do not know. What is certain is that his tomb in the church of San Flaviano in Montefiascone bears an inscription by his good servant Martin; "On account of too much Est!Est!Est! my master Johann Fugger died here."

MARCHES

This area on the Adriatic coast produces Italy's best white wine, Verdicchio. A dry but full, straw-coloured wine, it comes in an elegant amphora-shaped bottle. The best known one is from Castelli di Iesi: another comes from Matelica. Two good red wines from the same area are Rosso Conero, dry and robust, and Rosso Piceno, a softer ruby-coloured wine.

OTHER SOUTHERN REGIONS

There are another seven wine producing areas in the south of Italy but very few of their wines reach us in Canada. Ambrusio-Molise produces only two wines, a Montepulciano and a Trebbiano.

Campania on the west coast exports reds and whites from the island of Ischia, but the best known wine of the area is Lacryma Christi grown on the slopes of Mount Vesuvius. It is a medium dry white wine which can sometimes be excellent, dry and delicate with a hint of floweriness. The sweet, red, rosé and sparkling wines of the same name are all very ordinary.

Apulia, the area from the lock to the heel of Italy, is one of the largest wine producing regions. Once known mainly for its strong wines used in blending, with modern techniques it is now producing some very drinkable wines.

Basilicata, above Italy's instep, produces several local wines from the Aglianico grape unique to the area, and their one D.O.C., the Aglianico del Vulture. Calabria in the toe of the peninsula has been making wine since the days of the ancient Greeks.

The islands of Sicily and Sardinia also produce wines. The best known to us is the Marsala of Sicily, a sweet, fortified dessert wine not unlike Madeira or *amoroso* sherry. It does not deteriorate after opening, and makes a delicious dessert, zabaglione.

A New Respect for Chianti

by Kenneth Christie, M. W.

In the savage mountains of Tuscany, between the old world cities of Florence and Siena, lies the region of Chianti Classico producing wines of noteworthy quality. We used to see Chianti in its traditional raffia covered bottle that often implied an image of lower grade wines. Research some years ago by the consortium of producers revealed the startling statistic from an international sample, that an overwhelming number of wine drinkers identify the simple shape of the Bordeaux bottle with wine of high quality and prestige. What then more appropriate for the Consorzio Vino Chianti Classico than to adopt the bottle that has helped to raise the reputation of claret to the highest level.

What and who is the Consorzio Vino Chianti Classico? It is an association of growers both large and small, founded in 1924. The date of its foundation is some ten years prior to the introduction of the Appellation Contrôlée regulations in France, and this fact alone causes surprise to the Florentines who have for so long rigidly controlled their production. There are over 700 members of the Consorzio, including three co-operatives, but it is with those members who bring their production from grape to bottle, caring and nurturing their wines through the many stages of their development, the most interest lies.

If one factor alone demands attention, it is that almost every producer uses his own system to produce his final bottled wine. Traditionally Chianti is a wine of long maturation in cask, and touring the wineries one sometimes comes face to face with vast chestnut casks of wine which have remained in graceful solitude for over a decade. Unfortunately for growers who feel

CENTRAL ITALY
Pisa
Florence
CHIANTI
TUSCANY
MARCHES
Perugia
UMBRIA
LAZIO
Rome
ABRUZZI
Rome

that such long experience of the wood is essential to quality, the practice is now changing, and two years in cask has become the more usually accepted period.

Surely nothing is sadder than a vat of once fine red wine that has lain overlong in wood, with the consequent build up of aldehydes and acetaldehydes until the product is fit (in my opinion) only for the drain. Yet, if I can say that such cases are now fortunately rare, they nevertheless exist.

I had been invited to the region by the Consortium of Chianti Classico, and soon learned to look forward to seeing the black rooster which adorns the neck of every bottle of wine approved by test and taste in the Laboratory of the Consorzio. No wonder they say "Something to crow about!"

Tuscan farming is based upon the family unit, and in ancient times the landowners granted to each family a "poderi" - the amount of land a family could tend and cultivate. The landlord received from each poderi a proportion of the yield, which was taken into his home farm, known as a "fattoria." These ancient terms are still to be found on the labels of Chianti Classico although most of the tenant farms are now run by the landowners.

One of my hosts in the region was the genial and urbane Lapo Mazzei, whose family have owned, farmed and lived in the Castello di Fonterutoli since 1435, half a century before the intrepid Columbus discovered the New World. Perhaps if the softly spoken Lapo Mazzei feels that he has no pressing need to find fresh fields to conquer, his wine must of a certainty be an ambassador of considerable talent and penetration. By the normal standards of the region, Fonterutoli is a large estate with 130 acres of vines, producing about 220 gallons of wine per acre, which is but two-thirds of that permitted in the great wine producing villages of Burgundy.

The culture of grapes in Italy has, of necessity, taken its place alongside the raising of other crops. Thus it is commonplace to see vines sharing their vineyard with rows of maize, each vine clambering up olive or peach tree. Such vineyards may have been desirable when transportation of foodstuffs posed difficulties but these traditional, known as *promiscuo*, vineyards are now giving way to more specialized methods. However Fonterutoli is still at the crossroads between one method and the other and I felt sure that the quality of tradition was reflected in the excellence of Lapo Mazzei's wine. Passing days in the sun are normally cause enough to allow the daily workload to diminish, but when to the sunshine is added the richness and the generosity of the Tuscan cuisine, alongside the constantly replenished bottles of fine red Chianti, something has to give way - I suspect it was not my wish to continue to study the region, but my waistline!

At the Fattoria of Villa Cafaggio an ex-patriate Hungarian, Stefano Farkas has introduced modern viticultural practice, but this required the use of explosives to dislodge boulders which had been partly buried in the vineyards for centuries. This remarkable labour has resulted in the production of grapes of enviable quality. Although the sunshine is, in most years, ever present, spraying against disease is a constant chore, but in spite of the mountainous terrain, helicopters are being used more regularly to undertake this back-breaking task which is otherwise a tedious manual operation. To my surprise I learnt that the grapes are not ready for harvesting until mid-October, a full month later than is common in France and Germany, situated so much further north than Tuscany. If Cafaggio is set in idyllic surroundings, it's location several miles from the nearest metalled road perfectly exemplifies the communication difficulties of the region, which has remained relatively unchanged through centuries.

Chianti is the only red wine that I know well that is made of both black and white grapes, though with the new DOCG regulations the white grape content will drop considerably. But if such a blending operation lessened the intensity of colour, the growers discovered a perfect solution by adding a small proportion of almost pure black pigmented grapes to restore a rich garnet-ruby colour.

During a second stage of production, a unique process is introduced, through the addition of a sizeable proportion of selected bunches of dried-up grapes, which having been picked at the exact moment of their optimum ripeness and are hung in barns to dry. The effect of the late addition of these grapes is to heighten the alcoholic content of the finished wines, which is rarely below 12.5% alcohol and frequently reaches even higher levels.

There are so many wines of undeniable excellence in the Consorzio of Chianti Classico that I hold as great an enthusiasm for the region as any other wine producing area I have ever visited. Here is all the variety which distinguishes Burgundy, here too, the pride in property which has made the name of so many of the châteaux of Bordeaux world renowned. The difference is that whilst the French producers of Burgundy and Bordeaux have a well developed system of distribution, that of Chianti is embryonic. It cannot remain thus, and I shall (as I pledged when enrolled into the 700 year old "League of Chianti") do my best to carry the good word abroad. If the Consorzio feel that their black cockerel has something to crow about - they are right!

Germany

Main White Grape Varieties of Germany
Müller-Thurgau
Riesling
Scheurebe
Sylvaner
Traminer

The vineyards of Germany, which occupy only a small area of that great country, are the most northerly in Europe and represent less than two per cent of all European vineyards. Nevertheless, they produce more fine wine in relation to their size than does anywhere in the world, and the best wines of the Rhine and the Mosel are generally considered to be the equals of the great French Sauternes. The prime characteristics of good German white wines (there is little red wine made, all of it undistinguished) are a light, delicate taste and an astoundingly perfumed nose, like the scent of spring flowers. On the whole, fine German wines are best drunk, not with food, but by themselves as the Germans drink them, for apéritifs or evening drinking, and always chilled. Their relatively low alcoholic content and refreshingly light taste make them ideal for parties.

Despite their elegance and high quality, it is unfortunately the case that the wines of Germany are often relatively unknown and unappreciated in North America, even by those to whom the wines of France are an open book. The reasons for this neglect may have much to do with the apparent or real complexity of the names and labels. The 1971 German wine laws were designed to give the consumer better quality, more and clearer information, and greater security.

The laws seek to define labelling, control the harvesting and vinification, delimit accredited regions, establish minimum mustweights and serve the consumer by demanding a system of chemical analysis and organoleptic evaluation.

Three basic categories of wine were defined: *Tafelwein, Qualitätswein bestimmter Anbaugebiete* (*QbA*), *and Qualitätswein mit Prädikat* (*QmP*).

Tafelwein. This means simply "table wine," and indicates an ordinary quaffing wine of reasonable quality. If prefixed by the word *Deutscher* it is made from 100% German grapes, of any approved variety, from one of the four main growing regions (Rhein and Mosel, Main, Neckar and Oberrhein). If the label reads simply *Tafelwein* it will be a blend of German wine with wine from other Common Market countries, and will probably be marketed under a brand name.

In 1982 various new laws came into force including the introduction of the term *Landwein*, to stand in quality range between the original *Tafelwein* and the *QbA*. The residual sugar must not be higher than 18 grams per liter, making *Landwein* therefore basically *halbtrocken* wines.

QbA wines are quality wines from designated growing regions, a meaning quite close to *Vin delimité de qualité supérieure,* though the controls applied to the wines are far more strict than in France. The wines must come from one of eleven regions (Gebiete). They can only be made from certain grape varieties and from must with a minimum Oechsle concentration of 57°. Oechsle is defined as the number of grams by which one litre of must is heavier than one litre of distilled water. Most of the increased density comes from sugar in the juice, so Oechsle is a simple measurement of potential alcoholic conversion by fermentation. 57° Oechsle will develop a wine of 7° strength.

The QbA districts are Ahr, Mittelrhein, Nahe, Rheingau, Rheinhessen, Rheinpfalz, Mosel-Saar-Ruwer, Franken, Baden, Württemberg and Hessische Bergstrasse. The label must bear, in addition to the designated region, an official test number or Pruf. Nr. To earn this, the wine must pass a series of tests, checks and controls.

First, the Harvest Control. Officials examine the vintage during picking in the vineyard. Second, the Chemical test. One of the officially recognized wine laboratories measures the Oechsle concentration, the acid concentration and other indications of quality. Third, the Organoleptic Evaluation. A panel of tasters judges the wine in terms of clarity, colour, bouquet and flavour and rates it on a standard point system. Upon attaining the necessary number of points, the wine is awarded its A.P. No.

The label shown on this page illustrates a typical QbA wine.

These wines may be "improved" (verbessert) with sugar. Up to 28 grams per litre of sugar may be added to the must, an amount that would increase the alcoholic content by 3.5°.

Now, to cover the third category, the *pièce de résistance*, QmP. These quality wines with special attributes fall into six sub-categories, of ascending quality. The basic QmP Kabinett wine is a superior quality wine that deserves more than instant consumption at the table and is fit for laying away in the wine cabinet. Today, its must has a minimum weight of 75 (or 72 in colder areas such as the Mosel). It may not be chaptalized in any way and must pass stringent chemical and organoleptic test.

Spatlese, one rung up the ladder from Kabinett is a richer wine with minimum must weight of 80, and made from late harvested grape clusters that are over-ripe. Best drunk as dessert or after dinner wines.

Auslese, a refinement of Spatlese, is made by a laborious process in which the grower picks off those berries that will not over-ripen to leave for pressing a selected bunch of sugar laden treasures, frequently in the first stages of attack by *Botrytis.* This process can be contrasted with the *épluchage* of Champagne, where nimble-fingered pickers select out the over-ripe grapes from the bunches after they have been picked lest they tint the must. The German harvester must laboriously separate his two categories into twin baskets he carries slung from his shoulder while he tenaciously clings to the cliff-like vineyards lining his country's valleys.

Beerenauslese, a yet more select category. Here the picker must select over-ripe berries only (not bunches), the must weight should reach approximately 120, compared to Auslese's 90. His two baskets prove their worth in this category.

Trockenbeerenauslese, the top category, is wine made from the best of the selected grapes, which are left on the vine until they are like shrivelled raisins, full of sugar and the "noble rot," the same miraculous mould that attacks the grapes of Sauternes. A must weight of 150 or more, rich with full fruity flavour and the right balance of acid makes this wine a collector's treasure.

Eiswein. This sixth category of QmP wine is not a regularly obtainable class of

wine: it is, rather, a curiosity, an exception. "Ice-wine" is made from grapes in which the juice has been frozen, and concentrated, by the night frost on the vines. They are picked very early in the morning, sometimes as late in the year as December or January, and pressed while they are still frozen. Ice-wine has a very intense flavour. It is made only in the years offering ideal frost conditions and is extremely expensive.

In wines below the QmP category it is possible to chaptalize the must and raise the alcohol potential to the 8 - 10 per cent range that these wines traditionally feature. However, the acid balance can be thrown off, resulting in a wine that may be low in acid and flat. The balance of German wines is all-important, so you can understand the delicate touch that is required to maintain the uniformly high quality we have come to expect.

There are five principal factors that determine the quality of Germany's wines. The grape variety obviously governs the flavour. Traditionally, the noble Riesling and the higher-yielding Sylvaner have dominated. Today, we find many new strains being planted. The Müller-Thurgau, most successful of the Riesling/Sylvaner hybrids, yields about 20 per cent more than the pure Riesling, reacts better to the climatic uncertainity and shows off a bigger bouquet - all, however, at the expense of the style of the resulting wine. Generally speaking, quantity and quality are offsetting factors in a varietal's performance. Several new hybrids are gaining increasing popularity. Dr. Scheu's Scheurebe (Rebe means vine), the Elbling Morio Muscat, Traminer, Schönburger, Würzer, Kerner and Forta are all common.

The second factor is the soil. Just as Beaujolais' granite soil brings the best out of the Gamay grape, so the slate and dark brown calcareous soil of the Mosel and Rhein draw finesse from the Riesling. The geographical disposition of the vineyards is significant. The steep slopes of the majority of vineyards (perhaps you have been lucky enough to marvel at the dizzying outlook from Berkasteler's famous Doktor vineyard) tip the rainfall rapidly into the rivers below. In contrast to the vines of the Midi which reach fifty feet or more into the subterranean moisture that will succour them during a long dry summer, the German vines are shallow rooters, to take advantage of the all too brief dousing they will enjoy during the rainfall.

The climate, third of the quality determinants, is almost hostile to *vitis vinifera*. Danger of early frosts in the autumn and late frosts in the spring encourages only the hardiest of varieties. Relatively low statistical sunshine imposes a further hardship on the ripening of the grapes. Vineyards are carefully positioned on the sun-trap bowls of south facing slopes, with rows of vines planted across the prevailing wind direction to lessen the loss of heat when cool autumn winds whistle through the valleys.

Harvesting control is the fourth factor of importance. The German state control bodies determine and police the days on which the picking of various areas may begin, for each of the types of wine to be produced.

Fifth, the vinification processes affect the type of wine produced and the naming of that wine. This, added to the method of picking (bunches or berries) gives the German an opportunity to offer many differently styled products.

German wines are basically divided into two name-groups, Rhine and Mosel.

RHINE WINES

These wines, often called "hock" in England (the name comes from Hochheim near Mainz, and was popularized by Queen Victoria), come from the vineyards by or near the Rhine river, and its tributaries the Main, the Nahe and the Neckar. They come in tall, narrow sloping-shouldered brown bottles. The four main districts which produce Rhine wine are the Rheingau, Rheinhessen, the Nahe, and the Rheinpfalz, often called Palatinate.

The Rheingau

This small area, only 6,000 acres, ranks as one of the three fabulous wine growing regions of the world, with the Haut Médoc of Bordeaux and the Côte d'Or of Burgundy. Here the stylish, mature and noblest of Riesling wines are made, golden, fragrant and fruity. Some of the most famous names are Johannisberg, Geisenheim, Hallgarten, Rudesheim, Steinberg, Winkel, Marcobrunn and Vollrads.

Rheinhessen

A much larger district than the Rheingau, it produces softer, fuller wines of less distinction, mostly from the Sylvaner grape. Liebfraumilch, the name best known to foreigners, originally came from the town of Worms in this area, but is now a generic name for any blended wine from the Rheinhessen. The two villages of Nierstein and Oppenheim produce good Riesling wines.

The Nahe

Wines from this area are said to combine the characteristics of Rhine and Mosel, both flowery and robust. The best known villages are Kreuznach, Niederhausen and Böckelheim.

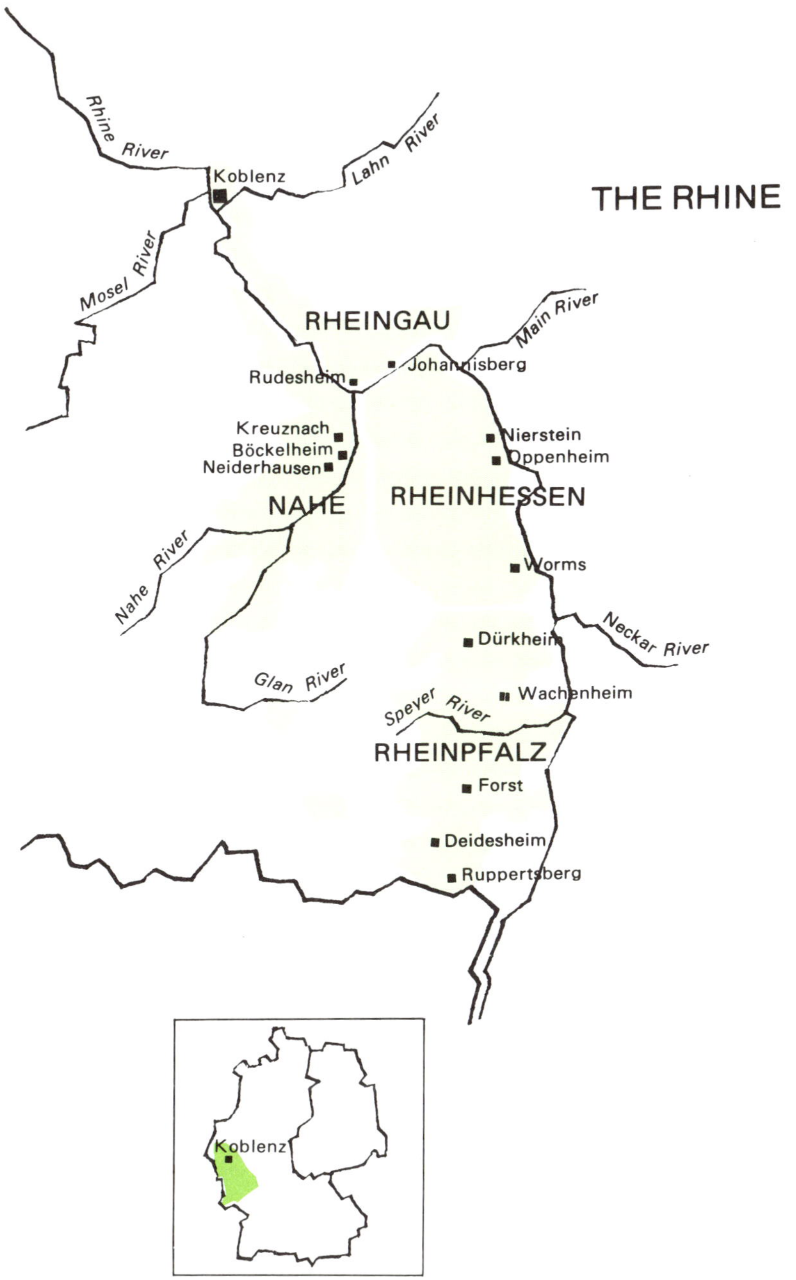

GERMANY
Mosel, Saar, Ruwer

The Rheinpfalz or Palatinate

The biggest wine-producing area in Germany, the Palatinate produces heavier, sweeter wines. The villages of Deidesheim, Dürkheim, Ruppertsberg, Forst, and Wachenheim produce excellent Rieslings, while much Sylvaner is grown elsewhere in the area. Forster Jesuitengarten is a very fine wine.

MOSEL WINES

Along the banks of the river Mosel and its tributaries the Ruwer and the Saar the Riesling grape produces fresh, light-greenish wines of great finesse and bouquet. Mosel wines come in long green bottles. They should be drunk young, within two or three years of the vintage, though some Ausleses of good vintages can last ten years or more.

Mosel

Along the Mosel proper the best and most famous winemaking villages are Piesport, Bernkastel (from which come the wonderful Bernkasteler Doktor wines), Brauneberg, Trittenheim, Graach, Wehlen, Zeltingen and Ürzig. A wine labelled Piesporter Michelsberg, Bernkasteler Braunes or Ürziger Schwarzlay will be a regional blend that, although not from the very best vineyards, will give a fair idea of the taste of good Mosel.

Ruwer

The villages of Eitelsbach, Kasel, Grünhaus and Avelsbach produce fine wine.

Saar

In good years the best wines of this district can surpass any other German wine for elegance and finesse. Scharzhofberg, Wiltingen, Oberemmel, Ockfen and Serrig are the names to look out for.

FRANCONIA

This region, which lies on the banks of the river Main around Würzburg, produces wines which are comparatively dry, less flowery in bouquet but earthier in taste than Rhine or Mosel wines. The wines of Franconia come in flat, oval green flagons of medieval shape called Boxbeutel, and should be drunk no later than two or three years. The most famous of these wines is Steinwein, from the Stein vineyard in Würzburg, and the regional name is Frankenwein. They are made from blends of Riesling, Sylvaner and Traminer grapes.

The Trend to Trocken

by Paul Marks

Germany is still, in the main, a beer drinking country, and if you have had the pleasure of drinking the country's best beer, you can see the logic in their taste. Nevertheless, because of the world-wide interest in health, nouvelle cuisine, jogging and so on, and a change in some aspects of the social lifestyle, Germany has become more of a wine-drinking country. In the past decade there has been more than an indication of a turn to wine with meals and private wine cellars are much more common now in affluent Germany.

The German winemaker then has been expected to fill a new need which he has found to have both advantages and disadvantages. I had occasion to try recently a Klüsserather Bruderschaft, a wine belonging to the new style of "dry" or *Trocken* German wines meant for the dinner table. I might say I found the new taste to be a qualified pleasure, but still something worth repeating, particularly at its reasonable price.

Certainly, the winemaker now has a new market for some acidic wines that in the past would have gone to make Sekt, or have been used for industrial alcohol; on the other side of the coin many great wines are probably wasted. In fact, in certain areas, say the Saar and the Ruwer valleys, in the most sunless years the majority of the wine would have gone to the sparkling wine factory. Then, too, the dry wines surely go against the grain, against the tradition of residual sugar to balance the acid that is almost always there in those northernmost vineyards of Europe that produce fine wines. The residual sugar has to be treated carefully so as to prevent refermentation in the bottle. Filtration, pressure tanks for bottling, centrifuges and sulphuric acid are the high prices that German winemakers and consumers have to pay for their traditional wines.

The most recently developed method for assuring an exact level of sweetness and acid balance has provided a ready-made technique, only slightly modified, for adoption to the needs of dry wines. The *süssreserve* is a batch of unfermented must (what the French would call *mute*), kept separate from the regularly fermented batch. The regular batch is fermented dry (with allowable *verbesserung*, or chaptalization, for Q.b.A. wines if necessary) and the *süssreserve* is then added, to reach whatever level of sweetness is wanted. (Usually, wines made with the *süssreserve* system have to be finely filtered to insure that no yeasts are left in the wine: there is also usually no wood aging in these wines.)

It is obvious that if the *süssreserve* were not added, the winemaker would be left with a fully fermented out dry wine. So all he had to do was add little or none according to the degree of dryness required in a given wine.

There are three categories of the so-called *Trocken* wines, differentiated by their very sugar-acid levels. The dryest (very dry) is called *Trocken-Diabetiker*, meant, obviously, for diabetics and less obviously for those of us who like mouth-puckering, bone dry wines. However, to protect the German government and the winemaker from some kind of malpractice suit, these wines have to carry the statement: *"Für Diabetiker geeignet - Nur nach Befragen des Arztes"* (Meant for diabetics - only after medical consultation). This is to ensure that the German wine drinker does not make the mistake of downing a bottle of *Trockenbeerenauslese* instead. Obviously, the German wine drinker is as likely to make this error as the non-German speaking imbiber. Just as you shouldn't confuse Pouilly-Fumé with Pouilly-Fuissé, on pain of eternal damnation, you should erase any mental connection between a Trocken-Diabetiker - the dryest - with *Trockenbeerenauslese* - the sweetest.

The *Trocken-Diabetiker* wines may have a maximum of four grams of residual sugar per litre, though they can go as low as .05 grams. The German Agricultural Association requires the *Trocken-Diabetiker* to undergo a special analysis for residual sugar and alcohol levels, and to carry the German diabetic wine-label (Deutsches Diabetiker Weinsiegel). Of course, all the dry wines are treated like any other wine, and must pass inspection for the A.P. number on all German wine bottles.

The second category is called simply *Trocken* (dry). This type of wine, most suited for use with meals, may have a maximum of nine grams of residual sugar per litre, but also must have the acid level within two grams below the sugar, for a respectable balance, and so the wine won't taste overly sweet. For example, if a wine had the maximum of nine grams of sugar, it would have to have seven grams of acid. There is no special analysis label needed, but it must have the yellow-gold, octagonal Trocken seal, showing a picture of Bacchus.

The third general category of wines called *trocken* are those labelled as *Halb-trocken* (semi-dry), which must carry a green *Weinsiegel* or label. The maximum allowable sugar level is 18 grams per litre, with the acid level never going further away than ten grams below the sugar's. This category is obviously meant as a kind of cop-out - it is dry without being really dry, and sweetish without being really sweet, meant to appease some of the less extreme purists and give the traditionalists something to drink with their meals. This halfway house, a stepping stone for the German connoisseur, has yet to receive any consistently favourable reviews.

Once a wine gets over 18 grams of residual sugar per litre, the wine is called *Lieblich* (mild). Obviously, there is a great deal of leeway for the winemaker, through the three categories of *trocken* and on into the *Lieblich* style. The normal variables of vintage, soil, region and climate will have an effect on the the control the winemaker attempts to exert. In fact, the variations reach into a kind of grey never-never land, with types that might be called either *Halbtrockenhalblieblich,* or further along the same spectrum, *Echtsüsslieblich* (an explicitly sweet wine, but only barely so.)

It is in fact possible to make a *trocken spätlese* or *auslese* (just as the Californians make late-harvest but fully fermented Zinfandels.) At the far end of the scale there is a 1976 *Hallgartener Schönhell Riesling Spätlese Halbtrocken*, picked at 96° Oechsle, with a botrytis flavour!, and described by American wine writer Frank E. Johnson as having a very unusual cinnamon flavour. Surely this wine, and others with grapes picked at even higher sugar levels (the Oechsle is one more scale for measuring the specific gravity of the grape juice, and thus the sugar level) are experiments, since they could have been made into excellent *Lieblich* wines, at least. However, the *trocken* categories are a real boon to the wineries, since these wines can be sold for considerably less. The marketing experts can push both the affordable prices and at the same time play on the prestige of their names (Schloss Vollrads, von Buhl, Graf von Schonbrun, H. Schmitt Söhne, etc.) and claim the better of their *trockens* as their "gourmet line" of table wines. In fact, the marketing of *trocken* wines has been so successful that a gouge has been made in the sales of the traditionally *Echt* or "sweet" wines.

Strangely enough, the German laws do not fully provide for an easy means of identification of the *trocken* wines; but that shouldn't be too surprising, since there is plenty of mystery built into the 1971 set of laws. Naturally, there is the usual A.P. number in the grade of *Qualitätswein*, but the yellow-gold or green labels of the *dry* and *semi-dry* wines are not absolutely required to be on the bottle. The seal must appear only on the *Diabetiker* wines. What *is* required is that the *trocken* or *halbtrocken* appear somewhere on the label, though there are no rules about word size or placement. It seems not to be a serious matter for the Germans, but you might need a magnifying glass and a kind of label-atlas before you'll find the words on some labels.

The two best values that I have experienced, both from 1977, are a *Johannisberger Ertenbringer Kabinett Riesling Q.b.A. Trocken* by von Mumm, and the *Klüsserather Bruderschaft* by H. Schmitt Söhne, the latter made predominantly from the Müller-Thurgau grape. Both are very good with food,

St. Urban, Patron Saint of Wine

their principle *raison d'être*. I drank both with the same combination: panfried trout and Swiss potato cake (Rösti). The *Bruderschaft* was accompanied by a few simply made scallops as well. I drank a glass of each first without the food, and both showed the basic problem of less than traditional sugar levels. The impression was of a hard, almost tasteless, chrome-steel quality, but with a heavy full body. They were not especially acidic in the sense of the zingy, tart quality of lemon juice, but rather the heavy, metallic acidity that the smell of battery acid leaves with one.

Nevertheless, with food the sugar-acid balance of both wines showed itself to better advantage. Just taste alone shows that neither wine was made toward the lowest end of the *trocken* scale, but each has sufficient sugar to ensure drinkability, a depth of flavour and a nice lingering aftertaste. The colour of both wines was very pale, though clear and clean. The nose was discreet, as they say, but with a nice flowery quality, and only the barest hint of the sugar level. I would recommend both wines for your first attempts at the style.

All this being said and done, it is my personal opinion that though these wines may help offset the tide of French table wines inundating the German market, they are in fact a contradiction, and are not "real" German wines. The essence of wines made so far north is that tightrope act necessary to fight greenness and acidity. Sufficient sugar means sweetness. To ferment most of the sugar out and then approach table wine style by a kind of *sauerreserve* means denying all the virtues of grape, soil, climate and style that are especially German.

Nevertheless, if this new style means more drinkable wines at affordable prices, well then ... Hats off, gentlemen!

Spain

Spain is the third largest producer of wine in Europe, after France and Italy. Most of this wine is red and white still table wine. Only two per cent of the total production is sherry, the most famous and the finest wine of Spain. Until the 1970's writers on wine confined themselves to eulogizing sherry, and more or less ignored other Spanish wines, merely mentioning in passing that they exist. But Spanish table wines finally became respectable and even sought after.

A brief summary of the wine laws of Spain will be in order here. In 1970 the statutes were revised, and a very complete and well organized system resulted. The Instituto Nacional de Denominaciones de Origen granted 30 delimited areas the right to produce D.O. wines, the rough equivalent of the French A.C. wines. Spanish wines come from seven main vine-growing areas, as follows:

Andalucía: Jerez-Xeres-Sherry, Manzanilla-Sanlúcar de Barrameda, Montilla-Moriles, Huelva, Málaga
Alto Ebro: Rioja, Navarra
Calalonia: Panadés, Alella, Tarragona, Priorato, Ampurdán-Costa Brava
Aragón: Cariñena
Galicia: Ribeiro, Valdeorras
Levante: Alicante, Jumilla, Yecla, Almansa, Utiel-Requena, Valencia
La Mancha: Valdepeñas, La Mancha, Manchuela, Mentrida.

SHERRY

It is traditional to begin any discussion of the wines of Spain with an account of sherry. This remarkable wine, one of the world's greatest, takes its name from the ancient city of Jerez, once pronounced Sheh-*ress*, then changed to Heh-*reth.* Sherry, which has been beloved of the English for centuries, is a blended, slightly fortified wine. Several varieties of grapes, of which the most important are the Palomino and Pedro Ximénez, are picked and exposed to the sun for differing lengths of time. They are then pressed and allowed to ferment twice. The fermentation takes place with the must exposed to the air, which permits the formation in some barrels of a yeast called *flor*. Wines attacked by this yeast will develop into *finos*, the very lightest and driest of sherries. Wine from other barrels will become *olorosos.* At the end of this period the wines are marked as belonging to one of three groups, *fino, amontillado* or *oloroso*. A little brandy is added to stabilize the wine, and the casks are moved into the *solera* system.

Main grape varieties used in Sherry
Albillo Castellano
Mantuo Castellano
Moscatel Gordo Blanco
Palomino
Pedro Ximénez
Perruno

This method, which ensures that the sherry maintains a consistency of style year after year, consists of series of barrels containing wines of the same style and quality, with the oldest wines at the bottom. When the blender draws off some of the wine from the *solera*, or final barrel, to be bottled, he replaces it with wine from the next oldest cask, which in turn is replenished from younger barrels. The top barrels are "topped up" with new wine from the *añada,* the wine of the year. No cask ever loses more than half its contents, so older wines are continually blending with and giving their character to younger ones. At the end of the blending process the wines are sweetened (or not) according to their style by the addition of sweet wine made from the Pedro Ximénez grape.

Real sherry can only come from the triangle in southwestern Spain formed by the towns of Jerez de la Frontera, Puerto de Santa Marıa, and Sanlúcar de Barrameda, where the chalky albariza soil gives to the grapes delicacy and distinction. There are four main types of sherry: *fino, Manzanilla, amontillado* and *oloroso. Fino* is the lightest and driest, pale gold in colour. *Manzanilla* is simply a *fino* made in Sanlúcar de Barrameda. It is popularly supposed to have a faintly salty tang, since it matures in sea air. *Amontillado* is a medium dry sherry, fuller and nuttier than a *fino*. *Olorosos* are sweet, rich, dark sherries often known as "cream sherries," best drunk as dessert or postprandial wines. González Byass' *Tío Pepe* is a *fino,* Williams and Humbert's *Dry Sack* is an *amontillado,* Harvey's *Bristol Cream* is an oloroso. And any dry sherry with Sanlúcar de Barrameda on the label is a *manzanilla* whether the label states so or not (it usually doesn't).

SHERRY REGION

OF

JEREZ DE LA FRONTERA

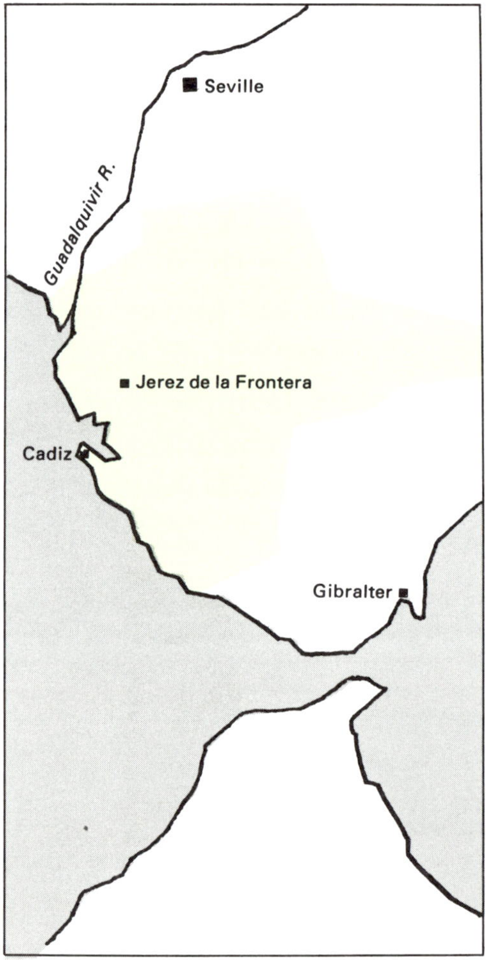

RIOJA

This region of northern Spain, in the old Kingdom of Aragon, takes its name from the little river Oja, a tributary of the Ebro. Before the 1970s these wines were relatively unknown and unappreciated but, since the Bordeaux crisis early in that decade forced wine buyers to look elsewhere for reasonably priced, good quality reds, the Rioja was discovered in earnest. The end result of the world-wide boom in Rioja wines has been considerable investment in the wineries of the area in recent years. Fortunately for the consumer, new vinification plants and processing equipment was not allowed to change the traditional way of making wine.

For the Rioja has a considerable history of winemaking. Documents dating back to the 12th century praise the wines of Rioja. In 1560 the first consortium of wine exporters was formed, and in 1785 Charles III founded the Royal Society of Vintners of the Rioja to maintain high standards. But it was the emigration to the area of Bordeaux vignerons during the phylloxera plague of the 1870's which resulted in the evolution of the rioja. Long vatting (which increases tannin and aging qualities) and long maturing in cask are the typical processes which produce the mellow, smooth, oak-and-vanilla tasting wines that are the pride of Rioja. There are two main types of red rioja, the *claretes*, dry, light bordeaux-style wines bottled in claret-style bottles, and the *tintos*, in burgundy bottles, which are darker, fuller and more alcoholic.

White riojas are less distinguished, as the traditional long barrel aging tends to make them somewhat flat and flabby, and the aromatic vanilla flavour imparted by the oak is not to all tastes. But younger, lighter and fresher white riojas are beginning to be made and exported.

The important thing to bear in mind about rioja wines is that they are almost always blended - equivalents of the châteaux and domaines of France simply do not exist. Wine is blended in bodegas or cooperatives, from grapes or wine produced by many small growers. In addition to this, the vintage years shown on bottles indicate only the year of the oldest, or best, or most preponderant, wine in the blend of several years. For all these reasons it is necessary to know the names of reliable bodegas or cooperatives: each bodega's reputation rests on its ability to blend and mature its wines. The best wines will be labelled *Reserva*, which means that they have been specially selected for additional aging in cask and bottle for a minimum of four years, but usually up to ten.

CATALONIA

As befits that most industrious and independent of Spanish provinces (some would say countries), Catalonia boasts an ever growing and improving wine industry. The centre of it is to be found in the town of Vilafranca del Panadés southwest of Barcelona. This ancient town (spelt Penedes in Catalán) possesses a fine wine museum housed in a 13th century royal palace, and a government sponsored wine college. The Panadés appellation is the most strictly controlled in Spain, and whites bottled under its aegis are always reliable and often remarkable. The foremost vintner of the region is Don Miguel Torres, whose ongoing experiments with new grape varieties and scrupulous methods of vinification have produced some excellent wines.

From the neighbouring town of San Sadurni de Noya comes 85 per cent of all

Main grape varieties used in Spanish whites

Viura
Malvasia
Macabeo
Xarel-lo
Airén
Garnacha Blanca
Parellada
Godello
Verdil
Merseguera
Albillo

Main Grape Varieties used in Spanish reds

Tempranillo
Graciano
Mazuela
Garnacha
Cariñena
Samsó
Mencía
Alicante
Monastrell
Cencibel
Bobal

Spanish sparkling wine, manufactured by the champagne method.

TARRAGONA

The other main wine producing area in Catalonia is Tarragona. This name is synonymous with a certain quality of wine that has become known worldwide, especially among wine traders. For these wines were the very first in modern times to be exported from the small city of Tarragona to the whole globe. Unfortunately this international reputation is only connected with bulk exports in cask, road-tankers and tankships. Huge amounts of wine exported to many countries were lost among unknown, untraceable and uncontrolled blendings. And yet it is an historical fact that it was the pioneering spirit of the people of Tarragona which first opened, in the 17th century, wide markets for Catalan wines.

In 218 B.C. Cneus Scipio, pro-consul of the Roman Empire, installed a small military base in the native village, named Tarakon. The fact that the small village already had excellent stone walls is probably why Scipio chose to remain in Tarraco (the Latin form) for a while. He never left it and from that time the town grew at such a speed that in a very few years, Tarraco was transformed into the principal city of Roman Spain. Finally the highest honour came: the city was entitled to use the word "Imperial" associated with Tarraco.

It was the Romans who taught the Iberian natives how to grow vines on the splendid soil of the hills descending softly to the sea. Very soon full amphoras of Tarragona wines were being shipped and disembarked at the port of Ostia to grace the tables of Rome. This trade became so intense that the Roman senate had to protect by law the interests of the wine-growers of Latium who were complaining of unfair competition from Tarragona wines. Thus the import of wines coming from Imperial Tarraco was prohibited in Imperial Rome.

Tarraco remained nevertheless a very important centre, and a prosperous agriculture had been developed thanks to Roman technical assistance and Iberian labour.

Tarraco was a big city with a rich bourgeoisie and the "Pax Romana" spread its protection over the inhabitants of this tranquil town. Unfortunately, this peace was interrupted quite suddenly. The barbarian invasions from 350 to 400 A.D. destroyed all these riches and with them all the vineyards of the countryside.

The Arab invasions followed and it was not until 1129 that Catalan warriors, descendants of the French aristocracy from the north and coming from the dynasty of the House of Barcelona, expelled the Muslims from the hills of Tarragona. Little by little, the fields were cultivated again. Not all the agriculture workers were Catalan peasants or newly converted Arabs. Among them were the monks who, with the rule of the "ora et labora," (pray and work) brought the vineyards back to their original splendour. Many monasteries like Poblet, Santes Creus and Scala Dei had splendid cellars to age the wines. So wine production began again with the same excellent results.

Phylloxera arrived in 1900 and the vineyards were annihilated. Many years were needed to recover from this disaster and the area returned to a mixed agriculture, growing almonds and nuts as well as vines.

Tarragona wines have recently become better than ever. They combine a unique soil, with the proper wine varieties, and experienced wine growers.

PRIORATO

To someone driving up from Tarragona, the mountains present a seemingly impenetrable snow capped wall. Then, almost magically, the road passes through a cut between two peaks to enter a valley 100 miles long and 30 wide.

This is Priorato - arid though laced with rivers and streams, all of them exotic. Even those travellers who cannot rejoice in the sight of vineyards and olive groves surely will find the scrubby landscape compelling. Hunting for wild boar is said to be excellent.

Priorato's name comes from a priory founded in the mountains by Carthusian monks in the 16th century. Their buildings have been in ruins since the early 1800s, but the vines they planted still survive.

The vineyards are stepped in terraces down to the red-earth valley of the Rio Ciurana. The ground itself is rocky and the slate of its volcanic composition and the vagrant, ticklish mistral, known locally as the "*seré*," combine to induce a rich harvest and a wine strong in alcohol.

Priorato wines are full-bodied and powerful. Some of the common ones come in at anything from 19 per cent to a rather intimidating 24 per cent, and none is ever less than 13.75 per cent. These Olympian heights of alcoholic content are reached naturally without artificial fortification.

The best prioratos are dry and coloured a brilliant, dark red. Not all the reds are table wines: some are "rancio" which means simply that it has been purposely oxydized to create an apéritif wine.

The people of the region, some of whom

CATALONIA

still speak the Catalan tongue, use the word black to describe their wine, and indeed sun is quite unable to penetrate its depths.

The highest wines in the district - physically, at least - come from Conca del Barbera. This area on the southern edge of Priorato, bears the Denominación de Origen in its own right. Its reds are vigorous and its spirited whites release an especially notable bouquet.

Priorato wines are disappearing. The reason is not hard to divine. In the villages which surround the market towns of Falset and Gandesa, almost everyone works among the vines. And almost everyone - over 90 per cent of the region's population -is over the age of 50. The modern Spaniard is not prepared to live in a region remote from civilization where work is physically so demanding. The harsh terrain is not suitable for mechanization. In some places it is so steep that plow mules must be tied to posts to prevent them from tumbling down the hillsides.

So those who can leave do. Even time seems to have passed Priorato by. Many of the villages are throwbacks to the 19th century. Some have houses dating from the 12th century, and a building erected in 1871 is regarded as a recent arrival. Equipment which would be preserved in wine museums elsewhere in the world is still hard at work in Priorato, and the small market for the region's wines makes it a nonpaying proposition to introduce modern production devices.

LA MANCHA

The wines of La Mancha and New Castile are made from a sea of miles and miles of short pruned vines, set three meters apart, with some olive trees for shade from the intense heat of the summer. The soil is reddish with some chalk and slate. It is a land of mud-walled farmhouses, outdoor ovens and Quixotic windmills. It is an area of mainly *vino corriente* wines for cafés in Madrid and blending in France. Much of the wine is also distilled. Long aging is not practiced, for the wine is meant to be drunk young and fresh. There are two La Manchas, alta and baja, the former in Alcabete and Cuenca provinces and the latter surrounding Toledo and Ciudad Real.

Valdapeñas is made in the southern section, about 85 miles from Madrid. There is a town named Valdepeñas, but it is not the centre of the wine trade. This is the country of the rather bizarre looking *pellejos*, the whole pigskin turned inside out and, retaining its original shape, used for shipping wine, and the *tinajas*, enormous Ali-Baba jars for fermentation and aging (these are nothing else than the ancient Roman amphorae). However, more and more casks and glass lined cement fermenting vats are used. The red wine is lighter than most Spanish wine but still of a full ruby colour.

The grapes of La Mancha are mainly Cencibel, Monastrel, Tinto Basto, Garnacha, Bobal, Aragon and Castellana for the reds, and the Arien, Jaen, Pardillo and Cirial for whites. All in all more than half the wine made annually is Valdepeñas. The latter is the most well known wine of the area so that, like Liebfraumilch before 1971, much wine is indiscriminately labelled as Valdepeñas.

THE LESSER DENOMINATIONS

Valdeorras and Ribeiro. These two small old D.O.C. areas produce very characteristic light, fresh white wines with a slight sparkle. There are also some quite sound red wines.

Navarra and Cariñena. The typical wines of this area are big, highly fruity reds with a high (up to 18°) alcoholic content. The best of them resemble Rioja.

The Levante. The Levante is on the east coast, between the ports of Alicante and Valencia, an area of dry, fairly mild winters. The inland part of the region, the alta, contains the D.O. of Cheste and the steeply mountained Utiel-Requena. All of the Levante's wines are simple, meant for quick drinking, more sweet than dry, more of them red than white. The wines are excellent for washing down paella, prawns, fish and game. The Valencia area makes sweet tintos, blancos, claretes and mistelas from the Malvasia, Muscatel, Planta Nova, Garnacha, Merseguera and Bobal grapes. Cheste wines from the Merseguera and Planta nova grapes.

Two newer D.O. wines considered as part of the Levante are Jumilla in the north, making ordinary, somewhat sweet wines from the Monastret grape, and nearby Yecla, a town of blending bodegas.

Andalucía. The sweet wine of Málaga was the favourite drink of Tamberlaine and of Catherine the Great of Russia. It was extremely popular in England under the name "Mountain wine" until the late 19th century. Made in a manner similar to sherry,

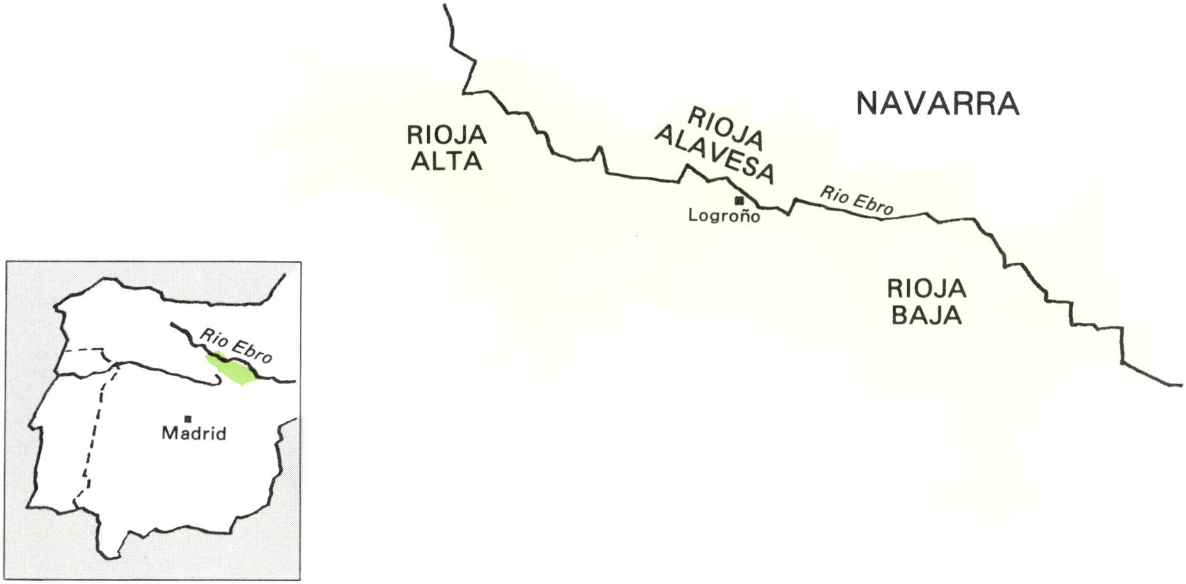

these rich dessert wines are fortified with brandy and given colour and sweetness by the addition of a dark syrup made from pure grape juice. Even "dry" Málaga is as sweet as, say, a tawny port.

The exquisite and elegant wines of Montilla and Moriles are first cousins to *fino* sherry - indeed, the sherry known as *amontillado* was thus called because it resembled the wine of Montilla. Like Sherry, Montilla-Moriles develops *flor,* and the end product, which is not fortified, is a pale, dry wine of between 14° and 17° of alcohol, with great perfume.

Most of the wine produced in the province of Huelva is red *vino común* made for distilling into Spanish brandy, but some of it is sherry-type wine with a *flor*, wines known as *generosos* with an amber colour.

And finally, some mention must be made of the greatest and rarest of all Spanish wines, Vega Sicilia. This remarkable red wine is made in a small bodega reminiscent of a Bordeaux château 40 kilometres from Valladolid in Old Castile. The vineyard's founder learned his trade in Bordeaux towards the end of the 19th century, and brought back with him two of the vines, Burdeos tinto and Burdeos blanco, which are blended with other Spanish varieties to make Vega Sicilia. The grapes are pressed only once and the wine racked once a year and left to mature very slowly in huge oak barrels. It is bottled only after 10 years in the oak, is expensive and very hard to come by, and has been favourably compared with the greatest French wines.

The other areas without D.O. wines include the Basque country along the Pyrenees, which provides cider and a thin local white wine called Chiclas, and Spain's island possessions. The Canaries (the colour is named after the bird, the bird after the islands, and the islands after its canine inhabitants) of course were most famous of their sweet wines, Canary Sack and Palma Sack, but over 100 years ago *Oîdium*, a type of rot, swept over the islands so that the wines are no longer of much importance. The Balearic Islands of Majorca and Benisalem make dark, heavy local red wines.

Impressions of the Rioja

by Kenneth Christie M. W.

My first visit to Rioja was from the south, by way of the valley of the Rio Iregua, a tumbling trout stream flowing through a wind-carved Arizonian landscape. Had a tribe of Apaches ridden through the mesas and buttes to surround my trusted and reliable Jaguar (what else?), who could have been surprised, for this was the era of John Wayne's and Clint Eastwood's greatest triumphs, when the best "cowboy and injun" flicks were made in Spain - genuine braves costing too much even for Hollywood! Thus the approaches to Rioja were immortalised in the celluloid canyons and plains of the Wild West, the hawk-featured Catalans doubling as the followers of Sitting Bull! This is but a description of the landscape which shortly opens into the wider fertile valley of the greatest river of Spain, the Ebro.

The vineyards of Rioja stretch for thirty miles on each side of Logroño, the regional capital, and for between five and ten miles to north and south of the river Ebro - vineyards covering over 100,000 acres (from an all Spanish total of 3.6 million). Of the rest of the area, the banks of the river are devoted to the softest, tenderest most succulent asparagus and strawberries ever tasted, while away from the river the soil is thin and rock strewn, composed from sandstone, chalk and limestone. Higher up the valley sides the gradient becomes steeper, culminating in sheer crags and cliffs. Within the valley one has a distinct impression of being in a small sheltered world, reminiscent of the country immortalized by H.G. Wells in "The Kingdom of the Blind" - but it could not be maintained that the Riojanos are blind to the quality of their wine and the grandeur of their towering landscape.

There are three clearly defined sub-regions within the valley - the Rioja Alta, the Rioja Alavesa, which lies exclusively on the northern bank of the river Ebro, and the Rioja Baja lying downstream from Logroño. One of the most essential factors of this celebrated wine is the difference in the wines between these three areas, that from the Alta and Alavesa districts being several degrees lighter in alcohol than that from the hotter, more arid downstream Rioja Baja.

Wine has been grown in the Rioja since long before the Romans conquered the Hispanic tribe to establish a garrison and settlement at Cenicero - meaning "ash-tray" after the Roman burial ground. In the Middle Ages, Spain was over-run by the Moors, the Rioja becoming known as "Veled Assikia." Happily for the cultivation of the vine the area was one of the first to be reconquered by the Christians who rapidly restored the viticultural tradition of the valley so that the thirst of the conquistadores might be better slaked.

During the 15th and 16th centuries the vineyards expanded relentlessly to the eventual detriment of the quality of the wine. So marked was this decline that in 1785 Charles III decreed that a "Royal Society of the Harvesters of the Rioja" be founded to protect and uphold the viticulture and viniculture of the area. This was to be one of the first vineyards which covered the quality of its produce with a standard similar to that introduced in France in 1935 under the Appellation Contrôlée regulations.

The Royal Society soon realized that the strength of the soundest agricultural economics is based upon the export of produce, and to this end a road was surveyed and built linking the villages of the Rioja to the ports of Leon on the northern coast of Spain. Further advice followed that "the export of your most abundant crops will not become a reality unless the wines (again) acquire the superior quality which they must have." The growers took this advice to heart and many visited Bordeaux and Burgundy to study the most up-to-date techniques.

The disaster of phylloxera struck Bordeaux many years before its scourge reached the Ebro Valley, but the fame of Rioja had already impressed many Bordeaux growers who abandoned their stricken vines and decamped through the Pyrenees to settle in Logroño and Haro. There they introduced the quality producing methods that had brought such prominence to the wines of the Gironde. One of the earliest results of this migration was the adoption of the oakwood barrica (cask) of 225 litres which is today universally used for the maturation of Rioja wines. By the early years of this century the style of Rioja had been standardized as a Bordeaux type wine - light in body, with a pleasant vanilla-like flavour.

The Rioja has a relatively mild climate, sheltered by the hillsides from the more extreme cold, and protected in the summer from the searing sun by moisture from the river. The springs are mild and wet, the summers short and hot - but it is the long warm autumn that seals the quality of the harvest, until picking begins in the middle of October.

The grapes grown in the cooler and more elevated Rioja Alta receive rather less sunshine than those from the Rioja Baja to the east. This less heated climate produces grapes with a lower sugar content, resulting in a more delicate and less alcoholic wine than the coarser, stronger wines of the Rioja Baja.

Taking the Rioja as a whole, the wines of the Rioja Alta and Alavesa are finer than those of the Baja. This is because, as the Ebro flows from west to east, losing altitude, the ratio of sugar to other grape ingredients increases, and it is sugar content that determines final alcoholic strength after fermentation. Wines from the two more western areas average 11 per cent to 11.5 per cent alcohol by volume, while in the east the strength can increase to the vulgarity of 17 per cent alcohol. At its best, Rioja is a magnificent wine by any standards. It is thus somewhat unusual to find a poor glass of Rioja; nevertheless some growers can be singled out for their extremely high quality. Perhaps the best of all the growers are the two Marquises - Riscal and Murrieta. (I once knew the third member of what was a Riojan aristocratic trio, the Marques de Vargas. This remarkable old man, straight as a barrel brush at well past 80, had decided upon his eightieth birthday to learn the English language, and had accomplished his goal by listening to gramophone records each morning whilst shaving.) Now both

Riscal and Murrieta are offered as red, white or even a good dry rosé, but it is more for red wine that Rioja is famous. Among the other ''greats'' of the region must be numbered the bodegas Franco-Españolas, Federico Paternina, Cune, and Bibaínes, whose viña Zaco is a special favourite of mine.

The Rioja varies from Bordeaux and other French vineyards in the manner in which the wines are commercialized. In Bordeaux many growers bottle at the estates. In Rioja the bottling is all in the hands of some 50 bodegas, who oversee the production from the purchase of the grapes to the sale of the bottled wine. Thus the entire economy for the 40 per cent of the total population of Rioja, who are involved in viticulture is in the hands of a diminishing number of bodegas as these are absorbed one by one by Rumasa and their ilk.

As long as the four red grapes of the Rioja, (the Garnacho - Grenache - giving lightness, the Tempranillo with its softness, the Graciano which contributes freshness and aroma, and the Mazuelo which imparts the ''backbone'' with its tannin and colour) continue to be blended, we shall enjoy this overlooked great wine. As with so many facets of Spanish life however, there is a danger of change, for many critics have pointed out that Rioja today is like the Bordeaux of a century ago. I hope change will not come too soon, so that I can continue to enjoy real ''class'' at a price I can still just afford. ¡Salud!

A Homage to Catalonia

by Gillian Gayton

"The Catalans," says the 11th edition of the Encyclopedia Britannica," are a frugal, sharp-witted, and industrious people, having much national pride, and a strong revolutionary spirit. They are distinct in origin from the other inhabitants of Spain, from whom they differ in their dialect and costume. In their great energy and love of enterprise they resemble the Basques."

Most Catalans would take violent exception to at least part of this description. The tongue they speak, for which they have fought hard over the centuries, is no dialect but a language in its own right, forged as were the other romance languages from late Latin. During the medieval period it came to rank among the great languages of western Europe. As the official tongue of the prosperous kingdom of Aragon, it was spoken by the end of the 14th century throughout an empire which comprised not only Aragon and Catalonia but Corsica and Sardinia, Sicily and the kingdom of Naples, and even at one point the duchy of Athens.

The military, maritime and commercial enterprise that carried the Catalan language far over the Mediterranean in the Middle Ages has remained a national characteristic. It is somewhat looked down on by the Castilians, who have always, unfortunately for their prosperity, despised trade. But Spain needs Catalonia much more than Catalonia needs Spain, which is one reason why the central government has tried for cen-

turies to stamp out the language that is such a unifying force among these fiercely independent people.

The vine has grown here since Roman times, Catalonia having been one of the earliest Roman provinces in Spain. Cicero spoke well of the wines of Tarragona and Catalonia, and clearly the Dark Ages did not put a stop to the wide cultivation of the vine, since the ninth century there was already well-established the particular system of land tenure which encouraged the spread of vineyards. The "Rabassa Morta" agreement between landlord and tenant, according to Jan Read, meant that the proprietor leased land to a tenant farmer on condition that the latter planted it with vines and gave a share of the produce back.

In the 19th century several developments took place which amply demonstrate the characteristic Catalan flair for invention and adaptation. They profited initially by the phylloxera plague in France by increasing their wine exports substantially, quadrupling them between 1876 and 1882. When the phylloxera began to invade their own vineyards, they were prompt to import immune American root stocks, and so they saved their acres under vine.

It was in 1872 that Don José Raventós, whose family firm of Codorniú had been making wine in the Panadés region since the 16th century, initiated the manufacture of sparkling wines made by the true champagne method. He brought to San Sadurni de Noya a French *chef de cave* from Charlemagne, and built the enormous underground cellars where the wine must lie for a least three years. Since that time Codorniú have become the world's greatest producers of sparkling wine made by the *méthode champenoise*, filling over 38 million bottles a year.

Three years earlier, in 1869, Don Jaime Torres returned from America, where he had sailed as a 16 year old cabin boy to make his fortune. He did, and when he got back he began to build up the 200 year old family vineyards into a wine making firm that is now one of the most respected in the world.

But wine making, like forestry, is a long apprenticeship.

Choosing the right grape varieties, finding the ideal location to plant them, waiting until they are producing well, and then discovering by trial and error the best techniques of vinification, such processes take time and patience, and the sort of attitude which thinks in terms of building for the future, not for immediate profit.

Which may be why the results of all this marvellous and typical 19th century experimentation and ingenuity took so long to be recognized in the big wide world outside Catalonia. Miguel Torres, managing director of the firm, is a French-trained oenologist with the true 19th century pioneering spirit. (He also from his photographs looks just like the late great Manolete, prince of bullfighters, but that's beside the point.) In the hills around Vilafranca del Panadés behind the Costa Brava he has been experimenting with noble grape varieties - Cabernet Sauvignon, Pinot Noir, Gewürztraminer, Chardonnay, Sauvignon Blanc and Riesling - as well as the native grape types.

Add to this the typically Catalan mixture of meticulous - ness and inventiveness in the vinification, and you get a series of wines which for quality and value cannot be beaten anywhere in the world. The prize-winning Gran Coronas, is 70 per cent Cabernet Sauvignon. The Gran Vino Don Miguel Torres, contains 45 per cent Cabernet Sauvignon and is a truly elegant wine of claret-like complexity and finish. Aged for 20 months in oak, it has great depth and flavour.

Almost as impressive are the wines made from purely native grapes, such as the Coronas, a blend of U11 de Llebre and Monastrell aged six months in new oak and six in second year casks. A delicately fruity wine with the bouquet of wild strawberries, it has a rich but gentle taste and a silky texture.

More aggressive, and perhaps more recognizably Spanish (hence no doubt the tiny fighting bull mascot dangling from the capsule) is the Sangre de Toro, made from Cariñena and Garnacha grapes. (These are respectively the Carignan and Grenache of southern France.) This is a big wine, full of power and spice, and showing more than a hint of its 18 months in American oak.

The white Viña Sol, a young fresh wine made from the Perellada grape, was one of the first Spanish wines to give the lie to the old truism that Spanish whites were always flabby or oxidized. Careful, slightly early, harvesting and cold fermentation ensure that every vintage has good fruit and acid balance.

The denominated area of the Panadés, is the centre of the sparkling wine industry, centred round the town of San Sadurni de Noya. Codorniú, the first of these wines, has already been mentioned. The Spanish have been drinking it with enthusiasm for years and, only 12 per cent of the enormous output gets exported. In lightness, freshness and persistent bubble the two sorts of Codorniú, the Corday (brut) and the Cremant (sec), are in no way inferior to Loire sparklers, though some connoisseurs find the bouquet a touch earthy.

Other firms within the controlled denomination of Panadés make admirable sparkling wine by the champagne method, notably Freixenet. (The word *cava* on Spanish labels denotes *méthode champenoise.*) In the D.O.C. Ampurdán-Costa Brava the district of Perelada produces good sparkling wine by the *cuve close* method, as well as red, white and rosé wines. And still within the Panadés the old-established firms of the Marqués de Monistrol and of René Barbier make balanced inexpensive red wine much preferable to many similarly priced products from France.

As champagne soars to an impossible price and even the mediocre vintages of Bordeaux are retailing at higher and higher prices, let us turn gracefully to the sparklers of San Sadurni and the serious (in the French sense) red wines of Vilafranca del Panadés, and thank heaven for those "frugal, sharp-witted and industrious people," the Catalans.

An Andalusian Success Story

by Kenneth Christie M. W.

The spectacle that summed up best the history and glory that is the sherry country was played out for me in the small township of Puerto de Santa Maria. I was the guest of the family de Terry, whose fame and celebrity belongs as much to their smokey Spanish brandy, traditionally wrapped in a golden silk stocking, as to their sherry. It was May, too hot for my Anglo-Saxon skin, already painful to the touch. We sat on hard seats in the shade of a stone cloistered arena, while high stepping pedigree Arab stallions were led one by one before our eyes by liveried grooms. If this was a backward glance to earlier more leisured times, I found this wherever I travelled in the sherry country, where it seemed that every one of my hosts walked with heavy limp or stiff leg from the latest fall on the polo ground.

Sherry, the wine of a small corner of Andalucia, has been greatly imitated and much envied for its success. It was the rich, white soil which originally inspired the planting of vines in Southern Spain, a natural wealth that led to many conflicts for the possession of the province, exchanging occupation from Phoenicians to Greeks, Romans, Moors and finally to conquest by the Crusader King Alfonso X in 1264.

The origin of sherry is scantly documented, but it is certain that wine has been made in the fertile triangle bordered by Jerez, Sanlucar de Barrameda, famous for its Manzanilla, and Puerto de Santa Maria for two and a half thousand years. The vineyards cover gently undulating slopes and hillocks, each crowned by a cheerless dwelling, sun-bleached and mean, built during the 19th century as a watch tower; today serving as presshouse, storehouse and home for the vineyard worker.

The predominant feeling in Jerez is dust and industry, in Puerto it is history and the fine horse flesh, in Sanlucar de Barrameda it is primitive - still the land of the absentee landlord, of high walled houses, windowless to the street, whose courtyards resound to the primitive rhythm of the flamenco.

The vine is the Palomino, producing its horde of greenish golden bunches. Amongst other varieties, the Pedro Ximenez yields a smaller harvest of munchingly sweet grapes, ideal for use in the making of sweeter wines. By September the grapes are ripe, and Spaniards who love pomp and splendour and any razzamatazz mark the beginning of the vintage with Fiesta - perhaps this great burst of gaiety is essential to buoy up the hearts of the pickers who bring in the crop. It is frightful work. The vines are not pretty hedge-rows as in Bordeaux but low growing bushes pulled down to the ground by the full and heavy bunches so that their gathering entails constant stooping and cutting. Women receive the grapes, and excluding any rotten fruit, pour them onto round *esparto* grass mats laid out in neat rows in front of the press houses. Now the broiling sun begins to dehydrate the grapes, which are covered by night against the dew.

I visited the press house built by Gonzalez Byass on the outskirts of Jerez. Here I found row upon row of hydraulic presses on two floors. With mounting amazement my calculations of the cost of the equipment alone became lost around the million dollar mark. However the use of modern processing equipment is very much a latter-day introduction, as until recently, payment of labour was considerably cheaper than the purchase of machinery. Formerly the pressing was carried out by foot in wooden troughs, the pressers using special soft leather boots into which rows of round-headed tacks were driven to trap the stalks and pips without crushing them.

As the juice runs from the presses, a violent fermentation

commences which lasts between three and four days, turning the sticky sweet grape 'mosto' into a young wine which continues to work slowly for several months.

A surprise to the first-time visitor to the sherry country is the apparent wealth of cathedrals and vast ecclesiastical buildings which dominate every urban view. Closer examination reveals that these edifices are the wine stores - the ''bodegas'' - which are unique to sherry - a wine needing a constant circulation of air to promote its development. Sherry depends upon oxidation, whereas exposure to air is normally mortal to young wine. At this stage the wine is stacked in seemingly endless rows of casks, one upon another, and left alone to mature.

For many reasons sherries are remarkable wines but for no more than the entirely providential manner in which they develop their various characters during early maturation. The wines produced, although from the same vineyard - even the same pressing, range from the light and elegant ''fins'' to the duller and coarser ''dos raya.'' The style into which each barrel of wines develops determines its future use, and during this period every butt must be regularly tasted and assessed.

Once the wine has attained its final character, it enters a further process, unique to sherry. This is the ''solera'' system; a method of fractional blending by the drawing of a few gallons from each butt of old wine and its replacement by younger wine, thus in each butt of wine ready for bottling is a blend containing a little wine from many vintages. The youngest wine taken into the solera system may be only nine months old, whilst the fuller bodied Amontillados use butts which have been in the bodegas for many years.

Today the brands of many of the sherry shippers are household names, but there can be no doubt that it is the uniformity of the wines blended in the solera system that has permitted brand development and has engendered the widespread appreciation of this remarkable wine. Sherry exports have grown by more than 100 per cent during the past decade - more than half the total going to the United Kingdom - and growth continues without any sign of curtailment. This causes no surprise to the Jereganos, who continue with manifold satisfaction in the long-established traditions which result in a product of constantly high quality.

Portugal

PORT

Until a decade or so ago, the name Portugal suggested only one wine to English-speaking people - port. Called after the city of Oporto, where the wine used to be aged in cask and whence it is still shipped abroad, port is a sweet, red fortified wine which originated in the 18th century. At that time shippers began to add brandy to the red wine they exported to England, in order to stabilize it for the long sea journey. Gradually a new sort of wine evolved, which has been popular with the English for two centuries, although nowadays France imports twice as much port as England.

Real port (called 'porto' by the Portuguese authorities in order to distinguish it from foreign imitation 'port') must be made in a strictly delimited area in the hills around the river Douro, and aged in the 'lodges' or low warehouses of Vila Nova de Gaia, opposite Oporto. The port-making process is unique. After three or four days of fermenting, the dark red must or grape juice, still full of unconverted grape sugar, is mixed with pure Portuguese grape brandy, which stops the fermentation process. The spring after the harvest, the new port is transferred to the lodges at Vila Nova where it is aged in wood 'pipes' or casks, each holding 116 gallons, for several years.

Port comes in several guises. *Ruby port* is a blend of young wines, a rich red in colour and fruity in taste. *Tawny port* is made from blended older wines that have matured longer in cask. It is lighter in colour and drier in taste than ruby. Genuine old *tawny port* is expensive, but tawny port can also be made from a blend of red and white wines. *Vintage port* is a wine made from a blend of one particular crop that has been declared a "vintage" year by the makers. It ages in bottle, reaches its maturity at not less than 15 years and can maintain its peak for 40 or 50 years.

TABLE WINES

There are many wines in Portugal well worth knowing that do not have a Denominacao do Origem (D.O.C.). Some are upgrading their quality for eventual appellations, while others are already more successful than any appellation could have made them. The most famous wines from Portugal (...we port lovers must be honest ...), if not the most famous wines in the world, and surely the most commercially successful, are those carbonated rosés from the edge of the Douro region. Of these, Mateus, Lancers and Faisca are the best sellers. In fact, according to the Portuguese Government Trade Office, the single most popular wine in the world is a Portuguese rosé. Most are sparkling or crackling carbonated pink wines, medium sweet, and both pleasant and refreshing when properly chilled.

The wines of Portugal with the D.O.C. are (aside from port): vinhos verdes, Dao, Colares, Bucelas, Carcevalos, Moscatel de Setubal and Madeira. The wines are award-

Main Grape Varieties of Portugal

Port
Mourisco
Alvarelhao
Bastardo
Tinta Francisca
Touriga

Reds
Touriga do Dao
Tinta Pinheira
Amaral
Ramisco
Preto Mortágua
Barrocal
Vinhao
Espadeiro

Whites
Arinto
Moscatél de Setubal
Dona Branca
Alvarinho
Azal Branco
Dourado

ed the D.O. seal after meeting the requirements of soil, climate, grape type and method of viticulture and vinification, and passing a tasting by a panel. Then the *estagio*, the capsule permit, is awarded.

Red Wines

Wines from the demarcated region of Dao (pronounced 'Downg') are full-bodied, flavourful wines which get even better with age and are one of the most consistent good buys on the market. The red wines of Colares, another demarcated region, are rarely seen abroad, but are reputed to be superb, up to the standard of the best Rhône wines and similar in character. They are made from vines which survived the phylloxera plague, and age well in bottle for up to 20 years.

White Wines

The Minho area of Portugal produces one sort of dry white wine, *vinho verde*, which is unique. The term means 'green wine', that is, young wine, and these wines should be drunk as young as possible. They are made from slightly unripe grapes, and undergo a secondary fermentation in the bottle, which leaves them slighly crackling or *pétillant*. There are also red vinhos verdes, but few of these are yet exported.

The Dao region also produces sound dry white wines with fair body. The white wines of Bucelas just north of Lisbon, are golden, perfumed wines relatively high in alcohol, and should be drunk well chilled. An aromatic dessert wine made from the Muscat grape is Moscatel de Setúbal, which can improve with age up to 25 years. Carcavelos is a wine of fine reputation that is fighting a losing battle against urbanization, particularly since it is made so close to the Lisbon suburbs and the resort of Estoril near the mouth of the Tagus River and the Costa del

Sol. The vineyards are literally being 'swamped' by Estoril. Both a dry and a sweet wine are made, red and white, but the sweet white version is the best.

MADEIRA

The island produces some of the world's greatest dessert wines. Prince Henry the Navigator in the 15th century transplanted the Malmsey vine from Crete to Madeira, and by the 16th century Shakespeare's Falstaff was addicted to the wine of Madeira. In the 18th century, brandy began to be added to Madeira, as with port, to preserve it on voyages. It was discovered that the wine improved after long sea travel in hot climates. This discovery gave rise to the present day system of "storing," whereby the wine, once fortified with brandy, is put into hot cellars or "stoves" and slowly baked for some months. This process gives it a pleasant burned taste. Madeira comes in four styles. The driest is Sercial, good as an apéritif. Next comes Verdelho, and then Bhal and Malmsey which is full, sweet and rich.

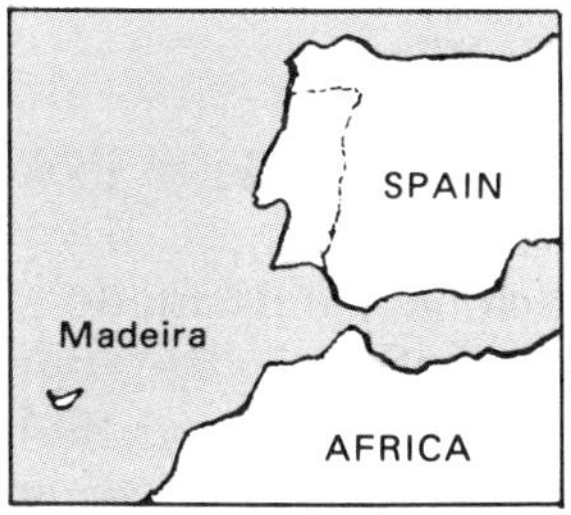

Vintage Port

by Kenneth Christie M. V.

For years students of wine have included in their rationale for the purchase of one bottle of wine in preference to another, the date of the preferred bottle's vintage. However as technological advances in the areas of viticulture and viniculture have gathered momentum, the differences between good and less good vintages have diminished. This has occurred to such a degree that the last really "off" vintage in Bordeaux was probably in 1968, whilst in Burgundy it was even longer ago.

One of the major factors in the claims that vintage differentials have narrowed, must lie with the producer's financial requirement to successfully commercialize and sell the wine of each harvest, rather than rely upon a higher price for better years, offsetting reductions for the less good. This trend towards the building of demand upon the reputation of a wine, or producing area, rather than upon the skill of the merchant who has selected it, is a relatively recent occurrence and is a direct result of the greater awareness of wine by the public at large, not only in Canada, but in all the major domestic and importing wine markets. Whether the trend serves the customer, or contrary wise, actually operates against his best interest is an argument without solution, as it depends upon which side of the market one is situated. Personally, I preferred the system that is passing, when a 'spade' was a 'spade' and a vintage was good, average or plain 'Off'!

In spite of these rather sour thoughts, I have to turn the readers attention to one wine, one special wine, made to look, by comparison with all others, a very particular paragon of virtue. This superb beverage, heady and luscious is only made in those unusual years to produce a vintage of the most exceptional quality. Indeed, so highly do the producers regard their reputations, and so proudly do they offer their unique product, that only in 25 vintages of this century has the wine been considered of sufficiently high quality to be called 'vintage'. The wine is of course, Vintage Port.

In 1979 the shippers, having waited as tradition demands for almost two years from when the grapes were pressed, declared that the wine of 1977 was sufficiently fine to rank amongst those special wines (the last were 1975 and 1970) to be generally regarded as Vintage Port.

What then is Vintage Port that so marks it out as being special, even amongst other port wines?

First of all it is a wine made from one harvest, unblended with wine of other years. The grapes are grown on unbelievably steep terraced hillsides up the River Douro from the Portuguese city of Oporto. After the fermentation has partially taken place, the fermenting juice is measured for its sugar content and when the moment is judged to be perfect with the correct degree of sweetness to alcohol the fermentation is stopped by the addition of grape brandy. Shortly afterwards the young wine is racked into larger barrels (called 'pipes') and taken down the river to Vila Nova de Gaia, the town across the river from the port of Oporto. Although most of the Port Wine companies keep their wine in Vila Nova, a few have storage houses in the vineyard areas, which are as hot and savagely beautiful as a lunar landscape.

Ports made away from Vila Nova have higher acidity levels combined with lower sugar content. They are known to 'Old Port Hands' as "Up the Douro" wines. Whether or not to declare a vintage has never been a question for any controlling authority for the Port Wine Trade, but it is entirely a question for each company (or "House"). Thus in some years of great quality only a few houses 'declare' whereas in others there may be many declarations. The ports of both 1975 and 1977 were of such outstanding quality that most Houses offered their wine as "vintage".

Although Vintage Port is not necessarily the finest red wine in the world, it is unique. It would be pointless to make comparisons with great Burgundies or the finest of red Bordeaux as each is made in an entirely different way. But a glass of this mature wine, with its deep colour an almost tangible quality, is enough to whet the appetite of even the most Philistine wine lover.

For over 150 years the Port Trade has been a peculiarly British tradition - like the Sherry Houses, most of the Portuguese companies were established by ex-patriate Irishmen and Scotsmen in the wake of Wellington's adventures in the Peninsula War. However, there had been a British Colony in Oporto since the beginning of the 17th century. The trade in Vintage Port is one of the most traditional of British customs, an exclusive base rapidly changing for a variety of reasons. On the economic front, wine lovers in countries outside the British Isles have now discovered Port in a big way. It is adored across France and Italy, where served chilled with a lump of ice and a twist of lemon it has become the "snob" apéritif. In Scandinavia, the affluent have developed a penchant for true old tawny ports (these are wines allowed to grow old within the pipes of oakwood; during the aging process their colour changes from deep purple to a garnet-tawny shade), whilst the Americans are taking to Vintage Port for the first time.

Thus after years of overproduction and dwindling demand the pendulum has reversed, and the British must take their place (as must the Newfoundlanders, who have always appreciated this great wine) with buyers from new markets. On the political front, the revolution in Portugal has led to the introduction of a changed approach, which has manifested itself in many ways, not the least important being the requirement imposed for the first time upon the 1975 vintage, that all Vintage Port must be bottled in Portugal. Whilst this regulation was passed off by the leftward leaning government as a control to combat "stretching" or adultery of the wine, in reality the reason is much more mundane and has more to do with the use of Portuguese bottles, cartons and labour, than with quality control.

For two years after the vintage the wine lies on its lees in the lodges of the companies in Vila Nova. During this time it is blended with other wines of the same year, but perhaps from other parts of the Douro Valley. Some shippers fine (settle the sediment with egg whites) the wine, others leave it on its deposit. This is a point decided upon by the individual blender or Master Taster, but after two years, give or take six months, the wine is bottled.

In the old days, this operation was a mystic ritual, and some bottlers rolled the pipes around their cellars to stir up all the deposit so that every bottle would be able to "feed on its lees." Others, having allowed the wine to settle, bottled it carefully before a guttering candle, and only stopped when the wine became so muddy that the flame could no longer be seen. The bottles too were specially treated, having their inside surface roughened by shaking granite chips or copper filings inside them. This drastic measure was to guard against a dreaded condition known as "slippery Crust."

Vintage Port, with all its remarkable fullness of colour, deposits a fine sediment made up of minute particles of pigment and the tiniest crystals of tartaric acidity. Although the particles are small, they are extremely bitter, and should not enter the glass when the wine is poured. Fortunately, as the wine matures, the deposit consolidates and forms a crust, which adheres to the roughened inside of the bottle. By tradition port bottles are made of the darkest amber glass. This is so that during the decades of life to be sustained in the bottles, the light will not affect the intense and vivid colour of the wine. Finally the cork. What a joy it is to feel the quality of a Vintage Port cork. They are made from only the finest material, mechanically cut into a rectangular shape and then rounded off by hand to ensure a perfect finish.

Now all the wine needs is time, a decade or two, perhaps even a World War will pass by before the wine needs drinking, for with Madeira, port is the longest living wine of all. This is not to say that it cannot be drunk a little sooner. The 1960s are now soft and fragrant, the '63s sublime - plenty of stamina, but soft and supple - even the '70s are now drinkable 'tho 'tis a crime to touch them before the age of consent. The '75s are be-

ginning to display their modesty as they mature. This is not to say that the vintage is inadequate, merely that it is not another 1963. Beginning to reach drinkability, they are full and fruity, and certainly more forward than the '70s: they are good but not exceptional.

On the other hand the 1977s will be outstandingly great. Without doubt the best year since '63, and to some experts ranking with the legendary '45s (which, in common with the '77s were all bottled in Oporto). The vintage coincided with Queen Elizabeth's Silver Jubilee - the wines will make appropriate partners to celebrate a golden year, or the beginning of the 21st century.

Yes, you have possibly guessed; I am a Vintage Port lover, and who could blame me, for not only is port a great wine, but it is also a wine for great occasions; at the end of the meal (Oh dear, must the ladies retire to the Drawing Room, it is so much more interesting having them here?) when the port - decanted with love and care an hour or two before the guests arrived - is passed around the table, always from right to left. Now the wine stands alone, not like a mere First Growth Red Bordeaux, purely used to wash down the meat and veg., no this is a wine to savour, discuss, elevate to a pedestal and remember for years to come - ''do you remember, my Dear, that marvellous dinner at the Embassy?'' - ''No my love, I only remember the Vintage Port'' - an unlikely scenario, but hopefully the moral is clear.

How Green was my Wine?

by Paul Marks

When the Portuguese, the Spanish, the Swiss, the Chileans or anyone else call their wines *Vinhos Verdes* (Vinos Verdes) they don't mean that the wines are green ... well, yes they *do* mean that the wines are green, but "green" as in young, inexperienced, new. The *Vinhos Verdes* - and we will use the Portuguese spelling because these wines are in fact a Portuguese speciality - may be practically any colour. Red wines can be green, too. In fact, the greatest percentage by far of Portuguese *Vinhos Verdes* is red, but we seldom if ever see any of those over here.

Only the white *Vinhos Verdes* carry abroad the image of northern Portugal. In Portugal all *Vinhos Verdes* are Denominacáo do Origem, simply because, as Hugh Johnson says, it *is Vinho Verde.* Johnson, however, may be doing the Portuguese a disservice since the wine, despite its simplicity and straightforwardness, is an "honest" wine at its best, perfect for summer thirst quenching.

Portuguese *Vinhos Verdes* are made in the northernmost region of the country, delimited on the north by the border with Spain, the Minho River (also the name of the province), and on the south by the lower section of the River Douro, before it gets to the mountainous region where port is made. In fact, the town Oporto is as much a clearing house for *Vinhos Verdes* as it is for port - probably the two most dissimilar wines in the world!

The Minho province is the most heavily farmed region of Portugal, a fertile country of Van Eyck-like streams and fields. The eucalyptus trees are the biggest things around. Though this is not a land of what in Italy would be called "promiscuous cultivation" (olive trees, etc., alternating and mixed with the vines), the Minho gives a similar impression. The grape vines, Vinháo, Borracal, Espadero and Azal Tinto for the reds, and Azal Blanco, Dourado and Alvarinho for the whites, are trained high on pergolas lined around the perimeters of the farm fields; there are no traditional-looking vineyards for *Vinhos Verdes*. Often the pergolas are supported by an oak or a chestnut tree. The leafy pergola and tree act as a surrogate for stainless steel fermentation tanks and controlled cold fermentation, as the foliage protects the grapes from the very hot sun. The height of cultivation allows little or no reflected heat from the ground nor any residual heat at night. The grapes grow as they might in a considerably cooler climate.

The wines are low in alcohol, about 9°, with an excellent acidity, which makes the character of the wine. But the Minho (and Spain's Galicia province across the border) makes cider as well, so that acidity is a kind of specialty here. As might be expected, then, there is a local strain of natural yeast that causes an especially intense malolactic fermentation (bacterial reduction of malic (apple) acid to the softer lactic acid, which takes place after the alcoholic fermentation.) The wine is bottled while the malolactic fermentation is still active, leaving a minimal but perceptible bubbly effect in the glass.

The white *Vinhos Verdes* can be guzzled endlessly, either for pure refreshment, or if with food, shellfish is a good choice. But don't eat anything too full, as the wine will taste much thinner than it really is. *Vinhos Verdes* go down so easily on a hot summer's day that a bottle each may not be enough.

The Portuguese *Vinhos Verdes* imported into Canada are all made by reputable firms, providing safe bottles, though there can be a significant variation of quality from one bottle to another, even among those drunk in Portugal. The Vinhos do Moncáo firm makes an Alvarinho cepa Velha, a vintage dated wine in a Mosel bottle! When *Vinho Verde* is thus pampered it ceases to be true to itself, and can hardly be called *Vinho Verde*. Most of the wine comes in stubby, bulgy green bottles which are very inconvenient for laying down, if one were so foolish as to want to.

Like the carbonated rosés by Lancers and Mateus, a *Vinho Verde* should appeal to friends who don't really like wine. By that I don't mean that these are not ''good'' wines, but that one need not pretend to any of the taste discriminations attendant on wine mystique, nor do they provide the qualities of those ''fine'' wines that would not appeal to the novice. Please though, drink them the same summer as you buy them.

CALIFORNIA
MENDOCINO
SONOMA
NAPA
San Francisco
ALAMEDA
SANTA CLARA
SANTA CRUZ
SAN JOAQUIN
MONTEREY
SAN LUIS OBISPO
SANTA BARBARA
Los Angeles
San Diego

North America

Fifty states of the union and three Canadian provinces grow some wine grapes, although commercial production is limited to 26 states and two provinces. A surprising 83 per cent of all the wine consumed in North America is domestically produced, the big leader being California which accounts for 70 per cent of the wine drunk. An even greater quantity of domestically produced wine will be consumed in the next decade, as the image of these wines being foxy-flavoured is overcome by new European hybrids and vinifera grapes replacing the labrusca varieties and North American hybrids.

After the repeal of prohibition, the wine industry was reborn and with California leading the way, low cost generic wines were introduced. A generic wine is usually a blend of different grape varieties that is given the name of a well known European winemaking area. (Burgundy, Chablis, Rhine and Sauterne are the most commonly used.) It should be noted that in most cases the flavour of those wines bears no resemblance to the area after which it is named. The demand for quality wine grew inexorably. Although Europeans initially satisfied this demand, it was only a matter a time before the Californians, in particular, imported the noble grape varieties from Europe. Aided by intensive research from the University of California at Davis they developed their own premium wines called varietals which must contain at least 75 per cent of the grape variety named.

The eastern states and Ontario have not been able to commercially produce varietals from vinifera due to the inclement weather. Instead they have successfully introduced the hardy European hybrid varietals. As the production of these wines increases the North American consumer will be able to reach with confidence for a domestic generic or varietal.

UNITED STATES

New York State

Average annual production of wine is 15 million gallons, second only to California's 350 million gallons a year. The weather is the primary limitation in New York, and other eastern states, with the growing season usually ending abruptly with a killing frost in October. Of the non-labrusca grape varieties, it is the European hybrids that flourish and these have been developed in recent years to give a wine of acceptable finesse and flavour, previously only identified with pure vinifera. Particularly successful are sparkling and fortified wines which are produced at very competitive prices.

Most of the best wineries are located in the Finger Lakes region at Hammondsport. The Taylor Wine Co. is one of the largest (it bought Great Western Champagne in 1961.) Best known as the largest seller of sparkling wine in the U.S.A., theTaylor company also produces an Emerald Riesling that is well regarded. Taylor itself was acquired by Joseph Seagram & Sons Inc. in 1983.

Fiercely independent of Taylor wine Company is Walter Taylor, grandson of the founder, who has created Bully Hill Vineyards, which devotes itself to making wine without the help of chaptalization or additives. The grapes grown are French hybrids, the best known being Chelois Noir and Awara Blanc.

Vinifera vineyards in Hammondsport, as the name implies, produce only the vinifera varietals - Cabernet Sauvignon, Gewürztraminer, Chardonnay and Johannisberg Riesling. The wines, produced in small quantities are excellent but difficult to find. Owner Dr. Konstantin Frank formed the company after a falling out and severing of connections with his former partner at Gold Seal Vineyards, Charles Fournier. Gold Seal started in the early sixties with the partners making champagne from French hybrids and more vinifera. Commercial considerations dictated the production of many labrusca-based wines as well and Dr. Frank, the purist, moved on to concentrate on vinifera. Gold Seal still produce Chardonnay and are experimenting with Pinot Noir. Other eastern states with notable commercial production are Ohio, Michigan, Vermont and Massachusetts.

California

California has provided one of the many second homes for the vines of Europe, a particularly hospitable home as regards climate for an enormous variety of vines and wines. The Californian is blessed (burdened, some might say) with approximately 600 varietal labels for table wines. In addition most of them make great quantities of generic wines from a total of about 300,000 acres.

The California winemaker has been more open to change and experiment than most. This brings to mind one immediate difference between the French and California industries: the French tend to keep their technology secretive, but share marketing and pricing practices, while the Californians tend to share their technology openly, and keep marketing practices and sales to themselves.

Along with his willingness to adopt any method that might improve his wine, the California winemaker (and his fellow enthusiasts) has been more than ready to compare his product with those of the traditional wine areas of Europe - in fact, the comparisons are made, in an increasing number of international winetastings, with the greatest of European wines. Most people agree on two points: 1) comparisons are odious and benefit no one, and 2) comparisons are fun. As Maynard A. Amerine, the retired dean of the faculty of Oenology at the Davis campus of the University of California, said "The best wines of France are made in France, and the best wines of California are made in California."

Over the past 30 years or so the University of California has devised a division of vineyards based on temperature study called "degree days." The mean temperature above 10°C is calculated for five day periods during the year. The sum totals of the difference between the mean and 10°C equals the growing season for a particular region. The state has been divided into five regions of degree days:

Region I:	2500 degree days or less
Region II:	2501 - 3000 degree days
Region III:	3001 - 3500 degree days
Region IV:	3501 - 4000 degree days
Region V:	4001 & more degree days

In its aid to wineries, the University recommends the appropriate grapes for each climate area: Chardonnay, Riesling and Pinot Noir for region I; Cabernet Sauvignon, Merlot, Malbec and Petit Verdot for region II; Zinfandel, Barbera, Semillon and Gamay for region III; and the grapes appropriate for dessert wines in the hotter areas.

Though these climate areas are in the main a relationship of north = cool and south/central = hot, in fact there are many micro-climates. The Napa valley, north of San Francisco, though mainly a region II area, has significant sections of region I and III. These micro-climates, especially in the newer vineyards in Monterey County, are being put to better and better use.

A small comparison of a few of California's climate areas with some of Europe's is revealing.

Micro-climate temperatures in "degree days"

California			France
Fresno(Central Valley):	4680•		
Livermore (Alameda County):	3260•		
St. Helena (Napa Valley):	2900•		
San Jose (Santa Clara County):	2590•	•2519	Bordeaux
Sonoma (Sonoma County):	2360•	•2400	Beaune
Aptos (Santa Cruz Mountains):	2110•	•1850	Auxerre
		•1730	Trier
		•1709	Geisenheim

A more traditional method of referring to California's growing regions is by county, several lumped together into larger regions.

North Coast Counties: Napa, Sonoma, Mendocino. These make up the best wine growing regions in the United States. Vines grow in the valley bottoms, on gently rolling hills and increasingly on the steep valley sides.

Napa Valley is the most important with fine vineyards and wineries stretching from Calistoga in the north to the town of Napa in the south. Here the cooling influence of San Franciso Bay inhibits grape development.

Sonoma Valley is separated from Napa by the Mayacamus Mountains. The valley is divided in two distinct sections. The south, around Sonoma, is the original development site. Further north is the more prolific area stretching from Santa Rosa to Cloverdale.

Mendocino starts north of Cloverdale and although the valley floor tends to be too hot for the finest grapes, the cooler mountain slopes are proving to be an emerging area for fine wine.

Central Coast Counties: Alameda, Santa Clara, San Benito, Santa Cruz and Monterey.

Livermore Valley is in Alameda County one hour's drive south of San Francisco and is famous for its Chardonnay and Sauvignon.

In Santa Clara the viticulture was started in 1977 by the Franciscan fathers but urban growth has forced many famous wineries to search for vineyards elsewhere. Much to their surprise they have found that Santa Clara is not necessarily the best location south of the Bay.

San Benito and Monterey. Both these counties, although further south, have cool micro-climates from the influence of the Pacific chanelling cold air through gaps in the mountains. Varietal wines are now being produced which are superior to those of Santa Clara. It is this area that appears to have the greatest potential for growth of premium varietal wines.

Coast Counties: San Luis Obispo, Santa Barbara. Again cool Pacific breezes in the high valleys have resulted in micro-climates which are ideal for the making of fine wine.

The Central and San Joaquin Valleys:with irrigation this area is the most fertile region of California. Grapes flourish with minimal maintenance and can be machine picked producing hundreds of millions of gallons of generic jug wines and dessert wines, and under highly controlled temperature conditions, some varietals. The vineyards east of Los Angeles concentrate on the sweet wine market.

The huge wineries such as Gallo and Lamont are continually experimenting with early picking and cool fermentation to heighten the acidity in the wine and lower the alcohol by volume. Their successes can be measured by the ever increasing sales they are having throughout the world.

Labelling:

Below are the important terms for understanding of the information on the label of a bottle of California wine.

1. The name of the winery, of course!
2. Vintage. If the wine is dated, California law stipulates that all the grapes must be of that year.
3. Origin. 100% of any wine made in California must be made from grapes grown in the state. If a specific area name is used, i.e. Napa, 75% of the grapes must be from that area. The better wineries use 100%.
4. A wine labelled as a varietal must have at least 75% of that grape, and the aroma and taste of that grape dominant. Again, the better wineries use as much as 100%, though this of itself is no guarantee of quality.
5. By California law, white table wines must be between 10° and 14° alcohol, and reds from 10.5° to 14°. Wines over 14° are considered dessert wines. Anything less must be called ''light'', e.g. Light Chablis.
6. The term, ''Bottled by...'' or ''Cellared and Bottled by...'' only means bottled by the winery. The term, ''Made and Bottled by..'' by custom and not law means that anywhere from 10% to 50% of the wine was fermented by the winery. ''Produced and Bottled by..'' or ''Produced and Finished by..'' means that at least 51% or more of the wine was fermented and finished by the winery.
7. Grown, produced and bottled by should mean that the wine is made entirely from grapes ''owned and controlled by the wine maker, in the vicinity of the winery...'' Since wineries have expanded to large holdings in widely separated areas, this term and the ones above are harder to define.
8. Several wineries label their bottles with cask number and specific vineyard - in California called a ranch. As yet these have no legal force.
9. Sparkling wine, called California Champagne (California refuses to bow to French demands, and continues to consider the word Champagne as a generic term) is made in every area of California, by the *méthode champenoise*, the charmat process, and carbonation, ranging from a very sweet *Moscato Spumante* to Hans Kornell's *Sehr Trocken*, a bone-dry *natur.* The terms to look for are:

Fermented
...in *this* bottle = méthode champenoise
...in *the* bottle = charmat process.

California is one of the important wine making areas of the world, and its potential for the future augers well for the wine lover.

CANADA

Ontario

Good wine can only come from good grapes produced in an area where several special climatic and soil conditions interact in their favour.

Like some of the great growing areas of France and Germany, the Niagara Peninsula is a bit of a geographic freak: a hilly pocket of fertile land temperately between Lakes Ontario and Erie and blessed with the wind block of the Niagara Escarpment. The soil combination of gravel, sand and clay, glacial deposits from the Lake Ontario side, could hardly be better.

So ends the good news. Constantly threatening the consistency of the Niagara grape crop are heavy September rainfalls and occasional severe winters; both spell disaster.

Niagara produces 45 different grape varieties on 24,000 acres (now 12,500 hectares) of prime vineyard land and that - save for two tiny grape growing areas in the southwest of the province near London and Blenheim and new research undertakings in Kent and Essex counties accounts for the wines of Ontario.

The wide variety of Niagara's grapes is a tribute to an industry which is growing, changing and intently trying to gauge the Canadian palate. The quality of the grapes and ultimately the wines has not yet peaked. Yet it's a far cry from the sad state of Ontario wine only a few years ago. The uneducated palate of many consumers helped stall the industry's progress in those days.

Ontario winemaking began back in 1811 when pioneer Johann Schiller first produced a saleable wine from vines he had planted on the banks of the Credit River. From that day to the 1950 s, Ontario wines were produced from those first labrusca grapes, a curse that world wine-watchers thought we would never shake off. The labrusca grape makes a great jam and a lousy table wine. For too long wine producers tried to believe otherwise.

Like a child going from pablum to real food, the Canadian palate in the last couple of decades expressed its distaste for the foxy labrusca wines and its craving for smooth European-type table wines, and the grape growers revolution was on. No less than 1000 independent Ontario grape growers began systematically ripping up their traditional labrusca stocks and replanting with classic European vinifera varieties and French hybrids (a cross between the vinifera and a native grape type.)

Today over half of Ontario's wine grapes are either vitis vinifera or hybrids and herein lies the future of this province's wine, indeed the country's.

White Table Wines

How good are Ontario wines? After a spurt of success in the early '80s, Ontario wines are again battling for market share against the imports. Their most noticeable market penetration has been with white wines, aided by the change in fashion to white table wines as the "in" apéritif in Canada. Over the last decade wines have become the 11.5% alternative to the cocktail or mug of beer.

When Canadian wines establish a good reputation at the world level - and they must if the next few years match the importance of the last few, Ontario white wines ought to be the star of the show.

Generally pale and clear the best of Ontario white wines come from the new varietals like Pinot Chardonnay, Seyval Blanc and Riesling. Of the white vinifera hybrids,

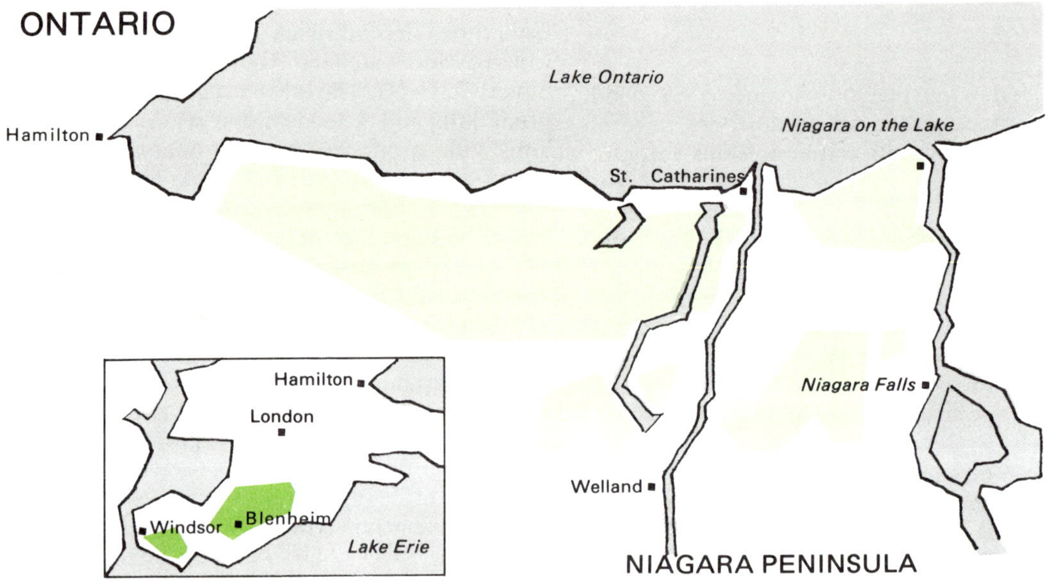

Vidal shows some promise of late, in producing some unique dry white wine. These new varietals which by law must carry at least 75 per cent of the named variety are in short supply and are fairly expensive. It is this area of the province's grape growing that most demands expansion as the replanting continues.

White American hybrids like Dutchess Delaware and New York Muscat are a big part of this replanting. As to varietals, Château des Charmes has been producing an outstanding Chardonnay from its own vineyard. The wine is fresh, perfectly balanced with a very clean finish. Château-Gai wines has recently introduced a Johannisberg Riesling with a good balance of fruit and acid and Inniskillin is showing great progress with its most recent productions from Seyval Blanc.

In the classification of proprietary wines (those specially-named by the producer) there are some fine blends appearing on the market, with more appearing each year. Sometimes a bit on the sweet side of dry, these blended wines are considerably cheaper than the varietals and are aimed at the thirst of the masses.

Volume is not a problem with these brand-name wines and one such blended wine stands out from all the others by sheer numbers alone. The amazing sales success of Château-Gai's Alpenweiss in a head on challenge to medium-priced imports like Black Tower is a boon to the entire Canadian wine industry. Alpenweiss grabbed an unheard of two per cent (100,000 gal.) share of the Ontario white wine sales market in its first year and followed it up with an eight per cent (400,000 gal.) share the next year. Alpenweiss was the right blend at the right price coming out at the right time.

The best of Ontario's white wines should hit their stride in the world market long before any of the reds reach such a plateau, if they ever do. The comparitively cold climate and very high acidity of the white grape is a winning combination known only to areas in northern France and Germany. As a first, Inniskillin in 1981 has shipped 180 cases of its limited edition Chardonnay and Seyval Blanc for sale in Germany. This history-making move means more than any awards Inniskillin may receive and is a giant step for Ontario wines and the recognition the industry seeks.

Red Table Wines

Unlike their white counterparts, Ontario red table wines do not have the ideal conditions that traditionally are associated with the production of great wines. Niagara lacks the intense sunshine and heat units of France and Italy that produce high sugar content in the grapes and an easy natural conversion to the desired alcohol level.

Hence, Ontario red wines must struggle to be good. So far, however, the struggle goes surprisingly well.

In the rush to leave red labrusca grapes like Concord, Catawba, Elvina and Niagara behind, Ontario growers have been replanting with American hybrids (an incestuous breeding of North American grape families) of which the best known are Vincent and Veeport.

Vinifera hybrids (crosses between European vitis vinifera varieties) have produced such outstanding red varietals as Maréchal Foch (an Alsatian hybrid derived from the Gamay grape of Burgundy,) Chelois (red vinifera of France's Loire Valley), Baco Noir (a Bordeaux cross), de Chaunac (named after Adhemar de Chaunac, a patron of Canadian wine) and Villard Noir (a vinifera hybrid from the South of France.)

Maréchal Foch, the red varietal that put Inniskillin on Ontario's wine map is still one of the best reds this province produces. Inniskillin has consistently produced since 1974, a full-bodied "Foch" that is fruity and hearty in the burgundian style. Inniskillin's recent Chelois looks as though it will repeat this success. More acceptable Baco Noir keeps appearing at provincial tastings and though usually still a bit strong, Bright's "Late Vintage" seems to have found the secret of softness. From the same winery, a very fruity blend of de Chaunac, Chelois and Foch grapes produces a good label in Entre-Lacs.

Though many think that Château-Gai's Princière Rouge, a blend based on the Gamay grape is their best red, even better is their Chianno Rosso, a very good house wine that is similar to, and priced better than the Italian imported sales it is aimed at.

A pleasant surprise, from London Winery comes Bellevista de Chaunac, an unusually robust but soft red that recently stood over the others at a Niagara tasting of limited edition Ontario wines.

Champagne

Ontario's champagnes are naturally fermented, artificial carbonation being outlawed. Most bottles of bubbly are made in the traditional *méthode champenoise*, and designated "Brut" (two per cent residual sugar), "Extra Sec" or "Extra Dry" (two to three per cent residual sugar) or simply "Sec" or "Dry" (three to five per cent residual sugar.)

Bright's produced the first Canadian champagne in this traditional bottle fermentation method in 1950 and today their President Champagne, a blend of Dutchess,

Seibel and Delaware grapes, is still Canada's largest selling champagne by a wide margin.

From Bright's, one of Ontario's oldest wineries, to Podamar, one of the newest, champagne has steadily increased in quality over the years. Podamar of Beamsville, in business since only 1973, crush French hybrid grapes from Niagara and use white oak casks to produce some very interesting champagnes, the Brut being above average and their Special Reserve remarkable. Almost all Ontario wineries produce a champagne.

Light Sparkling Wines

Otherwise known as "pop" wine, this gaseous phenomena of the 1960s has endured into the '80s. These wines are light and reasonably priced, most attractive to those who shun the complexity and dryness of table wines. These wines are under seven per cent alcohol and are made from native American or labrusca grape varieties. Andrés Baby Duck would be the best selling example of this type of wine.

Crackling Wines

Similar to their sparkling counterparts, crackling wines differ only in their alcohol content (usually 12 per cent, not less than 10 per cent) and effervescence. The big selling sparkling and crackling wines owe their popularity to their sweetness, informality and price. Crackling rosé seems to be the most popular of the latter. Propagating the "duck" family, Andrés followed their Baby Duck with an equally popular crackling Cold Duck.

Apéritif and Dessert Wines

Once again the Ontario labrusca grape proves its wine-worth in many places outside the category of table wines. From these grapes Ontario produces fortified wines like cream or golden sherries, port, tokay and muscatel. These are sweet, strong wines that have their place; after dinner or with dessert and their measure: one or two at the most.

Ontario's so called "dry" sherries still register about a "4" by the L.C.B.O. sugar code standard and are not dry. The sweet sherries are very much so and are best toned down by ice and lemon. Both dry and sweet are generally between 16 and 20 per cent alcohol and the better ones spend from four to five years in wood.

Ontario's vermouth, the dry containing between two and four per cent residual sugar and the sweet between 13 and 15 per cent residual sugar are usually used as mixes in Martinis or are gussied up with orange or lemon slices in a cocktail glass of crushed ice.

*

Even if you accept the date of 1811 as the beginning of the Ontario wine industry (many would argue that it really began in the 1950s) that still puts us more than 4,000 years behind the Europeans in the production of wine.

Through all the replanting of new and superior grape stock, with all the new and higher standards of production that the industry is adhering to, from all the elaborate and interesting wine tours being offered by Niagara wineries, with all the "limited edition" wines becoming common and the "estate bottled" wines about to appear on the market - one thing comes through clearer than a well chilled Chardonnay: the Ontario industry is immersed in an intensive educational experience in wine.

The student is eager and open minded; the funds are available for research and curriculum.

But is the effort being rewarded with high marks?

When an Ontario winery begins selling wine in Germany, when medals are being won in all the great wine countries of Europe, when time after time an Ontario wine is sneaked into a blind tasting of wines considered far superior and really rates well or wins - then Ontario is learning its lessons very well. If the pattern and patience hold, Ontario's products cannot be denied their rightful place in the world of wine.

British Columbia

The Okanagan Valley is the primary location of British Columbia's wine industry. This region lies in the southern interior of the province, nestled between the Columbia Mountain system to the east and the Coast Mountains to the west. The north-south running valley is the product of glacial action, which long ago gouged out the landscape to a depth up to 4,000 feet below the area's general elevation. A huge trench was created and filled by a post-glacial lake. After the ice retreated the lake shrank and left behind the present day Lake Okanagan and the Okanagan River. Evidence of the earlier lake may still be seen in the terraces of the Okanagan Valley and the light glacial soils.

The southern part of the Okanagan Valley has a long hot growing season of more than 200 days in a typical year. The climate is very dry, for easterly flowing winds which descend the Coast Mountains become warmer and drier as they move downward into the valley, soaking up moisture rather than dropping rain. This is known as the rainshadow or Chinook effect.

Grapes are grown from the Kelowna area, about midway north along Lake Okanagan, to the southern extremity of the valley, just north of the U.S. border. To the north soils are of the light, mountain variety, while in the south they are of shale and sand. Several varieties of grapes can be grown, as there are also micro-climates due to varying elevations of the terraces.

At the present time there are eight commercial wineries in British Columbia, of which six are located in the Okanagan Valley. The most remarkable thing about this industry is its relatively recent emergence and the current burst of activity.

Calona Wines is B.C.'s largest winery. It began in 1931 with the goal of producing wine from apples which normally would be left to rot on the trees. There were two years of struggle before the owners decided to switch to grapes for producing wine. The success of the venture is obvious today in the 3,000 acres of sunny slopes which are devoted to French hybrid and vinifera grape varieties. The company's emphasis is currently on European-style table wines, in keeping with consumer tastes which developed during the 1970s. The trend has been most successful and Calona wines have won over 100 medals of honour in international competition, mostly in Europe, in the last ten years.

Casabello Wines had its beginning in 1966, and completed its first crush even before the winery construction was completed. It too has rapidly expanded, and now holds its place as second largest in the province. All but one of the original seven acres of experimental vineyards have been given up to expansion of the winery and grapes are now obtained from vineyards contracted in several parts of the Okanagan.

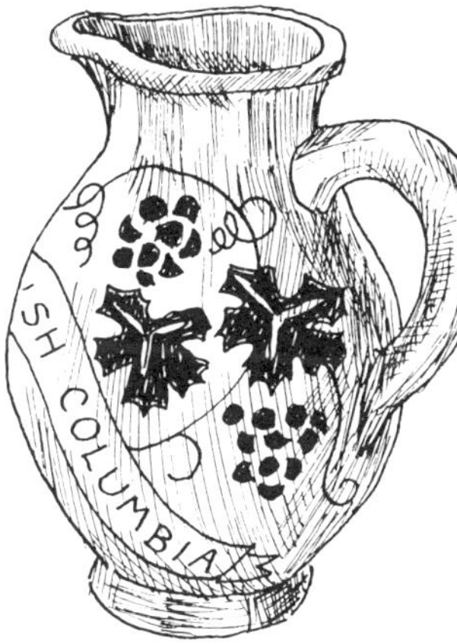

Another facet of the wine industry has emerged in B.C. In 1979 legislation was passed to permit the establishment of "cottage wineries" which are allowed to produce up to 75,000 gallons of wine yearly. B.C. grapes must be used for the wine, and 50 per cent of the crush must come from the winery's own vines. The cottage wineries may sell directly to the public from the winery itself or its wines may be sold through the B.C. Liquor Control Branch's specialty wine stores. They are allowed limited listings at regular liquor board stores and now have added their own shops in several locations. As an added incentive the mark-up on cottage wines sold by the liquor board in its specialty stores is 15 per cent rather than the 46 per cent which is normal for large manufacturers.

The purpose of the legislation was to upgrade domestic wines and compete with imports. That it is succeeding is obvious from the fact that six cottage wineries are now operating successfully.

Claremont Wines was the first and was established in the fall of 1979 in Peachland, B.C. Twenty-two acres of vineyards include Riesling, Rougeon and Foch grapes and have a southern exposure high above Lake Okanagan, where they are favoured by a rocky soil and suitable micro-climate. About 50 per cent of their production is sold right at the winery in a boutique-type operation oriented to the tourist trade.

Greymonk, Uniake and Sumac Ridge are cottate winery names that are becoming quite familiar in the British Columbia wine world.

However the industry is not without its problems. Provincial legislation dictates that the commercial wineries use 80% local grapes in the must by 1986; grapes which are often too acid and too expensive when compared with those of California. Growers and vintners are working together to achieve a quality standard that will make this feasible and hope to reach this objective by the 1986 specification.

Land prices in the Okanagan soared in the 1980 and 1981 development period but have levelled out as the industry matures.

Experts feel that the future is bright provided that the right grapes are grown. Some European grape varieties are not suited to the Okanagan's weather, which can give an overnight transition from winter's cold to summer's heat without benefit of spring. Agriculture Canada scientists are at work in Summerland, B.C. selecting hardy strains that can withstand severe temperatures, produce economic yields, and have good winemaking potential. A government program in Ontario has already created a virus-free collection of vines. There is also the matter of matching varieties and locations, taking into account soils and climate.

While B.C. is a relatively new entrant into the wine industry and lacks the long tradition and expertise of the European industry it has the advantage of new facilities, and an opportunity to utilize scientific knowledge in obtaining the best results from the region. It's progress is being closely watched.

The Many Faces of Zinfandel

by Paul Marks

Which grape variety can produce all of the following types of wine: a claret-style red, a Beaujolais-style red, a rosé, a still and a sparkling white, and a dry or sweet or dessert wine? The answer is Zinfandel, one of the world's most versatile grapes.

For this reason alone it would be a widely planted grape, even if it were not also able to produce wines equalling in quality the "noble varieties," the Cabernet Sauvignon and the Chardonnay. Zinfandel's aging capabilities have long been shown to equal that of the Cabernet Sauvignon, if made in the same manner.

There are still, however, two attitudes toward the Zinfandel among connoisseurs and members of the California wine industry. There is the approach to winemaking in the last decade in which wineries like Ridge Vineyards have treated the Zinfandel as a *cépage noble*, making the wine in a way that demands long periods of aging. Then there are those who hold the view that Zinfandel can only remain an *ordinaire* and can never demand prices beyond those of carafe ("jug") wines. Nevertheless, the best Zinfandels have indeed shown themselves capable of rising to greater heights than many Cabernet Sauvignons of less than the first rank.

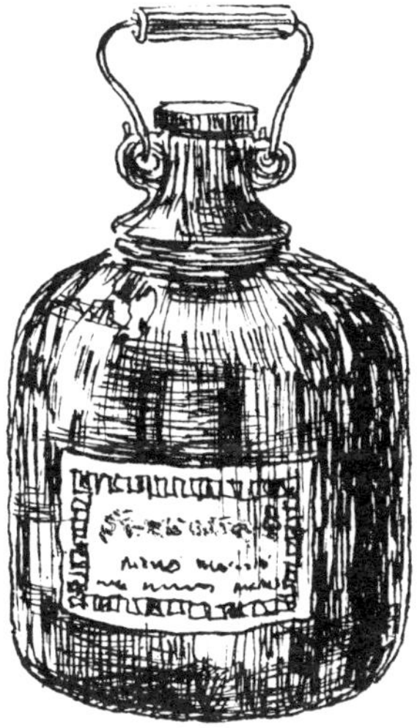

The Zinfandel is an uncommonly flexible grape, as it grows reasonably well in every climate, both in the very hot central valleys and the cool north coast counties, though it produces the best grapes in the moderately cool regions of the Napa and Sonoma counties. The vine bears well and the grapes usually ripen fully, nor do they need any coaxing to begin fermenting. Usually the Zinfandel has more tannin available than the Pinot Noir, but less than the Cabernet Sauvignon or Petite Sirah. The fruit flavour of the Zinfandel is tart, but it is never as astringent as a young Cabernet Sauvignon can be.

Out of this wealth of natural possibilities the California winemakers generally concentrate on five types of Zins (as the Californians call the wine). There is the most traditional style, with a light, fresh, blackberry-like quality. This type is usually the least expensive. One will pay a premium, approaching the price of the better Cabernet Sauvignons, for those Zins made in a heavier, deeper, wood-aged style, coming from the coolest regions. These need moderate to long cellaring.

The so-called "late-harvest" types, high in alcohol (14° to 17°, both with and without residual sugar), have become very popular recently. The Zinfandel breaks the rules by continuing to ripen practically indefinitely if left on the vine; the sugar increases to very high levels, yet the character of the variety never seems to be lost. Because of its long growing life the Zinfandel can in fact give two crops, the "normal" and the late-harvested.

In the mildly hot regions, Amador and Lodi counties (south and southeast of San Francisco) late-harvest types can be made every year, turning into clean, firm wines. Along with the Napa and Sonoma counties, the newer appellations of Monterey and Santa Clara can make Zinfandels in this style that are of fine quality. Though some are made into port-like wines with residual sugar, most late-harvest Zinfandels are table wines. Some recent vintages (1974 and 1975) are so well balanced that one is hardly aware of the higher alcohol (until it is too late). These wines offer exceptional aging possibilities.

Zinfandels can also be made into very good rosés, probably the best in the state, with much of the character of a full red. And, finally, the last of the five major styles is a direct result of the world craze for white wines. Though not much seen (it oxidizes much too easily) there is a Blanc de Noir Zinfandel.

No one knows for sure yet where the Zinfandel grape began. Its ancestry is lost - or it was. Recent and continuing investigations may have discovered its source. The legend was perpetuated until very recently that it was Colonel Agoston Haraszthy, the ''father'' of the modern California wine industry, who brought the wine to California. But there is no Zinfandel in Hungary, Haraszthy's birthplace, nor is there any mention of the vine in any 19th century ampelography.

Some say that the grapes arrived in California as a hot house table grape from England in the 1850s. Leon Adams in his *Wines of America* states that the Zinfandel was ''grown under glass by William Roberts Prince on Long Island, as early as the 1830s.'' Prince himself said that the grape came from Hungary. Nevertheless, 19th century evidence supports neither Prince nor Adams that this was the Zinfandel.

But another hot house variety, the Black St. Peter, arrived in California at about the same time. Early descriptions make it identical to the Zinfandel. There is a good deal of contemporary evidence that the two varieties were planted simultaneously in Santa Clara County; what is lacking is any evidence that the same thing happened in other parts of California.

The most controlled investigations, however, have led to an Italian connection. In 1967 an American plant pathologist discovered in Puglia, Italy, a grape called the Primitivo di Gioia that seemed identical to the Zinfandel. The Primitivo vine is now under study at California's Davis campus in the experimental vineyard, but real proof of the connection will take up to ten more years of research.

What encourages viticultural detectives is that both varieties give two crops, both maturing in the middle and late periods of growth. Even more exciting, though perhaps superficial evidence, is that the the Primitivo is also called the Zingarello!

Despite a generally recognizable character for the Zinfandel (a barrel-aged, fruity, strongly-flavoured, often tart wine) a problem arises as to how to pair bottles with food. In general it can be said that Zinfandels are best with the following food types: hearty meals with sweet spices, acidic dishes and vegetables (yes, indeed!). Among the simpler foods, pasta and pizza can be recommended. Zinfandels can also do well with cloves, curries, paprika, cumin, chili, allspice, and even hotter spices, but of course the fuller style of wine should be chosen.

The best combination of food and wine is obtained, however, with pork with any combination of spices and stuffings, and with tomato based dishes; chicken cacciatore, a tomato-immersed pot roast, and pasta. (Roast beef, plain roast chicken and cheeses seem to exaggerate the acidity of the claret-styled Zinfandels, though blue cheeses have some affinity with them.) Of course these recommendations are quite subjective, but they are based on a fairly wide-ranging acquaintance with Zinfandel.

I give below a list of wineries by region that produce models of the best types of Zinfandel (there are plenty of others.) The "shopping list" includes wines that have been highly praised in the wine press: I have marked with an asterisk those I know and like best.

Napa Valley
(*mainly claret-style Zinfandels*)

Louis M. Martini*
Robert Mondavi*
Sterling Vineyards*
Clos du Val*
Charles Krug
Heitz
Burgess
Château Montelena
Cuvaison
Raymond

Central Valley

E. & J. Gallo*
Guimarra*
Franzia
Setrakian

South of the Bay

M. LaMont
(Bear Mountain Winery)*
Monterey Vineyards*
Ridge Vineyards*
Bonesio
Fortino
Pedrizzetti
Thomas Kruse

Sonoma County
(*spiritual home of the grape*)

Buena Vista*
Sebastiani*
Kenwood*
Joseph Pedroncelli*
Joseph Swan*

Napa - the Promising Land

by Kenneth Christie, M.W.

Where's the most exciting vineyard in the world today? As a European I find it difficult to believe, yet difficult to dispute that it is in California. And if California, with its envied climate and wide agricultural valleys, is of passionate interest to wine lovers, it is in one special blessed valley that the greatest excitement is now generated.

Napa, the narrow valley lying to the northeast of San Francisco, is particularly pretty. In many ways it is similar to Chablis, with its landscape of gentle wooded hills, clear streams and old orchards, but even more delectable to the eye are the vineyards, standing with military precision upon both sides of route 29. Napa town is dreary, a settlement of 90,000 souls quickly passed by and remembered mostly for many petrol (in California, it's ''gas'') stations. If this judgement seems over-hasty, it is perhaps due to the anticipation of reaching the vineyards which lie two or three miles to the north of the town.

Once vines are seen, they tumble into one another, each vineyard with a sign to left or right of the road, and each named vineyard worthy of a detour. A visitor, loving wine, must consider this area as much a pilgrims' way as Chaucer's early travellers. I had heard little of Trefethen, the first vineyard to be approached, but before I could call a halt the car was past and on towards Yountville, distinguished by a special pub with bright gingham check tablecloths and great lunchtime food. (Don't miss the historic Burgundy House Country Inn nearby.)

Yountville is a mere dot on the map, but one in which dreams have been realised and in the passing of a few decades have transmitted their confidence to almost the entire community of the Valley. It was in this village, scarcely more than a crossroads, that George Yount planted the first of the vines that have begun to transform the established reputations of wine across the world. Just a stone's throw away to the east is the Stag's Leap Winery, which in 1976 sent wines to France, where in a great and perchance over-sung triumph they were tasted against and judged superior to the pride of France, the great first growths of Bordeaux. Stag's Leap, with many of its neighbours from the Valley, has gone on to new victories, and it cannot be argued but that there will be many more to come.

I first tasted Stag's Leap, along with a great Cabernet Sauvignon from Joe and Martha Heitz, their 1968 vintage, in South Africa. We were still shaken by their successes in Paris and decided to try the same tasting with the addition of the best Cabernets of the southern hemisphere making up the list. A dramatically dark wine from Chile seemed out of place amongst the elegant wines from France, Australia, South Africa and, of course, Napa Valley. In fact, it wasn't the American wine which won that day, but a fine mature Château Latour 1967. We learned much from our palates, the best lesson being never again to underestimate the quality of the (to me, newly discovered) Napa region.

I recalled the cynicism which surrounded the decision of the Möet and Chandon Company, when in the early 1970s, led by Robert-Jean de Vogüé, the French company bought and established a winery in Yountville. There were few who thought much of Bob de Vogüé's new winery plans, and many felt it was a commercial folly. How things have changed: no-one visiting the Domaine Chandon, today one of the most beautiful wineries in the world, with its attractive restaurant feels that the exercise was unwise. Domaine Chandon have not yet won all their spurs, but few harbour doubts that accolades will follow.

Before visiting California, I had tried to sell some of the best of Napa's wines in my shop. No success, though vineyards with exotic titles had impressed their personality upon me. Mayacamas, Silver Oak, Sutter Home, and Diamond Creek seemed redolent of a promise to tell their story of the development of the Napa Valley. That story was told for me by one of the new giants of viticulture, whose fame has spread far beyond the boundaries of the United States, Robert Mondavi. Forever talking about his wines and his vineyards, he has a well versed family to carry on his doctrine.

Robert Mondavi runs a moderate sized vineyard and winery, with perhaps a two million gallon capacity. It lies at the roadside 12 miles north of Napa, just a step through Oakville. The winery is pretty, surrounded by 200 acres of vines, mainly Cabernet Sauvignon. Mondavi's greatest assets are his boundless energy and the flow of innovative ideas which he applies to his winemaking. A tour of the winery with an enthusiastic wine-man, Bill Cadman, one of the Mondavi team, demonstrated many of their new processes at work. I was impressed by the experimentation with the Pinot Noir variety, where after some years of production without use of the stems, these are now being added back in changing percentages to determine which will make the best Pinot Noir in the Napa region. But as Mondavi explained, it is the Cabernet Sauvignon, grown between Yountville and St. Helena, which yields the greatest red wines of the area. This variety accounts for over 20 per cent of Napa production, and without a sustained consumption growth, overproduction will become a problem of a temporary nature.

Some of the most modern winemaking techniques are now in force throughout ''Bob'' Mondavi's winery. Grape fermentation is handled more precisely than almost anywhere else in the world; all wines (or musts) at this vital stage are held in stainless steel tanks with double jackets through which propylene glycol is circulated to maintain a perfect temperature for the development of finely perfumed wines.

After seven days of fermentation, the emerging wines are transferred to clean vats where, still on the skins, they are kept under carbon dioxide for a further seven days to ensure that all colour has been leached out into the young wines. They still showed the vivid concentration of colour which so frequently distinguishes great young wine from the mediocre.

Vineyards to the south of Yountville produce some of Robert Mondavi's finest white grapes, his delicate Sauvignon Blanc, less smokey than those from France, and the elegant Pinot Chardonnay, in my opinion one of the greatest realized promises of the Napa Valley. Once the white grapes are crushed in a bank of continuous screw presses, the mash is held in large (200 hectolitre/4400 gallon) horizontal rotating tanks for 16 hours. This period is sufficient to extract the golden green colour of the grapes, without loss of perfume. It is this attention to the detail of perfection which Mondavi employs within his handsomely arched buildings which recall the Spanish influence on the foundation of California.

If the Napa Valley is famous for its wines, the wineries have been the first to realize the tourist attraction that they have created. Many vineyards are open to tourists: one, the Sterling Vineyard near Calistoga at the northern end of the valley, is approached by a cable car ride. A rapid calculation of the receipts from the approach to Sterling reveals a total which matches the sales from the vineyard.

The mix of properties within the Valley is ideal. Few pioneers remain, and some of those who followed have constructed large modern wineries, yet there is an even greater number of smaller, premium wineries including Freemark Abbey, Chappellet and Clos du Val, each producing notable bottles.

One of the Napa Valley's potential problems is the possibility of urban encroachment from the cities to the south, whilst amongst its defences is the reputation that its wines deservedly enjoy. But a reputation rarely, if ever, grows without constant promotion, and here the region has been singularly fortunate in the early establishment of the Christian Brothers great winery at Greystone. Built in 1889, it is surely one of the most traditional producers in the region. Who could forget the motif carved by a brother upon an oaken beam, "Wine measurably drunk, bringeth gladness to heart and cheerfulness to mind (Eccl. 31-27). This is indeed the very message that Brother Timothy, surely the most erudite of the men of wine, proclaims throughout his tours of the wine loving world.

By 1981, the Napa Valley had a total of 23,710 acres of producing vines, and these are mainly the shy-bearing varieties that have made its wines famous. This substantial acreage produces almost 75,000 tons of wine grapes a year, a truly enormous total. Yet it is only in the Cabernet Sauvignon variety that any over-production is manifested, the demand for other types of Napa County wines being so firm that they are constantly over-sold. With the benefit of hindsight it seems staggering that so much has been achieved during the short history of this vineyard area. Napa has not been spared the dramatic difficulties of other regions. The vine pest phylloxera dashed hopes throughout the vineyards in the early years of the 1870s, yet only a century later, less than 120 years after vineplanting began in serious earnest at the instigation of the far sighted Governor John Downey, the Napa Valley ranks amongst the foremost of the world's winemaking regions. How the industry withstood the constraints of Prohibition and still survived is a fascinating story, but even this period is now passing into the distant past. Indeed, however one looks at the California wine industry, and Napa County in particular, its story borders on the incredible. A Hungarian nobleman, Agoston Haraszthy, developed the cultured European plantings at Sonoma. The Italian brothers Gallo, with their extraordinary high volume selling "Hearty Burgundy," brought respectability and stability to grape growers on the verge of financial ruin, and many others, whose names reflect the melting pot of nationalities that is the Americas, have raised a 20 mile long vineyard to the forefront of wine appreciation. From a European viewpoint it seems that it has been achieved too rapidly for the reputation to be durable, and yet without a doubt the prestige of the Napa Valley is universal.

Another carving at the Christian Brothers Greystone winery says it all: "Give me a bowl of wine, in this I bury all unkindness."

EASTERN EUROPE

Other Countries

CENTRAL AND EASTERN EUROPE

Austria

The ubiquitous Romans probably introduced the vine to the banks of the Danube 2,000 years ago. Yet the present area under cultivation in Austria is roughly only a tenth of what it was at its zenith towards the end of the Middle Ages, and today Austria needs to import substantial quantities of wine to satisfy local demand.

Most of the wine produced - 85 per cent - is white made from the Veltliner, Riesling, Traminer, Sylvaner, or Gewürztraminer grapes. The best way to drink Austrian wines is straight from carafes or barrels in local taverns. The whites, which are far superior to the reds, seem to lose their freshness and fruitiness when bottled. Whether red or white, Austrian wines should be drunk young as their staying power rarely exceeds two to three years.

The districts around Vienna and the Neusiedler See in the eastern part of the country are the chief wine-producing areas. Relatively few bottles are exported though some of the better known wines, such as the Kremser Schluck and the Gumpoldskirchener, can be found abroad. The regions of Krems and Wachau, on the banks of the Danube, produce what are generally regarded as the finest white wines of Austria. The Schluck is an excellent dry wine made from Sylvaner grapes, and the Kremser Kögl and Kremser Wachtberg wines can be compared to the Moselle Rieslings.

Main Grape Varieties of Austria

Veltliner
Riesling
Traminer
Sylvaner
Gewürztraminer
Müller-Thurgau
Pinot Noir

Switzerland

In addition to their superior watches and banks, the Swiss also produce about one million hectolitres of wine annually of sometimes excellent quality. The omnipresent Alps discouraged Hannibal and his elephants no more than they did the ancient viticulturalists, and many of Switzerland's best wines still come from the sloping vineyards above the Rhône River and from Lake Geneva's north shore. However, these are rarely exported and the Swiss who are great connoisseurs, also import considerable amounts of fine wines annually, particularly from France.

The most widely used grapes are Chasselas for the whites and Pinot Noir for the reds. The Chasselas wines which are light and fresh, can have a flinty taste. Dôle, the best-known wine of the Valais, is a mixture of Pinot Noir and Gamay grapes. The wines of Neuchâtel are among the most popular, and most available, of those found beyond the frontiers of Switzerland.

Main Grape Varieties of Switzerland

Pinot Noir
Chasselas
Fendant
Gamay
Riesling-Sylvaner

Hungary

With three per cent of its land under vine, Hungary ranks about tenth among the wine producing countries of Europe. Two fifths of its annual harvest of five to six million hectolitres is exported, mainly to Russia, West and East Germany, and the Scandinavian countries. The Romans (who else?) introduced vineyards to the vast Hungarian plains.

Main Grape Varieties of Hungary

Furmint
Hárslevelü
Muskotály
Budai Zöld
Ezerjo
Kadarka
Kékfrankos
Kéknyelü
Riesling
Szürkebarat
Zöldszilváni

Main grape varieties of Yugoslavia

Merlot
Plavac
Prokupac
Refosco
Riesling
Sipon
Smederevka
Sylvaner
Traminer
Vugava
Zilavka

There are 15 officially designated wine regions producing a wide variety of wines, from the rich Tokays in the north, to the fruity whites of Lake Balaton in the west, and the robust reds of central Eger. About 80 per cent of the acreage under vine belongs to the state, but there are still many private owners grouped into cooperatives.

For centuries, the greatest and most famous wine of Hungary has been the Tokay Aszu, a wonderful, sweet wine made from the same process of "noble rot" as French Sauternes and German Beerenauslese. Tokay Aszu was the favourite wine of Louis XIV of France.

In Hungary's northeastern region around Tokay, the overripe, shrivelled Furmint grapes, happily afflicted by *botrytis cinerea* are handpicked late in the year, often in snowy weather, and placed in *puttonos* or 25 kilo tubs. Tokay Essenz, the rarest of such dessert wine, is made only from the juice pressed out of the grapes by their own weight.

The quality of the Tokay springs from the harmony that exists between the soil and climate, the grape, and the process of vinification.

Hungary's full-bodied Egri Bikaver red wine, made mostly from the Kadarka grape, has been famous for centuries. Since 1552 the people of Eger, a town several miles northeast of Budapest, have claimed that it was Egri Bikaver, the "Bull's Blood of Eger," which gave their young men the strength and courage to fight off the Turks. Be that as it may, this wine, which is not unlike some of the better reds of the Rhône Valley in France, is a popular export product.

Main Grape Varieties of Bulgaria

Bolgar
Chasla
Dymiat
Gamza
Riesling
Mavrut
Melnik
Misket
Pamyt
Perla

The vineyards on the shores of Lake Balaton, the "inland sea" of Hungary also produce some good wines. Badacsony Keknylü is a moderately dry white wine with an agreeable bouquet and an unusual colour, bordering on green. The Badacsony Szürkebarat is a sweeter wine which shows a rich, amber colour upon maturity.

Yugoslavia

Yugoslavia is the tenth largest wine producer in the world. Much of its exported wine is bottled by large cooperatives, even though the vineyards themselves remain firmly in the hands of individual wine growers.

Serbia is the biggest wine-producing area, accounting for about half of total production. It makes mainly white wines from Riesling and Traminer grape varieties and a refreshing red table wine, Prokupac, which has been likened to Beaujolais.

Slovenia, which once belonged to Austria, produces good Rieslings especially in Lutomer. This region also makes Sylvaner and Traminer wines. Generally speaking, Yugoslavian Riesling is somewhat earthier than its Austrian or German counterparts.

Herzegovina exports Zilavka, a dry white wine from Kosovo and Metohija. The Adriatic coast produces mostly reds, including the ruby-coloured Plavac reminiscent of a French Rhône wine.

Bulgaria

On the southern foothills of the Balkans, and along the Black Sea, the vineyards of Bulgaria produce Mediterranean-type reds and whites, most of which are exported to other Communist countries and to West Germany. Vinicultural methods are perhaps the most modern behind the Iron Curtain thanks to a rebuilding of the Bulgarian wine industry in the early 1950's. The whites are regarded as being superior to the reds.

The Dimiat, a Riesling-type wine, is one of the better known Bulgarian white wines. The most common reds, from lightest to heaviest, are the Cabernet, Gamza, Melnik and Mavrud.

Rumania

Rumania was growing vines and making wine even before the Greeks got there. The country produces somewhat more whites than reds, with the bulk of exports being shipped to other eastern European countries and to West Germany.

Tirnave Riesling is Rumania's finest white wine, along with the Cotnari, a golden, sweet wine similar to a German Auslese. The Mufatlar, produced in the Black Sea region, has an orange-blossom bouquet that is quite rare. The Dealul Mare vineyards produce red wines from Cabernet Sauvignon and Pinot Noir grapes.

Main grape varieties of Rumania

Aligoté
Fetească
Furmint
Malbec
Merlot
Muscat Ottonel
Perla
Pinot
Riesling
Sauvignon
Tămîioasă
Traminer

Czechoslovakia

Although this country imports half of the wine it consumes, it does have a small, but flourishing, wine industry. The average Czechoslovak, it's well known, prefers beer.

Of the three main regions, Slovakia is the best developed from the point of view of viticulture, accounting for three-quarters of national production. A variety of reds and whites are produced in all three regions, Slovakia, Moravia and Bohemia, while Kosicé in eastern Slovakia makes a white wine similar to Tokay.

Soviet Union

Russia is one of the world's largest wine producers, making six times as many sweet and dessert wines as dry ones. Although few are exported, some Moldavian wines can be found in Western Europe, notably the Negrù de Purkar and the Cabernet, both red, and the Fetysk, a white wine.

The country's viticultural zone forms a vast semi-circle in the south of the USSR, stretching from the Rumanian border to the frontiers of Iran, India, Turkestan and Mongolia.

The Crimea produces a wide range of whites, reds and rosés. However, perhaps the best Russian wines, whether white or red, come from Georgia, thanks in part to its sub-tropical climate. Sparkling wines made from the Muscat grape also deserve mention.

EASTERN MEDITERRANEAN

Greece

The cult of Dionysus, the god of wine, began thousands of years ago in Greece. Homer sang the praises of wine in the Illiad and the Odyssey. More important still, the Greeks transplanted the vine to their colonies. Thus famous vineyards like those of Sicily, Malaga, Jerez and the Rhône Valley are in fact of Greek origin. Small landowners account for about 90 per cent of annual production. Greece is principally known for its Retsina, a wine flavoured with pine resin which has a bitter taste that is not to everyone's liking, but it is an excellent partner for typical Greek cuisine.

Main grape varieties of Greece

Saviatiano
Leatiko
Ketsifali
Mandilari
Malvasia

The Peloponnesean Peninsula produces the largest volume of Greek wines, the best being on the sweet side, such as the surprisingly flavourful red Mavrodaphne. Good quality wines are made on the islands of Crete, Samos, Santorin and Rhodes. The Muscat from Samos, especially, is a pleasant dessert wine.

On the mainland, Attica, a region of olives and wines from ancient times, produces a wide range of white wines made from the Saviatiano grape, the better known being the Pallini, Hymettus and Marco.

Cyprus

Main Grape Varieties of Cyprus
Mavron
Xynisteri
Muscat

The island of Cyprus began producing wines well before the Crusades. According to Greek legend, Cyprus was the home of the goddess Aphrodite who still graces Cyprus' wine labels.

Most famous of the island's wines is the Commandaria, named after the Knights Templar who guarded the Temple of Colossus. Made from a blend of red and white grapes, this dessert wine is produced on the sloping vineyards of the Troodos Mountains. Cypriot winegrowers also make robust red wines with high tannin content, such as Afames and Othello, as well as some white and rosé wines.

Turkey

Only a small percentage of the grapes grown in Turkey are used to make wine. The Turks like sweet wines, and their dessert wines tend to be too sweet for the western palate. The best of their dry whites usually come from the Narince, Emir and Hasandede grape varieties. A red wine known on the international market is the Buzbag, produced in Anatolia.

Israel

Thanks largely to the Rothschilds who in the late 19th century brought vines from France and established Israel's first winery, viticultural production has been steadily expanding, though it remains relatively small.

The Carignan and Grenache are the most common grape varieties. The climate is too hot to produce great vintages, but the winegrowers and co-operatives produce every conceivable type of wine, including a sparkling made by the *méthode champenoise.*

Egypt

Egypt does not figure in many books on viticulture and wine, but a small revival of wine production has been taking place since the start of this century, with sometimes surprising results. The Maryat region, west of the Nile Delta, notably produces two white wines, Clos Mariout and Crus des Ptolemées, as well as the red Clos Matamir. Cleopatra apparently found these wines useful for seducing Caesar ...

AFRICA

Algeria

Viticulture has remained an important feature of the Algerian economy since the country gained its independence from France in 1962, though the reputation for *vin très ordinaire* has stuck, if not worsened. Nevertheless, some excellent premium wines, developed from French grapes, can still be found.

In the past, hundreds of millions of gallons of heavy red Algerian wine were shipped annually to France for blending with the low alcohol *vin du midi* to create a palatable table wine. This trade, however, has declined considerably, partly because of a marked improvement in the quality of wines produced in recent years in southern France.

Morocco

Like Algeria, Morocco has suffered from a decline on the French market for its wine. Most Moroccan wines are either reds or rosés, with only a small quantity of whites.

The main viticultural regions are Meknes, Oujda, Rabat-Kenitra, and Casablanca. The reds are supple, generous and quite well balanced. The rosés are fruity and refreshing. But easily the most renowned wine of Morocco is its *vin gris*, a smooth, dry wine with a pale, rosé colouring produced at Boulaouane, El Jadida and Demnate. Those from Boulaouane in particular have a brisk following abroad.

Tunisia

Despite the departure of many Europeans after Tunisia's Declaration of Independence from France in 1956, winegrowing has survived and most Tunisian wines are exported.

The Tunisian vineyard forms a giant crescent around the Gulf of Tunis, with Carthage being the most well-known growing area. Tunisian laws protect three types of wine. First there is the Vin Supérieur de Tunisie, red, rosé or white, with alcohol content of 11° to 13° and aged at least one year. Muscat comes next, either with a simple appellation d'origine Muscat de Tunisie, or carrying an appellation d'origine contrôlée, in which case it is marketed under the name of the commune where it was produced. Finally, there are the vintage wines with an appellation d'origine contrôlée.

South Africa

Winemaking in South Africa goes back more than three centuries. Excellent wines, both white and red, are produced from European grape varieties under the strict supervision of a wine-growers' co-operative known as the K.W.V., founded just after World War I to cope with the problem of over-production.

The South African vineyards are concentrated in the southwestern part of Cape Province. Riesling is possibly the best Cape white wine, followed closely by Steen. The full-bodied reds are of the Burgundy type, and some are worth laying down for 10 to 15 years. The Pinotage, the result of a crossing of Hermitage with Pinot grapes, and planted quite extensively, has a perfumed bouquet which some liken to a top French Beaujolais.

South Africa also has a wide range of dessert wines and ports, the best of the latter being made in the coastal region around Paarl and Stellenbosch.

Palomino grapes have been imported from Spain to produce South African sherries, which now account for the bulk of the country's wine exports. The driest sherries, though less dry than their Spanish cousins, are fairly pale in colour and of a delicate flavour. Those aged by the *solera* system have much darker colour and are sweeter than European varieties.

Main Grape Varieties of South Africa

Riesling
Stein [Chenin Blanc]
Blanc Français
Clairette Blanche
Hermitage
Cabernet Sauvignon
Shiraz
Pinotage
Muscat
Sultana
Hanepoot
Gamay
Palomino

SOUTH AMERICA

Argentina

As in California, the first vines in Argentina were cultivated by Spanish missionaries, who produced wines in the 16th and 17th centuries chiefly for celebrating the sacrament. Today, Argentina is the fourth biggest wine-producer in the world after Italy, France and Spain, and much of the wine is of excellent quality. Viticulture is flourishing, having developed hand in hand with the demographic growth of the country.

Though there are six winegrowing provinces, Mendoza alone accounts for 70 per cent of Argentina's wine crop. The area of cultivation in Mendoza represents nearly two-fifths of the entire South American vineyard. Most of the wine from Mendoza is red and production is highly mechanized. The Cabernet Sauvignon tends to be the most consistent among the reds, while the Rieslings appear to have the edge among the

Main Grape Varieties of Argentina

Criollo
Malbec
Pedro Ximenez
Semillon
Pinot Blanc
Riesling
Malvoisie
Cabernet
Barbera

Main grape varieties of Chile

Malbec
Cabernet
Semillon
Riesling
Sauvignon
Pinot Noir
Muscat

whites. The wines of San Juan province are richer and have more body. Rio, on the southern tip of Argentina's viticultural zone, produces light reds, good whites, and sparkling wines.

The best Argentinian wines are classified as *vinos no communes*, these fine wines being mainly made from the Semillon, Pedro Ximénez, Cabernet, Barbera, Malbec and Torrentes grapes.

Brazil

The third largest wine producer in South America, Brazil is best known for its ordinary table wines, most of which are exported to Argentina, the United States and West Germany. The grape most used is the Isabella, an American hybrid. Brazil also produces sparkling (*espumante*) wines from Moscatel and Malvasia grapes.

Chile

The wines of Chile are widely recognized as the best in South America, in large part because French techniques in viticulture and vinification came to be generally accepted and practised in all the *haciendas*. Unlike nearly all of the major wine producing countries, Chile has never been confronted with phylloxera.

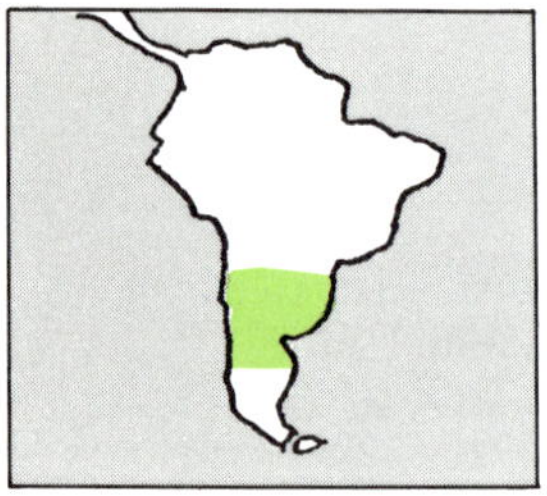

SOUTH AMERICA

Production, with reds representing 70 per cent, rose dramatically in the early sixties. It is closely controlled not only to meet standards of high quality but in an effort to curb alcoholism. For export markets, Chilean white wines must contain at least 12° alcohol and reds at least 11.5°. Fine wines bearing the *reservados* designation should be a minimum of four years old, while those designated as *gran vino* must have aged in casks for six years or more.

Ordinary wines are often a blend of those from the hot northern region and the colder, humid southern region. Most of the top wines originate from the central valley, where Cabernet grapes produce a particularly elegant quality.

Among other reds, one finds some Pinot Noir, Malbec, Cabernet Franc and Merlot. The best whites are made from Riesling grapes, although Semillon and Sauvignon are used as well.

AUSTRALIA

Winemaking in Australia dates back to the late 18th century, when British settlers brought grape seeds and vine cuttings with them aboard their ships. As the industry developed much of the export product was, of course, fortified wine - the big, rich port-style wines, sherries and muscats the Australians seems to love.

The Australians really only began drinking table wines in the 1960s, and now make some fine ones. The principal areas of production are all in the southeastern part of the country, the Hunter Valley, in Victoria, and around Adelaide in South Australia.

The two major red grape varieties are Shiraz (the so-called Sirah of the Rhône Valley) and Cabernet Sauvignon. Shiraz produces some of Australia's greatest and biggest wine styles and it is planted extensively throughout most areas. Cabernet Sauvignon plantings are also fairly extensive making different styles of wines in different areas. These vary from the light but longlived Cabernets of Coonawarra in South Australia to the firmer, bigger wines of the Barossa Valley, also in South Australia. Cabernet and Shiraz are often blended, in various proportions, to make a wine with the firmness of the Cabernet component, yet softened somewhat for earlier drinking by the Shiraz.

Many of the other European red varieties are planted and more are going in as winemakers search for added "fruit" and variety in their blends. The French habit of adding Merlot to Cabernet is gaining popularity, and grapes such as Malbec, Mataro and Grenache - not to forget the increasing popularity of Pinot Noir - are quite familiar to the industry.

The white varieties are more extensive, headed by Semillon, Riesling (called "Rhine Riesling" in Australia), Chardonnay and Traminer (sometimes referred to as "Gewürztraminer".) There are also large plantings of varieties, including those used for multi-purposes (dried fruit), such as Sultana, Doradillo and Muscat Gordo Blanco. Some other varieties are used for both table wines and for fortifieds and sherry: Chenin Blanc, Sauvignon Blanc, Colombard, Crouchen (sometimes called Clare Riesling), Frontignan (from which the "Muscats" or rich sweet fortifieds are usually made), Trebbiano and Pedro Ximénez.

Main Grape Varieties of Australia

Shiraz
White Hermitage
Pinot Noir
Cabernet
Semillon
Grenache
Riesling
Muscatel
Malbec
Chardonnay
Mataro

If there is no indication of grape varieties on a white wine label, it may be made from a blend of Sultana/Gordo and possibly some Riesling or Semillon. These are easy drinking whites with fruit and usually a little residual sugar and they may be labelled simply "Riesling" - opposed to the one-variety "Rhine Riesling." A wine labelled "Moselle" is intended to indicate more sweetness, the best example of these probably being Lindeman's Ben Ean Moselle, from Australia's biggest wine company. This is a non vintage wine with extreme consistency, probably the biggest selling bottled white wine in Australia, and now available in parts of Canada.

The Australians have recently made a major commitment to the North American market and hope to offer more of their enormous range of wines to Canadians in the coming years.

Mosaic Impression of the Capeland

by Kenneth Christie, M. W.

It would be simple to dismiss the winemaking of South Africa as flippant, but this would be manifestly unjust, as this sun-blessed country is the twelfth largest wine producing nation in the world, eleven times more prolific as a wineland than Canada.

Much of the credit for South Africa's development as a quality producer must rest with the remarkable organizational skills of the Cape Winegrowers Association (K.W.V.), whose role within the republic covers all aspects of winemaking throughout the Capelands. There is a very special quality about the atmosphere in the Cape Province, where the air has a certain aura of Champagne, but the beauty of the surroundings cannot overcome the lack of variety among South African wines. However, remarkable wines do abound and they are worthy of consideration and comparison with the finest of other countries.

Amongst white wines, most appear to be made from a versatile, though rather uninteresting grape known as the Steen, which has a familial relationship with the Chenin Blanc of Europe and California. The Steen is the most heavily planted variety but there are other *cultivars* (a term used in South Africa and California for grape varieties) grown in small parcels by dedicated innovators.

While white wines are limited in variety, there are three red grapes which force their attention upon the conscience.

Two varieties, Cabernet Sauvignon and Merlot, are recognized by all, for they are celebrated from Coonawarra in South Australia to California. The third variety is the Pinotage, which is little known although its name has a familiar ring. The Pinotage is a cross between the Hermitage and the Pinot grapes. The red table wines represent only two per cent of the total South African production. But, with a perfumed bouquet which some compare to a top French Beaujolais, others to a California Zinfandel, these wines are the most exciting.

The Cabernet Sauvignons of the Cape can be very great and epitomize all the virtues that have made this an attractive variety for planting from Bordeaux, to Italy, and now to many countries of the newer world. What then of the other varieties? Certainly the Merlot is easily recognizable, with its initial hardness developing into a velvety and subtle wine with a fine and complex character. A glass of freshly poured, strappingly black-purple Pinotage is a sight to remember. The colour of the wine of this grape is almost inevitably impressive and yet it is the wealth of its bouquet which dominates the senses. Similar to the Zinfandel of California, the Pinotage comes in many weights of alcohol and it is generally those of lower alcohol strength which are the most memorable. Usually Pinotage is drunk while still young, but when matured becomes as sensitive as an old wine from the Côte d'Or.

Wine growing in the Cape Province is organized on the estates whose settlement by the Dutch goes back over 300 years, to the days when Jan van Riebeeck was dispatched to South Africa by the Dutch East India Company in 1652. He was such a lover of wine that, within three years of arriving on the African Continent, he had planted his first vines and entered in his famous diary on the 2nd February 1659. "Today, praise be the Lord, wine was made for the first time from Cape grapes."

Praise be indeed, for from that beginning has grown a vast industry.

A large proportion of the architecture is based upon the homes and farms that the settlers had left behind in their native Holland. The buildings have a dominating central gable, ornamented, crenellated as a wedding cake. Within these old homes there is the quiet peace of long lived-in rooms, simply furnished with impeccable taste.

A few miles from Cape Town the land begins to rise along the road to Tulbagh, the site of a devastating earthquake in the 1960s. Beyond Tulbagh, nestling in the crook of a curve in the towering mountain wall, lies a typical farm, the home of the family Krone. Named Twee Jongegezellen, meaning "two young companions," the farm has passed from father to son, or father to daughter, since the first virgin turf was cut in the almost deserted land found by the Dutch settlers. Through good years and lean, including the disaster of phylloxera, the Krone family have harvested their vintage. Even when other farmers were grubbing up their vineyards, the Krones carried on, constantly upgrading the quality of their vine plantings. Today, some of the most outstanding white wines of the Southern Hemisphere are being produced at this farm, which is but one among many great wine estates of the Cape Province.

However, there are many vineyards which are badly neglected, their vines in poor shape, due to a basic lack of good husbandry. Too much South African wine is dull, fit only for the distilleries, where it inevitably goes, the South Africans being among the world's largest consumers of brandy per capita. There is a great reliance upon a few mammoth marketing organizations, whose skill is as dependent upon their label designers as upon the quality of the wines. Yet a version of controlled denomination has been introduced in South Africa. At the moment the system is more notable for what it permits than for what it prevents, at least it is a start towards the control of quality.

Yugoslavia's Motley Multitude

by John Baldwin

Prokupac, Kosovsko, Vrkink, Kraski: sibilant syllables and consonants that explode and crackle! The varieties of Yugoslavian wines number in the dozens but most are little known on North American markets. The names fall strangely on the ear and perplex the tongue, sometimes indicating a type of grape, sometimes a place name and sometimes both. Add differences in language between regions and a proliferation of names follows, even for the same types of wine.

Yugoslavia is among the larger producers of wine in Europe, ranking seventh or eighth depending on year selected and type of statistic used. Grapes grow in every province but Slovenia, bordering on Austria, produces the best wine according to most observers.

Northern Croatia, just to the south edging on Hungary, and the Istrian peninsula, adjoining Italy, are close behind in reputation. Serbia to the south and east, bordering on Rumania and Bulgaria, is the largest wine-producing region and naturally disputes the northern claims. The Dalmatian coast along the Adriatic and Macedonia in the south have grown their numerous small wines from a wide variety of grapes with little searching for international renown until recently. Many of these latter are earthy and robust verging on harshness, as fiery as the citizens of the mountains that stretch on through Montenegro to northern Greece, a fit complement for slivovitz, the pale plum brandy of Yugoslavia, that has burned its way to fame. Even the finer Yugoslavian wines tend to be aggressive rather than elegant, whether in bouquet or flavour, intruding boldly on the nose and palate. Domestically, the white wines tend to be slightly sweet (like those of Hungary) to better fit the type of food served although dryness is being emphasized for the export market.

Yugoslavia is associated with the communist countries of eastern Europe, but the considerable degree of independence it has shown in relation to its allies is reflected in the organization of wine production and sale. Numerous local co-operatives function, far more local names are permitted and export is not controlled by a single organization. All this leads to a considerable degree of competition compared to the monopolistic approach of their neighbours, particularly in marketing and export.

The foods relate to the wines, hearty and often heavily flavoured, again with Austrian and Hungarian influence apparent on northern menus, and Greek or Balkan in the south and east. Pork and lamb appear more often than beef; smoked meat and sausage are common; huge platters of mixed grills are popular. Soups are almost stews thickened with corn meal. Cheeses tend to be strong rather than gentle.

Riesling, Traminer, Pinot Blanc, and Sylvaner are the whites, and Gamay, Pinot, Merlot, Cabernet and Kadarka the best reds of the north in Slovenia and Istria. The whites tend to be a little softer than their Austrian counterparts. The reds vary, sometimes pleasant and easy on the palate, sometimes vigorous and sharp. The best-known Slovenian wine centres are Maribor and Ljutomer, both worthy of a visit.

Croatia produces similar types, but local red wine grapes such as Plavac, Postup and Dingnac become more noticeable. Along the Dalmatian coast these and numerous other varieties, and a tendency to give the wines the place names of small settlements, confuses classification. The wines are adequate for local drinking; a few merit even better treatment and are reaching the international market. One of these is the white Zilavka of Mostar, an old Turkish settlement in the Bosnian hills behind the coast above Dubrovnik. The wine has a strong rather unique bouquet and an earthy flavour that combines softness with a slight bite. It is a pleasant, not a great, wine that owes as much to successful marketing as to intrinsic merit, since Zilavka of equal or greater merit grows elsewhere - for example in the north.

In Serbia, on the eastern border, the Prokupac grape produces much of the red wine and Smederevka (Chasselas) is grown extensively for white wine although many other types are available.

To the foreigner, particularly the North American, the Dalmatian coast along the Adriatic is best known and most frequently visited. Even with a modest proliferation of modern hotels, the road from Split in the north to Dubrovnik in the south is one of the most attractive coastal drives in Europe. Craggy scenery, picturesque towns and villages of ancient tradition combine touches of east and west in architecture, mode, and menu. Climate is relatively mild and visiting can be pleasant at almost any season.

Most of the local wine types can be found only on the spot - and that is the best way to drink them. They are meant for consumption with the strong local fare and seem a little rough for our blander dishes or more delicate flavourings. In their native setting, they may taste well or they may disappoint. Quality is uneven, in Dalmatia and Macedonia particularly, but it is improving. There is only one good way to find out - by tasting. With such a multiplicity of choice, no external advice can serve well. In terms of cost, Yugoslavian wines are incredibly cheap. In terms of quality, some downright poor, some adequate for local use, and some quite good. But I have tasted none that are great. Those that have come on to the Canadian market are, in the main, good value for everyday use but not an embellishment for proud occasions.

Broken Vine to Tender Shoot

by Kenneth Christie, M. W.

Hambledon, Adgestone and Wootton scarcely rank among the most celebrated appellations d'origine in the wine lover's vocabulary, but at least in France, Germany and Great Britain they are no longer the butt of ridicule or selfconscious jest. Perhaps Wootton is the least known of these three great English vineyards, but during 1978 this domaine received three gold medals, two from France and one from Germany, which gave testament to the eminence of Wootton's Müller-Thurgau. Since then a shower of medals and accolades have been awarded to Colin Gillespie, the owner of Wootton. Other British vineyards have fared just as well in bringing home major awards from international contests at the world's wine festivals.

England is not a recently planted wine producing country. As one stands on the site of William Shakespeare's memorial in Leicester Square, London, it is hard to believe that 1,000 years ago it formed part of a flourishing vineyard. The meadows which ran down to the tidal banks of the Thames were long-planted and well-established vineyards. It is equally difficult to imagine the chill fields of Wiltshire, the limestone hillsides of the North and South Downs and the steep valleys of Somerset as the natural home of viticultural tradition.

The Romans brought wine to Britain. As their civilization spread north, six hundred and fifty years after Julius Caesar conquered Britain, the Venerable Bede listed cultivation of the vine alongside the planting of "willow, wattle and other crops." Alfred the Great wrote in his statute of law that "compensation shall be paid at an exact valuation by anyone damaging the vineyard." As the centuries unfolded the vineyards of England centred around the Church, until scarcely a monastery was unable to produce its own wine at table. But the ecclesiastics were not alone, for before the close of the 12th century, very few aristocratic homes lacked a vineyard.

It was never simple, even in the heyday of English viticulture, to ripen grapes in Britain and many vintages would, by today's standards, have been described as "off." In spite of mediocre summers, winemaking flourished until the great climate changes of the 14th century, when the ocean currents moved southwards.

Little by little, vineyards declined, but their absolute destruction awaited Thomas Cromwell, Henry VIII's "Hammer of the Monks," which effectively destroyed the monasteries, and their vineyards with them. By the beginning of Elizabeth I's reign only a handful of vines had survived to carry on a winemaking tradition more than 1,500 years old. Without a market for their produce, and without much enthusiasm the last of the pre-Revival vineyards was planted in Glamorgan, South Wales in 1875 by the Marquis of Bute. One of his descendants is today a member of Christopher's, a leading City of London wine merchant. The austerity that followed World War I finally killed off even this last brave venture when the small sugar ration was withdrawn completely.

There are now more than 150 commercial and 400 private vineyards in Great Britain, but the quality of their product is anything but uniform. There are far too many dull, overly acidic wines, and many others coarse and vulgar, but fortunately there are a few that fill the wine lover with delight. Among these are the vineyards of Hambledon, Adgestone, and Wootton.

In almost every vineyard one finds the Müller-Thurgau, a Riesling/Sylvaner cross which produces an average yield of between two and four tons per acre. In great years this vine is undeniably remarkable, although its wine matures a little too early due to its low acidity. Having learned much about the failures of the Müller-Thurgau, the vinegrowers are now planting two other exciting varieties. One is the Seyval, a French hybrid, which produces well even in ordinary vintages (the product is rather "sylvaner" in character.) The other, Schonburger, has all the aroma and spicyness of the Gewürztraminer of Alsace and is rapidly becoming a favourite with both growers and consumers.

Further plantings are being made by farmers across the south of England. While some will undoubtedly fail because of climatic or ground conditions, others will succeed and join those which are becoming increasingly popular and able to compete with any of the wines of France, Germany or Italy.

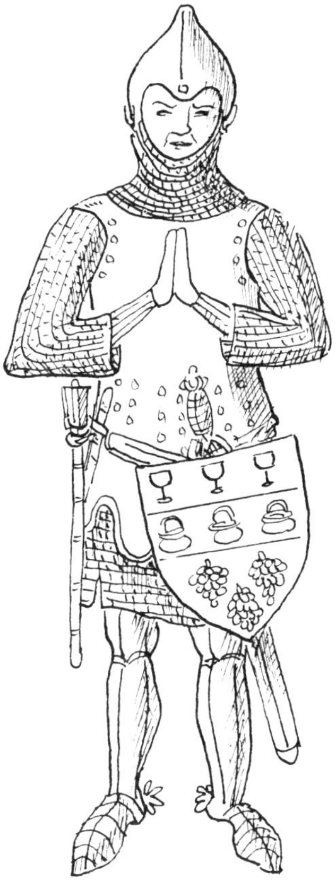

Growing the Vine

CLIMATE

The single most important factor in growing the vine is climate. Sunshine alone does not make fine wine, as soil, aspect, and the skill of the winemaker are vital constituents. However, the suitability of the climate will be the ultimate arbitor of quality. This is exemplified by wines of the Niagara Peninsula, where even the greatest efforts of the winemaker result in the best estate wines not being comparable with the best wines of the countries which possess more generous climates.

In an effort to relate ideal climate to specific grape varieties the University of California at Davis has developed a categorization of climate called heat summation as described on page 138.

This theory when applied to other wine growing areas of the world places them in the following categories:

Region I

The Rheingau, Rheinhessen, Mosel in Germany, Champagne and Chablis in France, vineyards surrounding San Francisco Bay in California, Niagara Peninsula and Okanagan Valley in Canada. Noble grape varieties that exhibit their best characteristics in this climate are Chardonnay, Pinot Noir, Riesling and Gewürztraminer, as they ripen early and show better acid to sugar ratios than in warmer climates.

Region II

This includes most of the temperate vineyards of France and northern Italy including Bordeaux, the Loire, southern Burgundy and Alto Adige; in California, parts of Sonoma, Napa, Monterey and St. Luis Obispo. Late ripening noble varieties thrive in the region including Cabernet Sauvignon, Merlot, Sauvignon Blanc and Chenin Blanc. Chardonnay is also grown and makes more full-bodied wines than in Region I.

Region III

This classic mediterranean climate makes up the rest of the coastal and northern regions of California as well as the Rhône Valley in France, northern Italy, parts of Rioja and Panadés in Spain and parts of Portugal. The noble grapes found in this region are the Syrah, Grenache, Gamay, Barbera, Zinfandel, Sangiovese and Malvasia.

Regions IV and V

These hot regions produce wines in large quantities with minimal effort. The resulting wines lack acidity, are high in alcohol and are rather dull but make up the vast proportion of wine drunk in the world. Areas include the Central Valley of California, the Midi in France, Valdepeñas and southern Italy. The most distinctive of the wines are the fortified wines such as port and sherry.

The above is a generalization. Within all regions are micro-climates, either cooler or hotter, which might favour an atypical grape variety for the region.

SOIL

After climate, soil is the most important constituent in wine quality, as flavour differences can be perceived even by relatively unsophisticated palates. Surface soil does not necessarily determine the flavour, as the vine has a main tap root which can extend 40 feet into the ground. In its progress downwards it can penetrate stones, gravel, sand and clay. Each level will contribute a characteristic to the resultant wine. Much of the Médoc has a heavy top soil, but due to a gravel subsoil the wines of the region have a renowned elegance.

Sandstone and Sand

Few wines seem to thrive in this type unless the subsoil has other characteristics. Its chief advantage is that the phylloxera vastitrix does not thrive on roots in sand and consequently vinifera rootstock can exist. Colares in Portugal is famous for its sandy soil and non-grafted vines.

Chalk

Easy for the vine to penetrate, this soil reflects the sun and is good for elegant, crisp and vivacious white wines exemplified by Champagne and Neuchâtel Swiss wines. Chalk drains well thus forcing the roots to penetrate further and further in search of adequate water.

Clay

Usually associated with full-bodied red wines it rarely produces great wines unless the subsoil is particularly porous (e.g. St. Emilion), as the vine is unhappy in a waterlogged topsoil.

Volcanic

With a great quantity of minerals in suspension in the water, the wines from this dark soil exhibit strong flavours which tend to overwhelm the more usual fruit and oak flavours. Southern Italian wines particularly exhibit this characteristic.

Slate

Slaty topsoil seems to be associated with very steep-sloped vineyards such as the Mosel in Germany and Priorato in Spain. The slate holds the heat of the day and, in the area of the northern Mosel vineyards, aids the maturing of fruit which is in a marginal climate. By contrast the Priorato has a very hot and arid climate and the cooking effect of the slate at night results in red wines of enormous alcohol (17% alc./vol.) and fruit which take many years to mature.

Similar effects to slate vineyards come from rocky topsoil vineyards such as Châteauneuf-du-Pape, whereas further north the rocky vineyards around Solutre (Macon) give a strong flavour to the wine.

The final determinate in the effect of soil and subsoil on the wine is the drainage. Vineyards on a slope, no matter how slight, generally produce better wines than those in a valley bottom or on a plain. Many of the earliest developed vineyards in California were on the flood plain, where cultivation is easy and very cost effective. However more and more winemakers are now developing vineyards off the valley floor, sacrificing ease and productivity in exchange for better wines.

VINE-WINE ANNUAL TIMETABLE

There is work in the vineyard or the winery every day of the year. The timing of the operations vary according to the geographic location. The timetable below is for a vineyard/winery located in a southern temperate climate in the Northern Hemisphere.

January. Pruning starts as early in the month as possible although traditionally it starts on the 22nd - St. Vincent's Day. The

vines are cut back and the number of canes per root are determined. If a high yield is required more canes are left. Vinifera canes one year old or more can withstand frost down to -18° Celsius. In the winery the barrels of new wine are inspected and topped up where necessary. Barrel stoppers are dipped in a solution of sulphur dioxide whenever they are removed and replaced.

Wines from previous vintages are bottled, and where possible labelled and packaged. Wines for export have to have special labels prepared which comply to the importing country's labelling regulations.

February. Purchase labrusca root stocks and graft them to cuttings selected from the vineyard. These fledgling vines are planted in sandy soil in an indoor nursery.

Overhaul vineyard machines - such as cultivaters, sprayers, pickers, and tractors. Order chemicals and fertilizers. During periods of high atmospheric pressure rack new wines by transferring to clean barrels or vats. Blending of different vats also takes place at this time.

March. In the first two weeks tie up all remaining canes and check bud development. Plough between rows. By mid-month the sap starts to rise; the brown sheaths on the buds fall off.

April. Clean up vineyard after replacing rotten stakes, brown cuttings, prunings. Plant one year old vines from nursery. If the growth rate in the vineyards is rapid beware of killing frosts and hailstorms.

May. This is a critical month as the vines are vigorously growing young tender canes, which are susceptible to frost at this time of year. Low-lying areas require smudge pots or sprinkler systems on clear nights to protect the vines. Weeds also grow prolifically and have to be killed. Mildew becomes a threat so spraying with copper sulphate is done after rainfall.

In the winery make a second racking and if necessary transfer wine into clean barrels.

June. Flowering is stimulated when the temperature exceeds 18°C. Calm warm weather is critical at this time. After the flowering each vine is inspected, the best shoots are tied and the rest cut off. This function is one determining factor in the size and quality of the ultimate harvest. Leaving more on the vine will result in a potentially bigger harvest of lower quality. Oidium (powdery mildew) is potentially at its worst and must be combated by spraying with finely powdered sulphur.

Although the temperature in the winery does not rise significantly, evaporation does increase (5% of total is lost per year) so all casks have to be checked and topped up. Older wines still in cask are racked.

July. Vines are trimmed so that the energy in the vines goes into making fruit. Soil between rows is tilled to eliminate the weeds which take moisture and nutrients from vine roots. Vines are regularly sprayed with a mixture of copper sulphate, slaked lime and water.

August. Berries develop rapidly, size being dependent on amount of moisture and sunshine. All grapes start the month green but black grapes turn colour during the month.

The winery is prepared for vintage. All winemaking machines and receptacles are cleaned and overhauled.

September. Hot dry sunny days are ideal as the final stages of ripening occur. Rain at this time means diluted extract and thin acidic wines. With lots of sunshine the picking time is critical because if the grapes

PRUNED 20 YEAR OLD VINE IN WINTER STATE

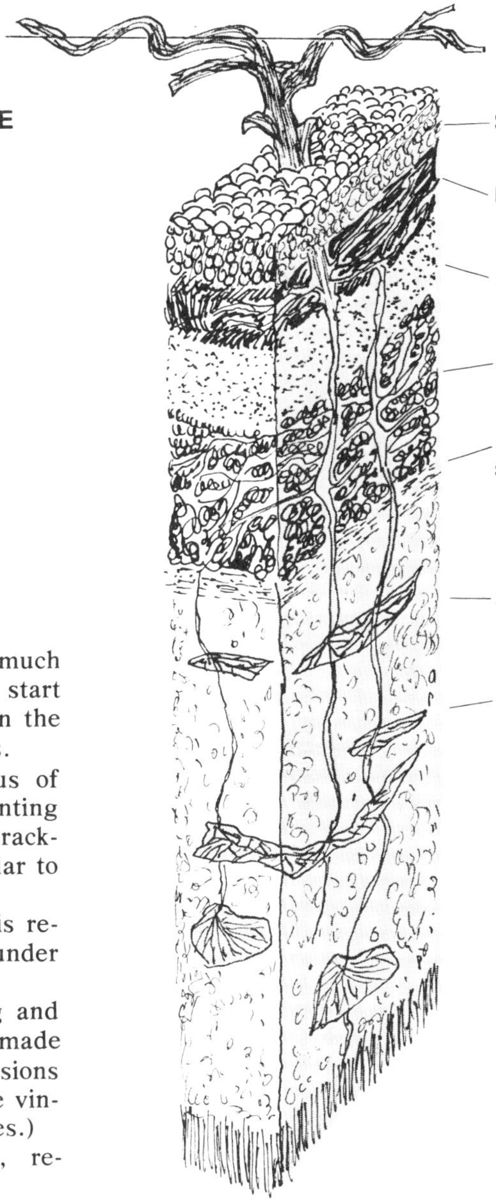

are left too long they develop too much sugar and lose acidity. Picking should start as edges of leaves start to dry out. In the winery crushing and fermenting starts.

October. The winery is the focus of attention where the new wine is fermenting and last year's vintage is given a final racking and moved to the second year cellar to make room for the new wine.

The pulp from the fermentation is returned to the vineyard and ploughed under with manure and fertilizer.

November. In the winery racking and fining continues. First decisions are made on quality of vintage and racking decisions are made accordingly. (The poorer the vintage the longer the wine is left on its lees.)

December. Bottle older wines, re-evaluate new wines and rack.

Making Wine

THE GRAPE

The basic constituent of a grape is water - 70 to 80 per cent in the stalk, skin and pulp, 36 to 40 per cent in the pips. But every part of the grape can contribute to the winemaking process. Tannin, which gives the wine its longevity, comes from the stalk and the skin, and from the pips if they are crushed. Colour and occasionally bouquet come from the skin. The bloom on the skin of the grape catches and holds the wine yeast. The sugar in the pulp is essential for fermentation. It is this that reacts with the yeast to produce alcohol. The pulp also contains tartaric, malic and citric acid necessary for freshness and preservation; nitrogenous material, certain minerals, pectins and pectioses afford the beautiful roundness to wines when the juice is reduced.

Grapes are often difficult to identify because local names have been given to them, and because they may, early in their development, have evolved several strains. Yet there are grapes from the vinifera vine which have an impact throughout the world such as Cabernet Sauvignon, Pinot Noir and Gamay.

Wines made from single grape varieties are not necessarily "better" than those to which many grapes have contributed. Different styles of wine can be created from the same grape, even on identical soil and depend on the skill of technicians and the application of modern laboratory facilities. An obvious example would be the Chenin Blanc produced by different California wineries. But before scientists found themselves able to control winemaking with such precision, it was the different grapes in different vineyards on which they relied to improve the resulting wine. The finest Mosel and Rhine wines are certainly 100 per cent Riesling, and the great red Burgundies all Pinot Noir. But in Bordeaux, up to five grape types are used to make the fine wines: the Cabernet Sauvignon contributes nobility, the Cabernet Franc fruit and vivacity, the Petit Verdot a certain type of acidity, the Merlot charm and bouquet and the Malbec for lightness.

For some wines, for instance Chianti, no single grape can provide precisely what is required, thus the tradition of growing a number of types together or growing them separately and then blending the fermented juice is justified.

In Europe there is no tradition for identifying on a label the grape varietal used to produce a specific wine. Choices are assumed, as certain grapes are customarily used in the making of specific varieties of wine. Government regulation confirms custom. For "White Burgundy" to be called "White Burgundy" it must be made with Chardonnay grapes without exception.

Accordingly, there are many important grapes few of us can identify, while there are also some which have become the names of the wines themselves.

THE PROCESS

The romantic, if unhygenic, picture of robust peasants, purple to the knees, stomping about on a mattress of grapes is one of those persuasive images of winemaking we retain despite our automated age. Commercial operations no longer employ people to press grapes with their feet although there is much to be said in scientific terms for this ancient method. The action of human feet marching across a bed of grapes ensures that the pips and stalks are not crushed. These contain acids which if released into the juice could render it hard and give it a woody taste which consumers would find unpleasant. Modern presses gently crush the grapes to break the skin and release the pale yellow juice - the "must."

The juice of both black and white grapes is pale yellow. The wine takes on its colour from prolonged contact with the skins of black grapes. Rosé wines result when the skins of black grapes are left in the vats with the must for about 24 hours. The yeast, that lives on the skins of the grapes as a bloom, feeds on the sugar in the juice once the crushing has occurred and converts the sugar into alcohol. Fifty per cent alcohol and fifty per cent carbon dioxide by weight.

Anyone familiar with the process of home winemaking knows that this chemical reaction is very difficult to control: temperature is critical - too hot and the yeast is killed, which stops fermentation; too cold and sugar has to be added to help the process along. The optimum temperature is 22°C. with an upper limit of 30°C. If the fermentation has to be restarted there is a danger that the residual sugar will turn into vinegar instead of wine. During this fermentation the level of sugar and temperature are constantly monitored and controlled for each vat.

Some vintners have gone over to modern thermostatically controlled steel vats, while others still employ the old oak cuvées with blocks of ice added to the must. An alternate method is to pump the fermenting juice off into pipes which are cooled and then fed back into the top of the vat. This process ensures that the head of skins floating on the liquid will be broken up and the juice will receive the air it needs to help the fermentation continue. In the old days workers had to break up this heavy mass of skins with long poles. The vats are open to allow the gases given off a place to escape. If the growing season has been particularly cold and rainy the must may lack adequate sugar so to help the yeast along grain sugar is added.

This is called chaptalization and is widely practiced in the marginal northern growing regions. The fermentation process continues until one of two things happen. Either the sugar is all consumed by yeast, the yeast now starved of nutrient dies leaving a completely dry wine of up to about 13% alcohol. Alternatively the sugar is present in sufficient quantity that after the yeast has converted the must to 14 - 17 per cent alcohol by volume it can no longer live in such an alcoholic environment and dies. The ensuing wine will have some residual sugar left in solution, which depending on the level of tartaric acidity will be apparent to the drinker.

The technique of the winemaker will determine the balance of the wine between the above extremes and various additives are used to achieve the balance of acidity, astringency and sweetness desired. Commonly used additives at this stage are tartaric acid, ammonium sulphate, magnesium sulphate, citric acid and potassium sulphate.

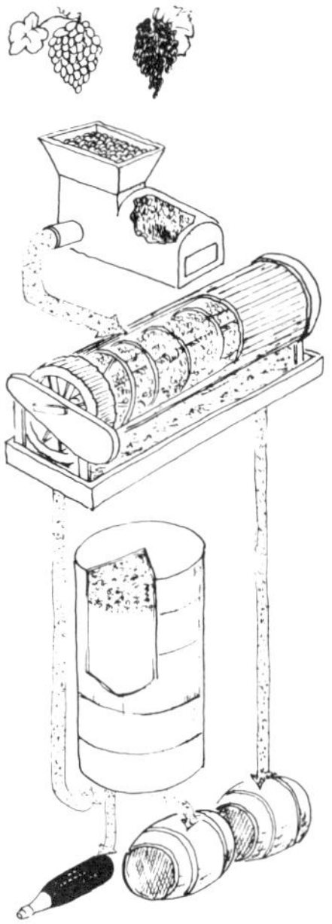

The longer the wine is left in the vat, in contact with the skins, stalks and pips; the more tannin is absorbed and the longer the wine will take to mature. Winemakers used to allow several weeks of fermentation. Todays market demands faster maturing wines so the fermented juice is run off within 15 days depending on the style of the wine.

Now begins stage two of the fermentation process which is much quieter than the vigour of the open stage. Temperature is maintained at a maximum of 15°C. in vats closed to the air. A layer of carbon dioxide pressure controlled by a fermentation lock keeps oxygen out. Flies and bacteria are also excluded. All fermentation activity ceases between three and five weeks. The yeast dies and falls to the bottom of the vat and is known as the lees and the wine is ready for racking.

The residue of skins etc. left in the open vat after stage one has meanwhile been pressed for a second time. The resulting wine is known as *vin de presse* and some of it may be added to the first pressing if the winemaker feels that it needs more tannin for longer life or to balance the fruit acid in the initial pressing. Many winemakers waste nothing. Part of this pressing may go to make marc, an alcohol distilled from the final pressing, and the pulp will be used as fertilizer.

The first run wine is now racked by having the clear wine siphoned off into clean vats. Temperature is maintained at 12°C. Racking is repeated two or three times every three weeks.

When the wine is clear it is transferred into wooden casks for a minimum of nine months. The casks are usually oak and are of various sizes and newness depending on the quality and style of the wine.

The method of white wine production is similar to that of red except that the skins of black grapes must not be allowed to remain in contact with the juice after the first pressing.

Wine is a living organism and it goes through three changes of life in terms of fermentation. The first fermentation when the sugar is converted to alcohol is a vigorous, dramatic event. The second stage is called the malolactic fermentation when malic acid is converted into lactic acid. This can occur along with the first fermentation or as late as six months after the vintage. A third fermentation takes place when the yeasts revive in the spring after the vintage. The renewed chemical activity could introduce carbon dioxide into the wine if the winemaker is not careful. (For Champagne and other sparkling wines this fermentation takes place in bottle so that the gas remains in the wine.) Once this third fermentation is over, the winemaker can begin the process of blending and bottling, depending on how long the wine is to remain in cask. The greater the volume of wine, the longer it takes to mature, so the winemaker may choose to bottle quickly in cool weather to have a wine which will be ready for the consumer much earlier than if it were left to mature in the vat.

After bottling the wine may be held for a further period or released onto the market immediately. Some wines benefit from aging in the bottle and some deteriorate relatively quickly. The potential longevity of wine can be determined by acquiring an acid testing kit and checking the wine in bottle.

Throughout the wine making process organic additives are sometimes used to enhance the quality and flavour of the ultimate wine. Use of these organic additives depends on the winemaker and the regulations of the controlling government body.

Sugar - is added when grapes have insufficient due to a lack of sunshine during the growing season (chaptalization.)

Acids - tartaric and citrus assist yeast and enhance flavour of finished wine.

Vitamins - B and C plus protein energize the working yeast.

Tannin - blends into wine naturally from skins, stalks, seeds and storage wood. Oak chips are sometimes added to wine matured in cement or glass vats.

Pectin Enzyme - removes the haze of pectin in the colour of the wine and gives higher yields of juice and flavour.

Non-organic additives are also used extensively.

Magnesium sulphate and ammonium sulphate - are used in small quantities as yeast nutrient. When used to excess the wine is spoiled.

Copper Sulphate - is used for spraying in the vineyard. Residue on the skins at the time of vinification does not harm the wine or inhibit the process.

Sulphur Dioxide - this common sterilant is used to prepare all vessels used in the fermentation. It is sometimes added to the grapes before fermentation to kill wild yeasts found naturally on the skin. Controlled yeasts are then added. During bottling it is used as an anti-oxident particularly in white wine. It is noticeable in the bouquet of many white wines but dissipates rapidly after the bottle is opened. Its function is to pick up free oxygen molecules in the wine thus inhibiting the enemy of wine oxidation.

Sodium Erythorbate - When mixed with sulphur dioxide it more than proportionately inhibits oxidation and does not have a residual bad smell and taste.

Tasting and Selecting

However grand or modest a wine, each one should be approached in such a manner that its properties may be intelligently evaluated, categorized and stored in the drinker's "taste memory." The purpose for evaluating any wine should always be to ensure first, that it is in good condition and, secondly that it is well made. Specific requirements may then be considered, particularly to determine whether the wine is at it's best for immediate consumption or for laying down for future pleasure.

Every wine selected should be enjoyable at the time of tasting even if its deficiencies or youth are recognized. Having tasted, evaluated and selected the wine, it may then be drunk in whatever context it was chosen.

The taster should develop a language of definition and it is this vocabulary that forms the basis of taste memory. Seventy-five per cent of tasting relates to the smell of the wine, so the taster should learn to identify the varietal characteristics of each wine, then the regional characteristics. Whenever possible, notes on the wine should be made immediately, as after the fact records have no long term relevance.

When purchasing in quantity, attempt to evaluate wines "blind," i.e. without seeing the label, and be comparitive by tasting a minimum of two similar wines. When tasting more than two, it is a good idea to include a known and previously enjoyed wine as a standard of measurement. If you are evaluating blind, be prepared to be completely wrong. Even the greatest tasters frequently make the most fundamental errors.

When selecting wines, remember an old adage of the wine trade: "Buy with bread, sell with cheese." Use bread to cleanse the palate between wines, not cheese, which flatters the wine and conceals its limitations.

When tasting a large number of wines, seriously reject any that have an unattractive appearance and smell. This reduces the number that have to be tasted. When tasting, spit out the wines, as ingestion of alcohol dulls the palate. Even when spitting, the tongue absorbs alcohol, so be prepared for a mild hangover later without having had the early glow.

As smelling is so important, avoid perfumes, smoking, and the consumption of acidic or sweet foods prior to tasting. Chocolate is the worst food for wine as it destroys the palate for hours.

The technique of tasting therefore, is to rate the appearance, bouquet, taste and aftertaste and make an overall summation by asking the following questions: Is the wine well made and if not why not? Is it enjoyable and if not why not? Don't force the issue by looking for positive characteristics. Simply learn to recognize youth, maturity and old age.

Appearance

Look for brightness and life but remember these qualities are achieved by filtration, which also tend to remove some of the character. Well-made, lesser wines therefore can be star bright but have little or no character.

When the wine is swirled in the glass, look for glycerol which leaves "church windows" or "legs" down the sides indicating body (alcohol and glycerine). Tiny bubbles can indicate youth and liveliness, but can mean an ongoing fermentation. This is particularly apparent in the spring.

To examine the colour, tilt the glass away from the body against a well lit, white background. Note colour tones from the edge and progressions of change and intensity to the centre. The better the wine the greater will be the spectrum of change. Lesser wines will show only about three distinct colour changes. Overall, red wines lighten with age and white wines darken.

White wines are very pale in youth, the palest coming from the coolest vineyards. Drier wines tend to be paler than sweeter wines, those of Mosel and the Loire being typical of cool climate, pale wines. Hotter climates impart a straw-colour to the wine and with aging, this colour intensifies to golden. A continuation of this process leads to maderization, when the colour darkens to brown. With the exception of some Sauternes, Tokay or Trockenbeerenauslese, which are delicious even when maderized, most over-aged white wines acquire a woody acetic flavour.

Many modern wines are blends of white and black grapes from many regions and, after laboratory treatments, have a colour determined by the winemaker and not by the grape or climate. This lack of pedigree only becomes apparent in the colour as the wine ages.

Red wines have a much more apparent range of shades than whites. Individual grape varieties exhibit much more specific colour characteristics, particularly in youth. Gamay is a vigorous, bright red with a purple edge. Pinot Noir is more plum coloured, and Cabernet Sauvignon has great intensity. Cooler climates produce less extract and alcohol and the wines appear light coloured when compared to those from mediterranean climates. With age the colour moderates to tawny with an apricot edge. Depending on the grape variety and climate, wines exhibit these mature qualities after different time periods.

Bouquet

To appreciate the smell of a wine a small quantity should be swirled in a glass. The nose should be placed an inch or so above the glass and then, breathing in gently, the nose should be inserted into the bowl of the glass. The messages conveyed to the olfactory organs should tell more about the wine than any other single action. The bouquet should be pleasant and attractive. The smells may not be familiar, but they should not be repellent or disagreeable.

The noble grape varieties have individualistic smells which vary depending on where the grape was grown. A standard for each should be established by familiarization with some classic examples of specific grape varieties. Thereafter these familiar smell characteristics will form the basis of comparison with all other wines tasted.

Only experience will indicate such things about the wine as the climate of the vineyard, the heat of the fermentation, the quality of the vintage, the style of the winemaker, and the age of the wine. Many of these impressions will have been stimulated

by the appearance, then further emphasized by the smell. Very old wines have complex smells which change subtly glass by glass.

Some unpleasant odours disappear in a short time and relate to "bottle stink" which is contained in the bottle between the wine and the cork; this and various sulphurous smells rapidly dissipate when the wine is swirled in the glass. Other possible odours are "woody," "chemical," or "chlorine" which relate to poor, unclean winemaking techniques. "Corked" wine does not have the smell of cork but is a musty smell due to the wine being invaded by bacteria resident in the cork.

Taste and Aftertaste

Having analyzed the appearance and smell, the actual tasting of the wine should fulfill the preliminary impressions. A small quantity should be taken into the mouth, run across the tongue, squeezed to the roof of the mouth and literally chewed before swallowing. The constituent flavours are enhanced if a quantity of air is drawn in with the wine. This physical activity gives an opportunity for the shape and texture of the wine to be appreciated. A well-made wine will confirm in flavour the promise of its appearance and bouquet.

After swallowing (or spitting) breathe out through the nose and note the intensity of the lingering flavour. A great wine will reward this effort with an ongoing sensation of taste. This is known as a long aftertaste or finish (the echo of the wine). The finer the wine the longer and more complex will be this souvenir of its time in the mouth. Lesser wines leave little or no aftertaste, much the same as the echo of a glass of water.

Be sure to learn the difference between the lingering souvenir and the roughness in the mouth caused by excessive acidity or tannin.

Acidity

Particularly prominent in young dry white wines, it sharply effects the tip of the tongue and inside of the lips. Chilling the wine enhances the sensation. It acts as a preservative of the wine and, when inadequate, leaves the taster with an impression of dullness. When the acidity is in balance with the fruit, the taste buds are stimulated and the wine is enjoyed to the fullest. Wines with pronounced acidity in youth, if stored in a cool place, tend to deposit tartaric crystals during their first winter in bottle and taste much softer in their second year.

Tannin

Tannin is a preservative and is particularly apparent in young red wines. It is perceived by a sensation of furriness on the sides of the tongue and cheeks. As the wine matures, the tannin breaks down and is assimilated, giving an increasingly complex flavour.

Fruit

Each grape variety has its own smell and taste, which is then modified by soil, climate and vinification. The basic characteristics should however be identifiable. Wines should be drunk when the fruit is in ultimate harmony and balance with acidity and tannin.

The diagrams on the following pages were inspired by Clive Williams, M.D., who uses something similar in his wine school in London, England. They attempt to express how the constituent parts of wine change in the bottle in relation to one another over a period of years.

TASTE DESCRIPTION INDICATING IDEAL DRINKING TIME

A wine's constituent parts under certain combinations give a taste profile which is described under **A**, **B**, **C** or **D** as they evolve. The charts represent wines produced from an average vintage and kept in cellars in Canada at an average temperature of 60°F. Above average vintages and cooler cellars would extend the duration, particularly for the better quality wines.

- Optimum drinkability will vary according to the drinker's appreciation of youthful characteristics.

A. Still youthful. Tannin/acidity apparent. Fruit beginning to show.

B. Mature colour. Good balance of fruit/acidity/tannin.

C. Colour fading in reds, deepening in whites. Long fruit flavour, soft with relative complexity.

D. Faded colour in reds, browning in whites. Losing balance. Volatile acidity becoming discernable.

1. **High Quality Red Wine**

Cabernet Sauvignon, Merlot	Bordeaux, California
Nebbiolo	Barolo, Piedmont
Grenache	Rioja
Syrah	Côte Rôtie

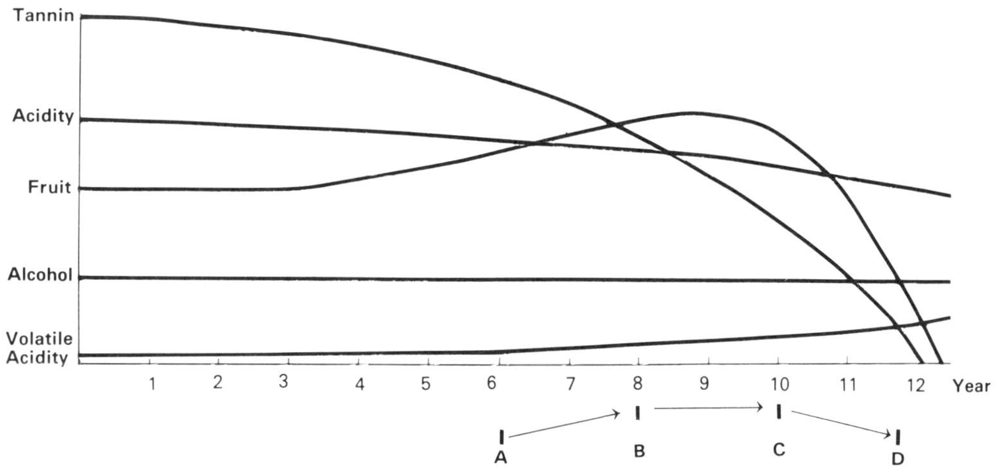

With the above wines, fruit development is discernable from "A" as tannin declines. As fruit falls (C) acidity becomes increasingly apparent; then volatile acid is discerned (D).

2. **Average Quality Red Wine** made from noble grape varieties.

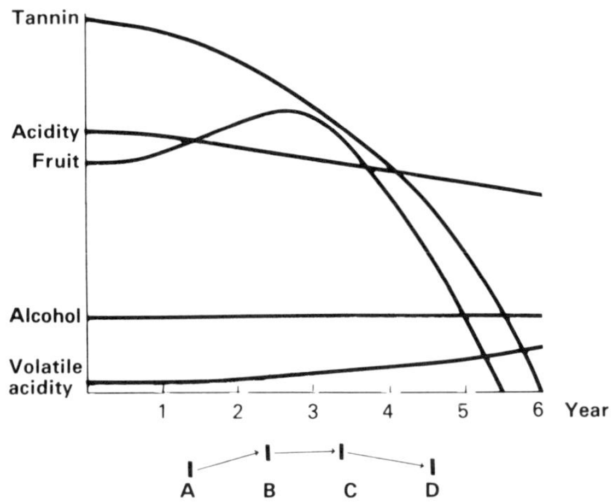

Within two years tannin has declined and fruit has increased. Wine is at its drinking peak for less than a year then declines rapidly.

3. **Well-made Light Red Wine** such as Beaujolais or Bardolino made from high acidity grapes such as Gamay.

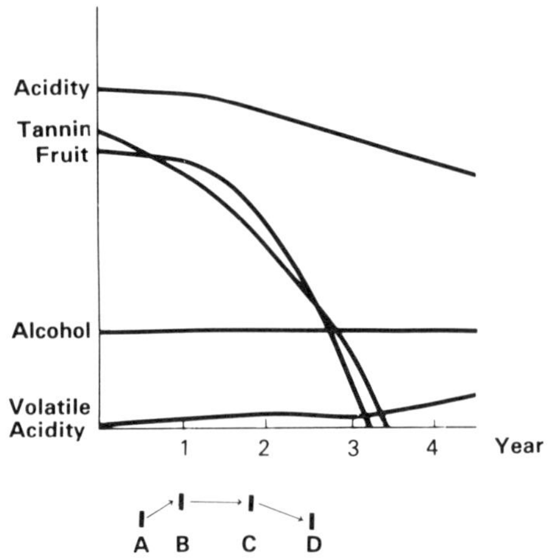

High acidity is the characteristic of this wine. The wine tastes fresh and fruity between B and C after which the fruit declines faster than acidity and tannin.

4. **Inexpensive Red Wine** for everyday drinking.

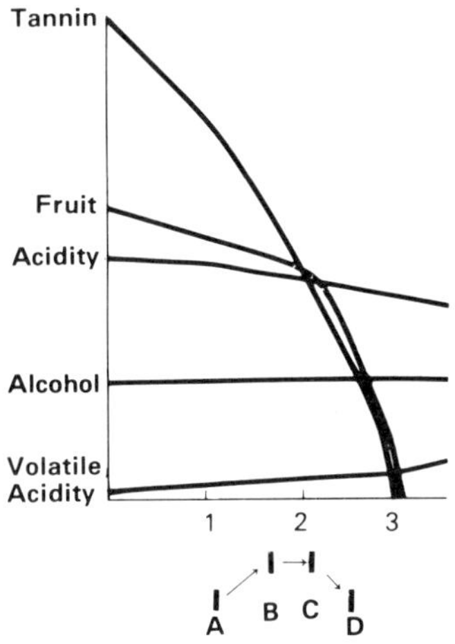

Fruit is everything in this wine. When it declines nothing is left except acidity and alcohol.

5. **Long-lived Dry White Wine** is a rarity. Chardonnay improves in the bottle as do Gewürztraminer and the finest Graves made from Sauvignon Blanc and Semillon. The finest sweet wines from Germany and France also follow this pattern.

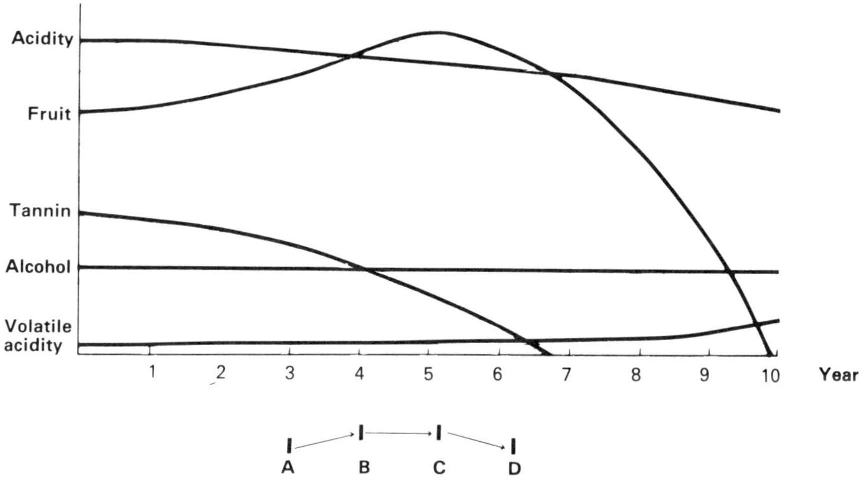

In youth up to A + initial wood maturation is evident by tannin. Thereafter fruit dominates until, as it falls off, acidity and volatile acidity become increasingly perceived (D).

6. **Inexpensive Dry and Semi-dry White Wine** made using modern cool vinification techniques. Hotter fermentation gives wines of lower acidity and higher alcohol.

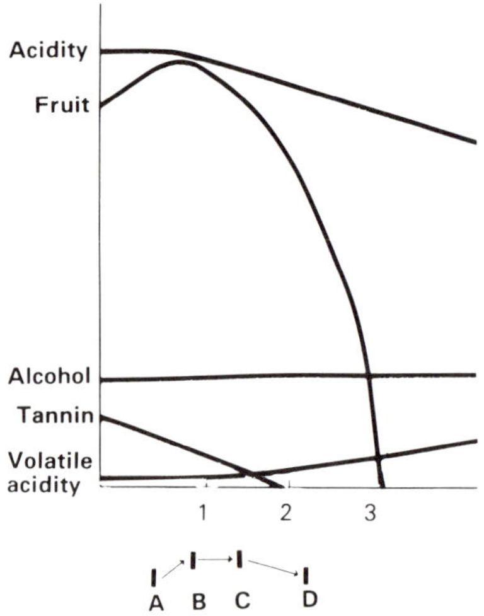

The attraction of these wines is the fresh, fruity crispness. They are at their best in youth and lose their attractiveness as the fruit falls out.

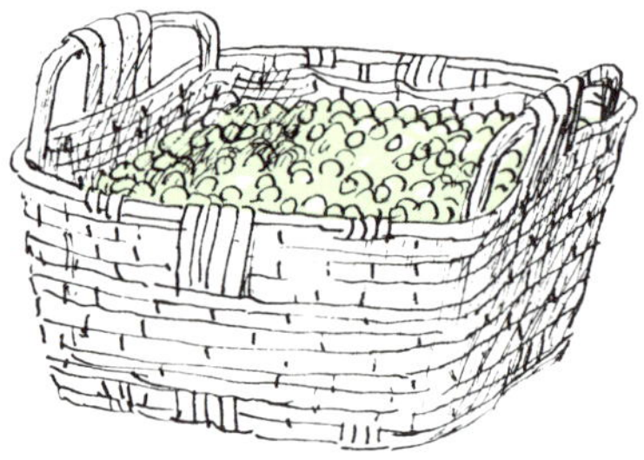

The art of Winetasting

by Kenneth Christie M. W.

The great man of food and wine, André Simon, was reported to have said "Let me taste the wine and I'll tell you if it's good, let me see the label and I'll tell you if it's great; for a glance at the label is worth 20 years experience!" So, why taste?

One good reason for tasting is that some wines are so extremely expensive, that their very cost deserves more than a passing acquaintance with the tonsils, and if purchases at high prices are going to have any justification a reasoned judgement of the sensitivity and delicacy of the wine is necessary. Now, I am the last person to dictate how others drink their wines. Indeed if drinking red wine in the form of ice cubes is the way you get your kicks, then so be it, however I believe that there are more worthwhile ways of consuming wine. Great knowledge is unnecessary but experience may make tasting more pleasurable.

Remember that wine is a product of paramount agricultural importance to many countries in both hemispheres; every drop made has but one final objective, to be consumed, but not all in the manner described in Charles Walter Berry's doggerel. "Over the lips, round the gums, look out stomach - Here it comes!". Wine made by sufficiently conscientious vignerons to be worthy of more than just swiggling is worthy of a deliberate and conscious act of review in order to assess its quality. Readers who wish wine to be nothing more than a mild and pleasantly flavoured beverage, take heart, for that is what millions of gallons of wine is best suited for, but this article is particularly directed to those who wish wine to be something more than that, who wish to share in the delight that a careful and systematic approach to winetasting can bring.

Once set upon a determined course to 'taste' wine, rather than merely 'drinking' it, there are a few basic rules that should be followed. The first is, be Honest. This is an absolute necessity and though it appears obvious, we are a very impressionable lot. We only have to hear one comment, complimentary or otherwise, to find our own opinions subtly changing to agree with what we have overheard.

The second law of the tasting room is - Don't drink when tasting! This is particularly important if more than three or four wines are to be tasted at one session. Tasting wines to build up a taste memory is one thing, enjoying a bottle with a meal or with friends is another, and once the alcohol in the first wine is absorbed through the throat, the vital sensations that make a winetasting more than a cocktail party are doomed to temporary amnesia.

Another firm rule should be to taste 'good' wines. It is pointless lining up a row of glasses of branded red Bordeaux, for at certain price levels below the exceptional, the maxim that "all cats are grey by night" holds true. This is not to say that the modest wines that bear branded labels indicating that Baron Phillippe de Rothschild had a hand in the selection of the cuvée or, perhaps even the Prince Noir himself chose the blend, are not commendable, but they are all too frequently indefinable, and rarely is their character clearly cut. If you want to set in your memory that true character and flavour of a vintage or district, this can only be done by tasting a wine of sufficient quality that it will demonstrate its virtues for you to store away in those strange grey cells that make up the miracle of memory.

Although tasting sensations must be personal and one should not depend on other people's vocabulary, here is a system of guidelines which may be helpful in evaluating and accurately identifying wines.

This system depends upon separating the qualities of wines - colour, bouquet and taste - from each other and marking them numerically. For ease of operation one can group colour and bouquet together with a maximum mark of 10 points; the same mark can be applied to the taste. Thus the greatest wine experienced would perhaps merit 10/10, being 10 for colour/bouquet, and 10 for taste. By the same measure an average wine would merit "5/5", being half way between zero and the maximum. Finally, a product of absolutely no merit would receive a zero marking "0/0". One should never be afraid of marking a wine below average, but the cardinal sin is to give a wine a high mark based on a previously known reputation or a rather grandly designed label.

Balance, the degree of equilibrium between bouquet and taste, can be shown by a varied mark, say *7/6* for a wine with a more attractive perfume than a flavour. Further, we can even describe the relative maturity of a bottle by a small appendix to the system, by the use of the mathematical signs. Thus "+" indicates a hard young wine requiring longer keeping or long keeping potential, "=" denotes a wine that is 'ready to drink,' "-" (do I need explain?) for a wine that is over the hill and on the way down.

Now everything so far evaluates quality, nothing for identification. This is much more difficult and can only be gained by experience; buzz words which conjure up personal experience must be used. I always find the Cabernet Sauvignon (the noblest grape of Red Bordeaux) recalls the childhood memory of sweeping my father's garage floor - not fashionable, I grant, but an honest and personal memory. Could anything be more foolish than the pundits who parrot-fashion describe Pouilly Blanc Fumé as 'gunflint' - do they mean before or after firing?

Try the system - or another. Stick at it for a while. Even better, write down your impressions and next time the same wine is tasted, do it again and compare your results. I promise that it will not be long before your marking becomes remarkably consistent, your ability to recognize really good wine from others of less virtue will develop apace, and your enjoyment of wines both good and less good will be considerably increased.

With these few basic pointers to the way in which wines are best examined, there are a number of other points worthy

of consideration. Remember that tasting is best done in the company of others with whom one's conclusion can be compared. It matters not if they seem more skillful or knowledgeable, their opinions will help to firm up your own. Try not to smoke: it may be great to you, but it could ruin the occasion for others. Finally, don't try to taste more than a handful of wines at one sitting.

So, out with the corks and into the glass, and suddenly all our senses come into play. The touch of the bottle, evocative of good times, leads to that sudden shock-sound as the cork plunks out to free the way for the wine to be poured, and then, that magical glug-glug-glug as the glass is filled.

One of the greatest problems associated with winetasting is the application of words which the newcomer finds completely meaningless in the context of wine drinking - such words as 'precocious' or 'shy', 'mousy', or 'noble.' The difficulty is resolved once the newcomer to tasting has become a little practised and finds that these words tend to fall into their own place. Thereafter the jargon of the tasting room becomes acceptable and understood. I use many words which have particular interpretation to me and which are misunderstood by others, nevertheless if one is to build up the taste memory which makes wine drinking so much more enjoyable, words must only be used which particularly grab and describe what is happening inside the mouth.

There is a close relationship between how good a meal looks and how good it tastes, but with wine there is a middle arena where the nose comes into its own to assist in the preparation of the palate. On pages 226 and 227 are glossaries of terms used by many wine men to describe the bouquet and the palate. They are not intended to subvert or replace those of a personal nature, however they may be helpful in interpreting the often senseless descriptions of wine used by many wine merchants (such as the writer!), journalists, and all too frequently 'wine snobs'! . . .

The Davis System

by Margaret Swaine

Margaret Swaine is a journalist and executive vice-president of The Taste Guild, Canada's first consulting company specializing in wine and gourmet food promotion.

For those who like consistency and defensible results, an objective approach to winetasting is necessary. There are several methods of looking at wines analytically to give them numerical rating out of a total such as 10, 20 or 100.

Before taking these systems to heart, we should keep in mind that though professional judges do exist, most tasting panels in Canada are ad hoc groups of fellow imbibers.

Every individual has a different threshold level or physical capacity to detect certain flavours. The threshold levels for detection of sugar, for example, can vary from below 0.5 per cent in wine to above 2.5 per cent.

There is also the problem of taster fatigue and overload. Much as you may like sniffing wine, your nose quickly tires of the game. It is wise to keep it out of the glass for 15 to 30 seconds in between attempts to analyze. Overload can only be avoided if wines are served in the proper sequence. After smelling highly sulphurous wine, it is nearly impossible to detect sulphur in the subsequent samples. In the same vein, after a very tannic wine, every wine following will taste tannic.

Most experts do not advise non-professionals to taste more than five wines at a time. If the wines are not being swallowed then ten is a good total. Professional judges are stoic blokes, able to taste more at a single sitting, though there is a limit to how much even they can sample effectively. A certain German expert suggests 300 a day. Americans take a considerably more relaxed position, recommending as few as 50.

Training is very important to identifying odours. The human nose can detect as little as a ten-millionth of a gram, but can only recognize what is familiar. With experience, one can identify 1,000 or more different odours at different times and detect smaller differences between the levels of a given odour. There are no shortcuts to acquiring this ability. Pity.

Typical wines contain more than 300 organic compounds, 200 of which are more or less odorous, though some may be sub-threshold.

Dr. Maynard A. Amerine, Professor of Enology at the University of California at Davis, worked with the staff to develop the Davis 20 point score card in 1959 as a method of rating the large number of experimental wines that were being produced at the university.

There were some defects in the scoring system as it overemphasized some factors and underemphasized others. Modified Davis score cards are often used now, though the total of 20 points remains the same.

The Davis system is straighforward with a certain number of points given to ten separate criteria. It works well as a technique of tasting for production control or production selection. Only minimal personal bias can enter. For this reason and others the Liquor Control Board of Ontario changed over to the Davis System from their former 100 point system.

The Davis system works well for buyers such as the LCBO because it determines whether a wine is technically correct, however you should use it with caution if you are trying to lay down the ultimate in cellars.

It not only does not leave room for you to imprint your own likes or dislikes on a selection, but it also denies red wines of medium-full to full tannin the two points for normal astringency. This liberates the evaluator from assuming responsibility for determining the aging potential of a wine, but could create havoc for the collector of fine Bordeaux.

These comments are not meant to slay the Davis system for the general consumer. It is great for choosing non-offensive wines for dinner guests. Those who are wine cellar addicts might well modify this system with a touch of the romantic.

On the opposite page can be found an outline of the Davis evaluation system for those readers who might wish to try it.

UNIVERSITY OF CALIFORNIA AT DAVIS
20 Point Scale System
Organoleptic Evaluation
SCORING GUIDE FOR WINE

1. *Appearance (2 points).* The wine is given 2 points if it is brilliant, with no dullness, murkiness or particles of sediment. If it is clear, but not flashing with light reflections, it rates 1 point. If full or cloudy it gets 0.

2. *Colour (2 points).* Acceptable colours for white wines are varying shades of yellow, gold, straw. Flaws are any amber tones, indicating oxidation. A rosé can be a true pink, or by reason of its grape source, tinged with deeper red or orange. Overly violet tints, brown tints of amber or deep red are faults. The colour of red wines depends greatly upon the grape variety. Pinot Noir may be light enough to verge on transparency. Cabernet and Zinfandel will be deep red. Newer or younger wines will often have blue-purple edges, as older wines will show bronze edges.

3. *Aroma and Bouquet (6 points).* Aroma is the sensory impression arising from the mouth with the assistance of the sinus chimneys. Bouquet is fragrance detected by the nose. Either may be vinous, smelling like wine, but without any grape variety characteristics. The intensity may be light, medium, or high. Negative factors are odours that can be described as alcoholic, excessively woody, mouldy or corked.

4. *Vinegary-acescence (1 point).* This is the term for volatile acidity. Does the wine smell of vinegar? If not, it rates 1 point. If it smells of vinegar it rates 0.

5. *Total Acidity (1 point).* Felt in the mouth, around the edges of the tongue, it is wine's refreshing zing. If low, the wine is flat, flabby or soapy. It can be too high with unpleasant sharpness.

6. *Sweetness/sugar (1 point).* Sugar and total acidity go together. Overly sweet for the wine's type is a fault, as is overly dry.

7. *Body (1 point).* This is the wine's viscous nature identified as mouth-feel, also the bigness, or alcoholic strength.

8. *Flavour (2 points).* The flavour should correspond with the bouquet and aroma, being clean, fruity, full or balanced. It should not be metallic, stemmy or alien in character.

9. *Bitterness (2 points).* Tannins give a wine astringency, and so does the wood in which wine is aged. Younger wines will be more rough than older wines. The ideal is mellow softness, velvet, roundness. A young wine is not discounted for a natural tannin.

10. *General quality (2 points).* The only category for subjective appraisal, adjusting the score on the basis of the wine's total performance.

17 - 20	Outstanding quality - fine wine
13 - 16	Sound commercial wine
9 - 12	Commercial, noticeable defect
6 - 8	Common, poor
1 - 5	Unsatisfactory

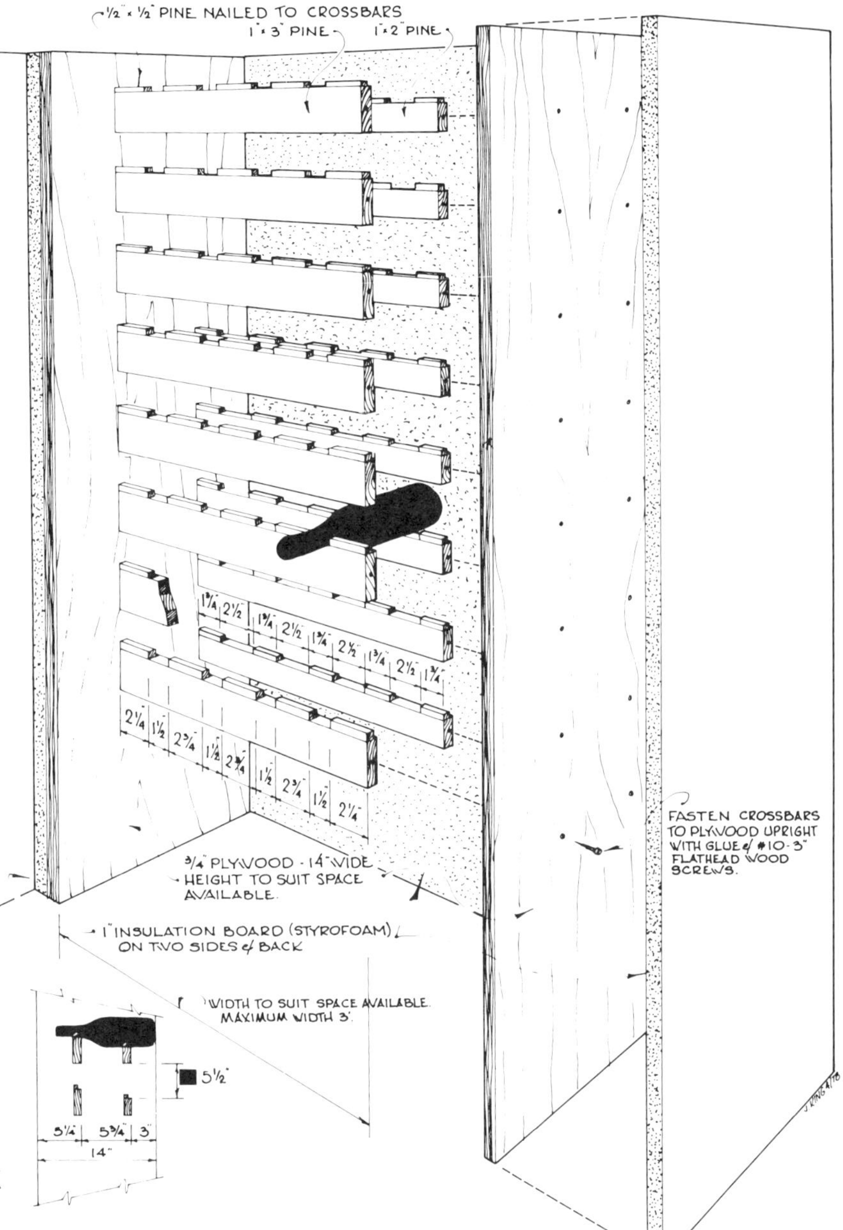

CLOSET WINE STORAGE RACK

Storing and Serving

Occasionally one hears the maxim that ideally you should not open any bottle of wine until you have had it at home resting for six months. There is also the advice that you should buy good wines while they are young and hold them to maturity, rather than paying a premium for well aged wines because the shipper has stored them for you. This could mean a significant stock to lay away for the person who wishes to have wine with dinner several times a week. Whether storing a lot of wine for several years or just keeping a few bottles on hand in a small apartment, there is still the problem of keeping them in good condition.

In this day and age, in our country, "cellar" can mean any adequate storage space in the coolest part of your house or apartment. Ideal temperatures however, are hard to achieve in our climate.

Whether you are using a chest of drawers (provided you don't use it for anything else) or stacking a closet with commercial racks; light, temperature and atmosphere are of fundamental importance. The following seven major points are the basics for a first-class wine "cellar."

1. The wines should be kept in a reasonably dark area. The light of an ordinary light bulb won't cause any problems; it's sunlight or ultra-violet rays that are to be avoided.
2. Ideally, the temperature of the sleeping wines should be around 10-12°C, but 20° won't hurt even the best wines; they will just age faster.

3. The main concern is constant temperature. Any fluctuation should be small and gradual. The temperature should definitely not go down to near freezing. Below 5°, flavours are definitely affected.

4. No vibration, if you can help it. Wines are living things, and the ride home on the back seat of the car, with the wine ebbing and flowing in the bottle like the tides in the Bay of Fundy, can be a very traumatic experience for any wine, ordinaire or classified growth. Keep the bottle upright in the car. It will still need a rest, but not for as long; perhaps a week or so, instead of two or three.

5. Ventilation of any storage area is advisable, and don't store your garlic on the same shelves as your Lafites.

6. Humidity is a good thing for your cellar, to help keep the corks moist. Don't worry about the mould that builds up on top of the cork under the lead capsule. It won't hurt the wine, and it looks appropriately romantic. Excessive moisture can only make the labels fall off. If your wines are in an apartment closet, a humidifier in the room should do the trick, especially if you bored holes in the door. For a basement storage area, such as a closet under the steps, or a separate room, you could fill the floor with a layer of gravel or pebbles, which you could water regularly. The evaporation usually provides good humidity.

7. Put a strong lock on the closet or basement "cellar" door, and don't label the door with the word 'wine,' especially if you leave for an extended period.

Temperature is probably the most important of these points, for slow maturing will retain the delicacy of the fine wines. Air conditioning, in the shape of cooling units that can cool spaces up to an insulated 600 cubic feet, or cabinets equipped with racks and trays to hold hundreds of bottles at 12° C, vibration free, are available. Just plug it in - but it can be costly. Don't use an air conditioner that brings in outside air, but one that cools and re-circulates the same air in the basement cellar. And don't try and adapt an old refrigerator for wine storage. An ordinary refrigerator is made to extract moisture. The ullage would be disastrous. If the only convenient place in your house is in a basement room or under the steps to the basement, the most important thing is insulation against the heating system. A partition may work, but thick styrofoam panelling on the door of the wine closet, and some on the inside wall can work very well, even if the furnace is only a few feet away.

Artificial cooling, however, needs one more word of warning. Aside from the expense of the electricity and the installation (and each of us has to decide whether our wines are worth that to us) there is the common occurrence of power failures, especially during the summer. A 72 hour blackout at high summer temperatures, or even blackouts for only a few hours, can put your fine wines through a routine of torture.

Our illustrated Closet Storage Rack was designed to solve the wine storage problem in a small mid-town apartment. The average temperature in the apartment was 20° to 22° +C., mainly because our wine lover is also a plant lover. However, the apartment also had a humidifier keeping things at a normal 60 to 65 per cent relative humidity. The wines would perhaps have liked things a bit more moist, but in this case plants and humans came first, in that order.

Our tenant had ruled out boxes of wine exposed in the living room; anyway, the heat coming up through baseboard elements wouldn't provide the best environment. There were no kitchen cupboards that would hold more than a bottle or two, and there was no available space in any chest of drawers. The only available and appropriate space was in the corner of one of two hall closets, the kind with folding doors, this section of the closet running along the wall beyond the door hinge.

The main problem to be solved was that the end wall of the closet, the wall against which he wanted to place the wines, was also the wall containing the plumbing for the shower. The only solution was styrofoam or something equivalent, against the entire width, breadth and height of that inner wall, but not flush against it. An air space of an inch or two provides very effective insulation against hot showers. The plans shown here can be used for building the bins to fit in practically any closet.

The front of our apartment cellar need not have its own door. Another piece of insulation board, cut to fit snugly in the space in front of the wines, but still easily removable, in case you'd like to drink a bottle once in a while, will work effectively. This, of course, is only one possible solution to closet problems. But simple insulation against direct heat is the basic plan of attack no matter what the special problem.

The very simplest of storage units is just to leave the wines in a cardboard case (your local liquor store will usually oblige), lying on its side. Slightly more sophisticated are the home-made bins - several designs are shown on these pages. These are not meant to be aesthetic but are strong and functionable. You would generally use one inch boards, anywhere from 10 to 14 inches deep, depending on whether or not you want the necks of the bottles to protrude. Sizes must be adjusted for magnums or half-bottles.

BOX WINE RACK

REPRESENTATIONAL PERSPECTIVE VIEW ONLY

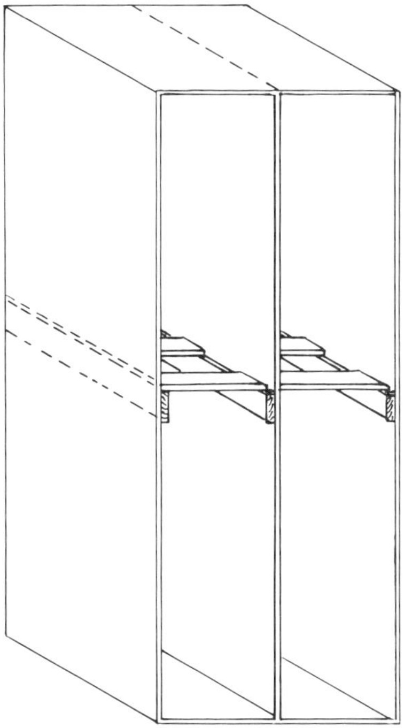

NOT TO SCALE

SIDE VIEW

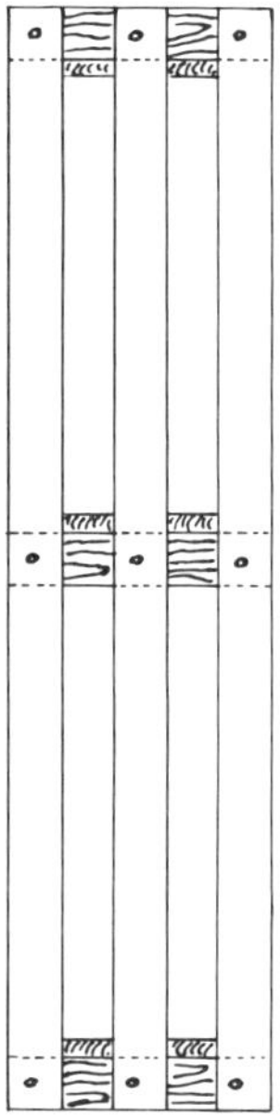

Material:
1'' X 2'' dressed lumber, type of wood and finish optional.

Construction:
Slatted, with cross-pieces glued and pinned to uprights. ''Shelves'' are two horizontal interspersed pieces of 1 X 2.

Size:
Vertical height - up to ceiling. Front to back - 5 X dressed lumber width, or about 9 3/8''. Left to right - two claret bottles diameter clear between uprights. Number of bays as required.

Note:
Some form of diagonal bracing will be required to retain squareness. The vertical height between shelves should not be more than six bottle diameters, or bulging is risked.

SOME DESIGN CONSIDERATIONS

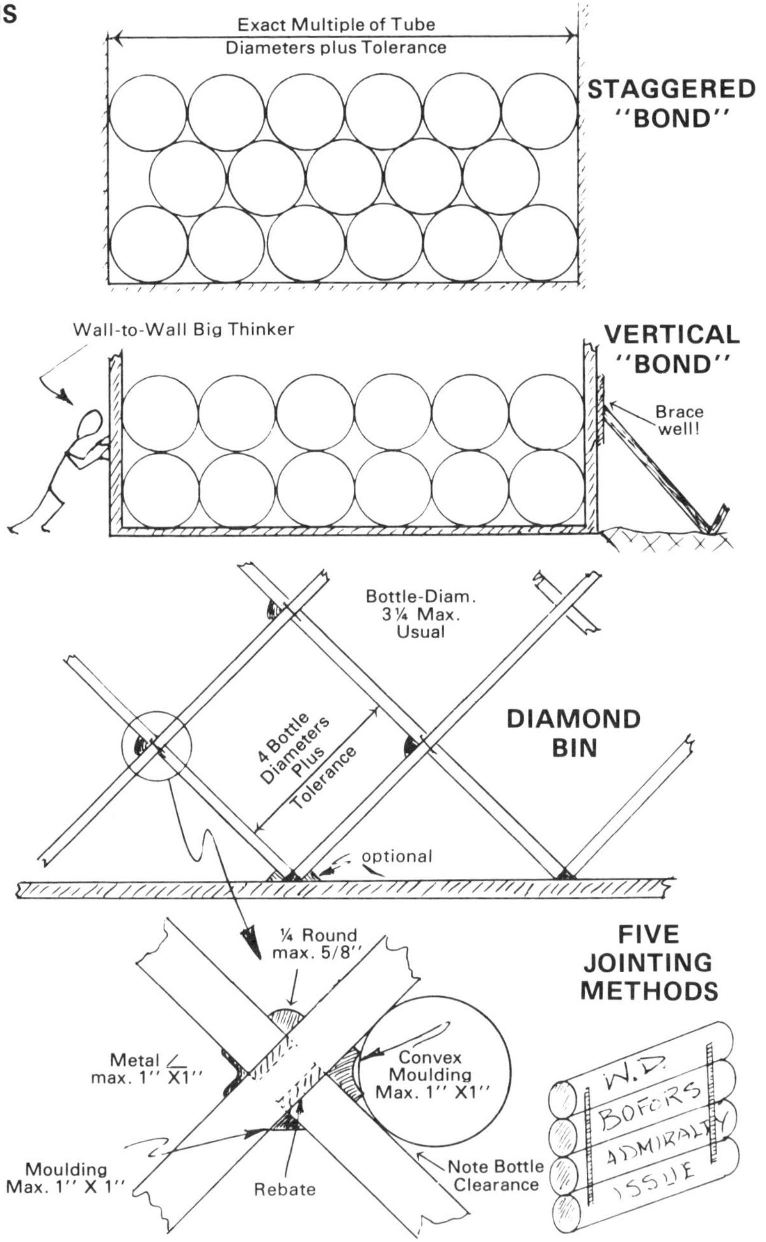

- When looking for tubes made of cardboard, tile or plastic, be sure that the interior diameter will accommodate the largest bottles you anticipate storing. Excluding the magnum sizes, you will be fairly safe with an inside diameter of 3½".

- Those of you embarking upon new cellar construction will no doubt want to build in a relatively permanent form of racking or binning. There appears to be no currently available modular rack that looks attractive, is built well, interlocks securely and is affordable. Hence the pipe or tube approach which requires relatively little do-it-yourselfing, or the bin approach for the carpenters among us. When using non-interlocked modules (e.g. pipe or tube), firm buttressing of the sides of the stack is essential. If you have an alcove, obviously your problem is solved. Or if you are a wall-to-wall big thinker and your foundations won't give way at the seams, the undertaking is simple.

- "Pipe" racks may be dry-wall constructed or cemented. Your choice of "bond" - staggered or aligned vertically. "Tube" racks will probably be more stable when laid up diagonally. Once the bottle containers are laid in place and securely buttressed at the sides, no further finishing is required.

- For bin builders there are two approaches: the metal-angle gussetted construction method and the triangular-wood moulding technique. Bins must carry a considerable weight, as they are usually set up to hold at least sixteen bottles per bin. This is quite convenient; a dozen bottles will fit into one bin, leaving a three bottle space above.

- Some suggested joint details of metal - and wood-gussetted bins are shown opposite.

DIAMOND WINE BINS

24'' X 60'' Unit = Holds 100 Bottles +
(Use any number in combination)

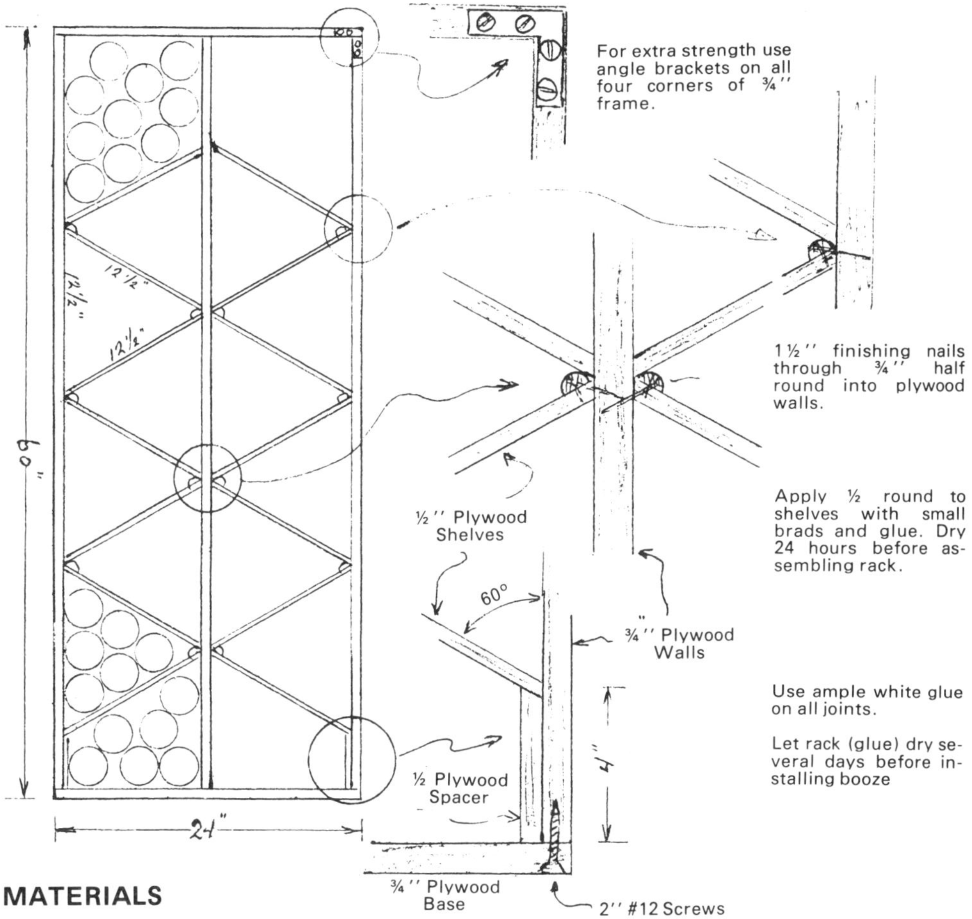

MATERIALS

3 - Walls 58½ X 8'' - ¾ Plywood
2 - Ends 24'' X 8'' ¾ Plywood
14 Shelves 12¾'' X 8 ½ Plywood
12 Pieces 8'' X ¾'' Half Round
2 Spacer 4'' X 8'' ½ Plywood

Screws, Nails, Glue, Angel Brackets

Brace Sidewalls Securely.
Use Exterior Grade Plywood

SELECTING THE WINE GLASS

Of course, there cannot be such a thing as "The" wine glass. There are many types and variations just as there are many wines, however, there are certain characteristics that one should look for in choosing a good wine glass.

INAO glass

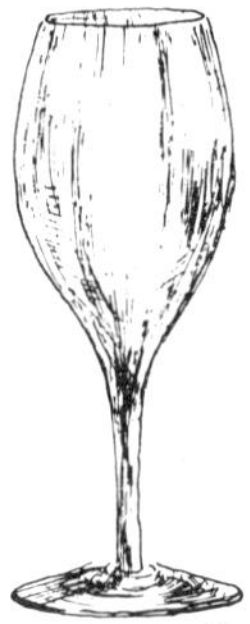
Champagne flute

Burgundy ballon

A clear-stemmed glass properly shows off the colour of the wine, does not impart any taste or odour and, if correctly held by the stem, prevents the heat of the hand from affecting the wine's temperature.

Visual appearance is an important part of the pleasure of a wine so the bowl of the glass should be as clear as possible. Raw materials other than glass (metal, china, clay, etc.) can be shaped properly, but these all have flaws related to transparency, taste or odour. Thus, clear glass rules.

Quality would seem to be a simple item to deal with. We have all been told for years that full lead crystal, with 24 per cent lead oxide in it, is the best. The Canadian government must agree because it is against the law to advertise anything as crystal unless it contains at least 24 per cent lead oxide. However one of its main weak points is its brittleness and its low resistance to sudden temperature changes, such as in a dishwasher.

Thus, though full lead crystal does offer greater transparency than ordinary glass, it is not a necessity. A good compromise is semi-crystal (the French call it *cristallin*) which is used by Rosenthal, Orrefors, Koster-Boda, and others. This was the material selected by the Institut National d'Appellation d'Origine in France when they developed the INAO standard professional testing glass, known in England as the International Standards Organization or ISO glass.

One of the very precise list of specifications for that glass was that it contains 9 per cent lead, not more, not less. The percentage of lead ensures proper transparency, yet the strength of the glass is improved somewhat because of the lesser amount of lead.

If you decide you want even more variety, then it becomes open season on additional formats. Some available in Canada are: 7 ounce white wine, liqueur, port/sherry, Sauternes, green-stemmed Moselle or Alsace, square-shaped clear-stemmed Alsace, clear thin-stemmed Roemer (for Rhine wine) or flared and amber-stemmed Roemer.

Whatever the glasses, there should be a balanced relationship between the size of the bowl, the length of the stem and the weight of the foot or base.

The ideal glass for sparkling wines is the champagne flute, not only for its aesthetically pleasing shape, but the length of the bowl and narrow closing retains the bubbles that the winemaker has worked so hard to nurture.

For other wines the size of the bowl is really a question of personal preference. There is a strong trend toward a much larger bowl than has been traditionally used, especially for serving a good red wine. A full-bodied red from an "oversize" burgundy ballon (they come in 7 to 88 ounce sizes) can be a special pleasure.

These are only suggestions. If you prefer heavy cut crystal glasses then by all means use them. They may not be ideal for wine drinking and you are possibly sacrificing something of the wine for the sake of the glass. However, like wine drinking, your choice of glassware should be the one that brings you the most personal pleasure.

A Story of Sickness

by Kenneth Christie, M.W.

Bottle sickness sounds like a malady from the days of Charles Dickens, and one might guess that it is caused either by too much intake of gin, or by the injudicious prescribing of those liquids of which Dickens remarked that "the worse the taste, the more efficacious its result." The tar-water with which Aunt Betsy dosed young Copperfield was a wholly benevolent remedy for coughs and cold that plagued Dickensian infants, and the sulphur that cleared their "tubes" is of the greatest assistance in the making of wines. But alas, bottle sickness, that strangest of ailments, rarely responds to either sulphur or tar-water.

A few weeks after completion of the yeast fermentation that converts grapes into young wine, a change takes place which renders the recently delicious juice undrinkable. The cause is a necessary but sometimes inconvenient bacterial form, which breaks down the vegetable acidity of the young wine and converts it to a less bitter acid form.

Within the bottle, the effect is seen in the taste of verjuice, the crab apple bitterness of abnormally high acidity, and the sharp prickling on the tongue which is seen in the glass in a corona of tiny bubbles that ring the border of the wine like a circle of small diamonds. But this common sickness is due more to lack of skill than other factors, and can be avoided by allowing the malolactic fermentation to terminate before beginning the transfer from vat or cask to bottle. Although this process involves a number of cataclysmic alterations in the chemistry of the wine, there is little outward effect upon flavour or taste unless the bottling takes place before the bacteria have completed their feast upon the malic acid in the newly made wine. Unfortunately there are few guide lines for the vigneron as to how he should deal with his wine during the time of malolactic fermentation. The wiser men wait, whilst the impatient pulverize their wine through savage filtration and fining processes, hoping that these activities will so sterilize the liquid that it will show no further signs of life or rebellion. If it were not for the current pace of our society, this frenzy of activity would not be required, but so great are the needs of the winemaker that he is forced to make and sell his wine rapidly. Thus practices once shunned are now commonplace.

What then of the other forms of bottle sickness? Nathaniel Johnston, doyen of the Bordeaux wine trade, has strong opinions on the reasons and cures for bottle sickness. He believes that wine matures as a result of its exposure to temperature, and relates this to the constituents that make up a bottle of wine; tannin and acidity, glycerol, sugar and aldehydes, and most important, alcohol. These are present in a continuously changing relationship and should one fall to the bottom (in the form of sediment), the remaining balance is changed. Depending on which component is precipitated as sediment, the wine becomes either harder or softer - but definitely altered.

Red wines, in particular, need an extensive period to settle down after bottling. Similarly, movement from one climatic area to another often inflicts a detrimental, if temporary, shock when wines are described as "dumb" or "shut in." With newly bottled wines this fault often lies in the relationship between sulphur, which is added to wine at the time of bottling, and the free oxygen which is accidentally taken into the wine solution by the pumping and bottling processes. Until the molecules of free oxygen have been contained by the action of the sulphur dioxide, they exert a substantial and degrading effect upon the wine which only time will repair.

It is not unusual, when tasting the first bottle of a newly arrived wine, to find it less than pleasing. With a second test after a few months, the wine is often found to be much better. The first judgement may have been too hasty, or perhaps, the newly arrived wine was suffering from a case of bottle sickness.

The Delight of Decanting?

by John Kalbfleisch

John Kalbfleisch, longtime amateur wine lover is deputy editorial page editor of "The Gazette" in Montréal.

When applied to wine (decanters can, after all, hold other liquids) the term decanter means a stoppered bottle of flint glass or lead crystal, often incised with an attractive design, in which wine is brought to the table and from which glasses are filled. The wine is decanted, that is, poured from its original bottle to the decanter, in order to separate it from its sediment. Hence, it is more likely that a decanter would be used with an old wine. The cork from the original bottle should properly be brought to the table for inspection by the host and any interested guests. The best decanters are made from clear crystal to show off the wine's colour to best advantage.

Decanting is probably as old as the art of crushing grapes to make wine. However, modern decanters, at least for English-speaking oenophiles, probably trace their descent back to the white-enamelled earthenware serving bottles in which wine was brought to the table in Stuart times. They had handles, feet, and loops for a string around their short necks. Often a blue inscription declared the bottle's contents. They were small and few were manufactured later than the 1680s - a good thing, too, as they often leaked, were liable to taint their contents and, being rough about the mouth, were difficult to cork.

In 1675, George Ravenscroft evolved flint glass, a term commonly used for any sort of clear glass (lead crystal is the modern equivalent), and serving bottles or decanters were among the tableware he manufactured. From the very beginning, elaborate decorations were available. So popular did decantation become that by the early 18th century "decanter" was a word thoroughly imbedded in the English language.

By the middle of the century, the growing wealth of England was reflected in an increasing refinement in many households. Flint glass tableware became increasingly popular. Decanters in particular were seen as things of beauty. The cruder vessels they replaced were relegated to the kitchen, and the hard use they received there has ensured that few of these earlier pieces have survived.

Eighteenth and nineteenth century decanters often have beautifully ringed necks, globular bodies and decorative stoppers. The rings - there may be one, two or three - generally had spaces between them so that fingers, directed by increasingly wine-befuddled brains, could be ensured of a secure grip.

Champagne became widely popular in the middle of the 18th century, prompting one ingenious craftsman (presumably with little appreciation of the wine's *sine qua non*, its effervescence) to invent a shouldered decanter with a cylindrical pocket for ice extending from its side into its body.

Decanters were not exclusively enjoyed by those with refined or even bourgeois tastes. In 1880, one Isaac Craig wrote, "I recollect distinctly seeing both tumblers and decanters made of green glass. In old times these decanters were used in every house, mostly by the poor families who could not afford cut glass. Whiskey was set out to every visitor in these decanters, and before and after every meal. Although of green glass they were not cut, but ornamented by beads around the neck."

That decanters are lovely examples of the glassmaker's art few people will dispute. But what of decantation? To decant or not to decant - that is the question.

Alexis Lichine, the winegrower and former wine merchant, maintains that sherries, ports and other wines which deteriorate, however slowly, once the cork is pulled are too often held for too long in decanters. However, Canadian author and newspaperman George Bain counts himself among the decanterers. Not only is decanting useful in ensuring that a wine is free of sediment, he writes in *Champagne Is For Breakfast*, but in addition there is "an even better reason ... A pair of graceful decanters filled with rich red wine - somehow, the same does not seem so true of white - just plain look good on the table."

I for one would disagree, albeit mildly, being prepared as I am to risk some unsightly sediment in my glass in return for the almost limitless variety of bottles and labels which can grace my table. The overwhelming majority of wines I drink are - sadly, I suppose - relatively young anyway, so that sediment for me is really not a problem.

However, if you must decant, here is how it is done. Gingerly bring your last bottle of Château Lafite-Rothschild '29 up from your cobwebbed cellar, taking care not to jostle or even rotate same. Having eschewed the former, you will allow any sediment present to slide down the length of the bottle to the punt, the funny part at the bottom of the bottle created by that mysterious dimple; in eschewing the latter, you will ensure that any sediment which does not slide down will nevertheless remain attached to that under side of the bottle which has been its home since first you laid the bottle down. Now the moment of truth: with a steady hand, pour the precious liquid cleanly into the waiting decanter. And always stop the instant the first sign of sediment appears. Even though sediment is an utterly harmless result of the wine's advance toward a glorious old age, that last murky ounce, as George Bain notes, should be poured over the turkey as it cooks. Such an end for even an ounce of so noble a wine, however murky, need not be mourned. Think of the snob points that can be scored off your guests: "Oh, of course, I always baste the turkey in Château Lafite-Rothschild '29."

The Taste of Wine with Food

by Paul Marks

There are chemical constituents of wines and of certain foods which create effects that for the "normal" European or North American palate are just plain bad tasting, experience, conditioning or training aside.

The natural iodine components in most fish react harshly with red wine that is significantly tannic. White wines with meats, red or white, cause nothing basically unhealthy or bad tasting; the traditional taboo is based on aesthetics more than anything else. Why not highlight your Montrachet with something equally rich in glycerine, malic and lactic acid, and buttery, apple-like esters, instead of the grey background of most meats. Meats on their own are basically bland foods, weighty perhaps, but generally not pungent, piquant or savoury.

Chocolate and wine, any wine, is tantamount to murder and suicide. If the taste sensation of wine is your goal, then try to put on weight some other way. Curry will kill most wines, too, but some whites, Gewürztraminer for instance, put up a brave fight. For me, grapefruit or cantaloupe as appetizer will kill any succeeding wine, white or red. I also recently discovered that artichokes and red wine are a disastrous combination, causing a terrible metallic taste.

The addition of sauces with food creates another problem altogether, and is of such importance and complexity that it can not properly be covered here. Let it be said that very often the choice of a wine to go with food will be determined by the sauce rather than the dish itself, which explains some traditional combinations such as the Bordelaise eel of the Dordogne with St-Emilion.

Nevertheless, even with combinations that are primarily

poor, for either gastronomic or aesthetic reasons, there are situations that might prove the rule by the exception. It comes again to a matter of individual perception. Beyond that, there are the variations based on time, place and condition.

Now for a few wine and food suggestions. Probably the handiest little list of wine and food combinations is in Hugh Johnson's *Pocket Encyclopedia of Wine* (London:Mitchell Beazley, and New York:Simon and Schuster, 1981.)

Basic no-nos are those I've listed above, but I might add that dry red wines with sweets generally tend to emphasize the wine's acidity. On the other side of the coin, red wines for table or dessert probably taste best with fine cheeses, and best of all will be the last half glass. It seems to me that the best part of any fine wine comes just as the wine is about to disappear, and you want more. Most desserts don't take any wine. You might want to try wine with a chocolate mousse just because I said it won't work - but then, if you like the combination, you probably don't like wine in the first place.

Traditionally, most fish and shellfish need dry, light, acidically balanced white wines. Fatty, oily fish like salmon are best accompanied by heavier whites, with more glycerine. In the same category of classical style, your good, plain roasted chicken deserves your best claret or fuller white; anything, in fact, not too heavy. The same may be said for veal, but in both cases if there is a sauce things work differently. Then you have to match the sauce, depending on how spicy, hot, bland or mild it is.

When it comes to pork I differ with Mr. Johnson. Despite the English tradition of (sauceless) pork with your best red or white, it seems to me to deserve a good beer, or perhaps a sparkling wine instead.

The bigger birds and game birds, turkey, duck, goose, and so on, give greater choice for me: medium to full reds like St. Emilion, Pomerol, California Cabernet Sauvignons, a white Hermitage, or the best white Graves, with Kabinett wines of the Rheingau or Alsatian Rieslings working best of all. The whites of the Côte de Beaune are perhaps not the most appro-

priate, but nor are they altogether out of place. And if your guest happens to have a weakness for them then nothing else will do.

Lamb ... ah! remain true to your best Bordeaux. As for other meats: roasts and the best steaks, just empty your bank account, as they cry out for Burgundy, northern Rhône wines, and the like. But, again, these are optimum choices. Anything big and red is what to look for. If you want breed, class, style, finesse and all that rot, well, there goes the budget.

On the more prosaic side of things, your homemade version of the Big Mac had better sit alongside a coke or a beer, but the summer barbeque works famously with a generic Côtes du Rhône, an ordinary Chianti, or a jug of "Hearty Burgundy." Speaking of Côtes du Rhône and Chianti (including Chianti Classico) these seem to me to be the best bets for most of your foods that need red wine; from my experience they work well with a greater range of food than either Bordeaux or Burgundy, except the lightest, plainest or blandest dishes.

Of course it helps to know beforehand the style of wine types and how they work with food. But the experience of trial and error works wonders for your memory bank. Many St. Estèphes, for instance, just don't have enough dry extract or glycerine to go with a fatty stuffed duck. Or, as I more recently discovered, some California Cabernet Sauvignons are too soft to go with spaghetti and meatballs. Yet, as I have implied, bottle variation can change the picture entirely. A recent trial of 1971 Ghemme, made from the Spanna grape, another name for the Piedmontese Nebbiolo of northern Italy, surprisingly didn't work with a spicy minced meat; it would have been better with chicken. But, that isn't true of most Nebbiolo wines (Barolo, Barbaresco, and others of Piedmont.)

As you see, then, wine and food combination is, in fact, a casual kind of folk art. Just as whatever suits your taste is the best choice, so you can choose whether to play this game by intuition or reasoning. You will have reached a fine-edged level of expertise when you know exactly what is required but decide not to give a damn.

Living with an Oenophile

CONFESSIONS OF A SPOUSE

by Judith Posner

Judith Posner is a sociologist and teacher at York University and occasionally does freelance writing as a hobby.

It's not that I don't like wine. I do. I even believe that no respectable meal is complete without it. And I know the difference between Bordeaux and Burgundy, although I must confess that my gift for analytic discrimination often ends there. Neither do I begrudge my spouse's obsession with the grape even though it eats heavily into our finances. (Of course he convinces me that wine is a good investment. How can it be a good investment when you drink it all?) What bothers me about wine is the way it works its way into every nook and cranny of our life. It pervades our relationship with others. In short, it is insidious.

In fact, I think I have been quite tolerant over the years. For example, I never complain about the fact that our dinner parties are arranged around wine. Guests are invited according to their level of wine appreciation so that my husband does not have to get into a quandary about what vintage (or non-vintage) he should be serving. And although in traditional sex role fashion I am in charge of the food while my husband sees to the liquid refreshment, I am not *really* in charge of the food. I merely cook after my husband choses the menu. And as you have probably guessed by now he chooses the food according to the wine he intends to serve. I have put up with all of this as though it were quite ordinary. I am used to going shopping and having to pass up some wonderful looking salmon because my husband feels like a Bordeaux evening. What irks me is the fact that I knock myself out preparing an accompaniment befitting one of his finest Côtes du Rhône only to find that he is so concerned with the wine that he barely notices my elaborate provençale stew. Occasionally I nudge him under the table, or with closer friends I verbally remind him to eat. But to my chagrin he is usually so busy gurgling and swooning into his glass that his food is stone cold by the time he gets around to it. And when the guests leave I solemnly swear I will never cook for him again, but of course I do. Sometimes he is so excited that he actually excuses himself from the dinner table to retrieve his grey looseleaf notebook into which he records his most intimate oenophile impressions. Not surprisingly, he is frequently so preoccupied with the wine that he completely forgets to interact with his guests - unless of course the topic is wine. This is the most insidious aspect of it all.

Night after night, the most interesting sorts of people can be at our house, and a variety of subjects could arise at the dinner table, were it not for the topic of wine which overshadows everything. I would like to be able to tell you that he bores everyone to death, but strange as it may seem this does not appear to be the case. Perhaps for some it is such a novelty that they enjoy it. While others, our oenophile friends, think nothing of spending the greater part of an evening discussing food and wine. Such discussions generally culminate, for first timers especially, in a small visit to the wine cellar. I use the time to great advantage - clearing away the wreckage from the entrée and preparing for cheese and dessert. Meanwhile I can hear low murmurings from the bowels of the basement as he displays his prize possessions.

Did I say basement? I really shouldn't be mentioning in a public forum exactly where he hides his collectables. Lately his obsession has turned to paranoia. He has been muttering about putting in a burglar alarm and he gets very twitchy when the meter man or service people find it necessary to poke around down there. And upon returning from holiday the first thing he does when he comes through the door is run down to the cellar to check on his bottles. Personally, I can't believe he would know if any were missing, but he claims he would. Once, when he was out of town and I was invited out to dinner, I grabbed a bottle of Médoc to take with me. I wasn't quite sure about it and, horror or horrors, it turned out to be a little on the young side, but *we* liked it. Anyway it took him some three months but he did eventually notice its absence. I broke down and confessed in shame, and was relieved to find that it wasn't *terribly* young nor was it very expensive. But now when he goes away he instructs me about the various untouchables and makes the appropriate suggestions for my cruder palate.

Recently I suggested that if he was so concerned about his finer wines and since he is increasingly short of storage space, that he place some of the better bottles in out of the way corners that are relatively inaccessible behind our ordinary table wines - which we affectionately call "plonk." But of course this suggestion didn't go down very well. Aside from the public aspect of such an arrangement during his renowned guided tours, such a presentation would be aesthetically repugnant during his private meditations. He would not like to enter his cellar and find himself face to face with some ordinary Chianti from the LCBO.

In spite of all my complaints, the time we enjoy wine the most is during the weekend at home, puttering about the house. After returning from the market on Saturday we begin with a little cheese, paté and Beaujolais and never look back. Sometimes we even get to a few tasks that are long overdue, but overall I have concluded that wine and house maintenance don't really mix. And then suddenly in the middle of the afternoon my husband mysteriously disappears and I know exactly where to find him. He is in his cellar, bottle-gazing and rearranging - moving each bottle more gently than a newborn so as not to disturb the sediment.

And speaking of babies, our son and heir to this great wine obsession - what does he think about it? Well, at three months we were dunking his pacifier into the stemware to ensure his non-interruption of our repast. At six months we had a tasting in his honour - a magnum of Corton Charlemagne '64 given to us by a fellow oenophile as a baby gift. Eric, bless him, slept through the entire tasting. Now he is eight months and shows a distinct preference for reds, Bordeaux in particular, but he is not at all fond of Cognac. Actually, I think he prefers beer but I wouldn't dare mention this to my husband.

Vintages

"To drink or not to drink, that is the question." Had Shakespeare lived today, he might well be muttering this when faced with deciding whether or not his best bottle of wine was ripe enough for a corkscrew. Indeed, now many of us serious wine drinkers have had the experience of opening a bottle of expensive claret only to find out, to our horror, that the wine was not at all ready to drink. If only each bottle had its own best-time-to-drink timetable printed on the label!

Actually, if in a liquor store you picked up five bottles of wine at random, chances are good that four of them would be ready to drink anytime. That's because many of the world's wines are made so as to be near mediocre best by the time they grace our liquor store shelves. Such wines include most of the whites, rosés, non-vintage reds, various blends, American "jug wines," Beaujolais, light Chiantis and Valpolicellas; in fact the majority of inexpensive wines fall into this category. Just give these wines a few months' grace, to give them a chance to recover from whatever travels they were subjected to, and drink away.

With most vintage wines, though, we have to play guessing games as to their drinkability. Not even the vintner himself could predict with any certainty when his wine will reach its peak and for us, the consumers, the task is much more formidable, for we have only the labels to go by. Such important factors as the winemaker's degree of skill or how the wine was previously stored and shipped are usually unknown to us. Also, vinification methods have been changing in the last decade, favouring faster aging by imparting less tannin to the wines. This may vary considerably among winemakers and from region to region. However, the single most important fact to know, and this information is often available to us, is the quality of the vintage from which a given wine was made.

In a great vintage, a warm spring with just enough gentle rain induces early flowering on vines which in turn, providing the sun was kind and persistent during the latter part of the summer, produces fully matured grapes early in the fall. In such years, often low on yield, the grapes contain a high level of sugar with concentrated flavour resulting in wines of very high quality and long life. In a poor vintage, cold, damp weather retards flowering, with a wet summer providing the *coup de grâce*. The resulting grapes are unripe, with very low sugar content, making wines which are thin and acidic and which if they have to be drunk at all, might as well be drunk early and so be done with. Such wines won't improve with age. In between the two extremes, there are of course infinite variations. During each year, though, a few winemakers, for whatever reasons, buck the trend and produce wines of contrary quality to the average rating of the vintage. In poor years such wines are a bargain.

VINTAGE CHART

	BORDEAUX						BURGUNDY						ITALY		CALIFORNIA Napa & Sonoma		
	Reds		Whites (Graves)		Sauternes		Reds		Whites		Beaujolais	Rhône	Rhine/Mosel	Piedmont	Tuscany	Reds	Whites	
YEAR	Vintage Value	Time to Drink	Vintage Value	Time to Drink	Vintage Value	Time to Drink	Vintage Value	Time to Drink	Vintage Value	Time to Drink	Vintage Value	Vintage Value	Vintage Value	Vintage Value	Vintage Value	Vintage Value	Vintage Value	YEAR
1961	**100**	**7-25**	**95**	**3-10**	**95**	**5-20**	**95**	**5-20**	**75**	**3-7**		**95**						**1961**
1964	**80**	**4-15**	**80**	**3-8**	**50**	**3-7**	**85**	**4-14**	**80**	**3-8**		**80**		**100**	**90**	**85**	**85**	**1964**
1966	**85**	**6-18**	**80**	**3-8**	**65**	**3-9**	**85**	**4-14**	**85**	**3-9**		**90**		**35**	**60**	**75**	**65**	**1966**
1967	**75**	**3-12**	**80**	**3-8**	**90**	**4-15**	**65**	**3-8**	**75**	**3-7**		**85**	**75**	**85**	**75**	**60**	**60**	**1967**
1969	**60**	**3-9**	**75**	**2-7**	**70**	**4-9**	**85**	**4-12**	**85**	**3-9**		**85**	**85**	**70**	**85**	**70**	**60**	**1969**
1970	**90**	**4-16**	**85**	**3-9**	**85**	**4-15**	**70**	**3-9**	**75**	**3-7**		**90**	**75**	**80**	**80**	**90**	**80**	**1970**
1971	**80**	**3-11**	**80**	**3-7**	**90**	**4-15**	**85**	**4-12**	**90**	**3-10**		**80**	**100**	**95**	**95**	**65**	**65**	**1971**
1972	**50**	**3-8**	**60**	**2-5**	**60**	**3-8**	**75**	**3-9**	**50**	**2-5**		**80**	**60**	**30**	**50**	**45**	**65**	**1972**
1973	**70**	**3-9**	**65**	**2-5**	**65**	**3-8**	**65**	**3-7**	**75**	**3-7**		**65**	**70**	**70**	**60**	**70**	**85**	**1973**
1974	**65**	**3-9**	**60**	**2-5**	**50**	**3-7**	**55**	**2-6**	**65**	**2-6**	**70**	**60**	**65**	**85**	**70**	**85**	**75**	**1974**
1975	**85**	**4-15**	**85**	**3-9**	**90**	**4-16**	**40**	**2-4**	**70**	**2-7**	**45**	**40**	**85**	**65**	**85**	**65**	**85**	**1975**
1976	**75**	**3-10**	**65**	**2-5**	**65**	**3-8**	**90**	**4-13**	**85**	**3-9**	**85**	**90**	**90**	**50**	**55**	**60**	**70**	**1976**
1977	**60**	**3-8**	**75**	**2-7**	**50**	**3-6**	**50**	**2-5**	**55**	**2-5**	**65**	**65**	**55**	**50**	**85**	**60**	**65**	**1977**
1978	**80**	**4-11**	**70**	**2-6**	**70**	**3-8**	**80**	**4-10**	**80**	**3-8**	**85**	**85**	**50**	**90**	**90**	**80**	**70**	**1978**
1979	**70**	**3-9**	**65**	**2-5**	**75**	**3-10**	**70**	**3-8**	**75**	**3-7**	**70**	**70**	**75**	**80**	**80**	**50**	**60**	**1979**
1980	**60**	**3-7**	**65**	**2-5**	**70**	**4-9**	**65**	**3-7**	**70**	**3-6**	**60**	**70**	**60**	**70**	**75**	**75**	**70**	**1980**
1981	**75**	**3-9**	**70**	**2-5**	**80**	**4-12**	**70**	**3-8**	**75**	**3-6**	**80**	**85**	**70**	**75**	**75**	**70**	**70**	**1981**
1982	**80**	**3-11**	**75**	**3-4**	**65**	**3-7**	**75**	**3-8**	**80**	**3-7**	**70**	**80**	**70**	**80**	**80**	**60**	**60**	**1982**
1983	**80**	**4-12**	**80**	**3-5**	**80**	**4-10**	**85**	**3-10**	**75**	**3-6**	**75**	**80**	**85**	**75**	**75**	**80**	**75**	**1983**
1984	**60**	**3-8**	**65**	**2-5**	**70**	**3-8**	**55**	**3-6**	**65**	**2-5**	**70**	**75**	**75**	**70**	**60**	**85**	**80**	**1984**

This vintage chart is only a guide. However, in making it, creator Frank Prazak consulted many different sources as well as drawing upon his own experience. As a result it may be more reliable and offer more information than most other vintage charts, and should provide you with a good base when making an educated guess before subjecting a bottle to a corkscrew.

Vintage Value

Numbers indicate an average quality of the vintage for the region. 100 - best, 10 - lowest.

Time to Drink

The numbers here indicate the suggested average waiting time in years before drinking the various wines of a given region. As a rule, the better the wine, the longer one should wait before drinking it, the longer it is likely to keep its peak and the longer its overall shelf life. The lower number of the column applies to inexpensive regional blends, the higher number indicates probable waiting time for the top wines. The very best wines of the region would probably need still more time than indicated. As an example of how this may work, let's look at the pecking order of the Bordeaux reds from the fine vintage of 1970 where our listed time to drink is 4 to 16 years.

4 to 7 years: regional blends (appellation Bordeaux or Bordeaux Supérieur Contrôlée) and district blends, e.g. Pomerol, St. Emilion, Médoc, etc.

5 to 8 years: commune blends from the Médoc, e.g. Saint-Julien, Margaux, etc.

6 to 9 years: châteaux (estate) wines of lesser districts of the region, e.g. Côtes de Bourg, Blaye, Fronsac, etc.

8 to 12 years: most minor estates of major districts (called Crus Bourgeois in the Médoc).

10 to 14 years: top Crus Bourgeois, better estates of Pomerol, Graves, lower Grands Crus of Saint-Emilion, the Médoc.

12 to 16 years: the greatest estates of major districts. Top Grands Crus, Premiers Grands Crus, best Graves. A few of these may need more than 16 years.

If one doesn't know where a certain wine would fit into the above order, its price tag may give a good indication of relative quality. For Bordeaux the various regional, district and commune blends, will be at the lower end of the scale, minor estates and Crus Bourgeois next, and Grand Crus and the top estates of Pomerol and Graves much higher.

Premiers Grands Crus, the very best Graves and Pomerols will start from $40 and up. Here one pays a good portion of the price for the prestige of a given label, for it is doubtful that the actual difference in quality between this exalted group of châteaux and their nearest neighbours is worth the large gap in price.

The other major wine regions may not have such a wide range of quality and prices (although the Burgundies and California wines come very close) but they all have ranges of their own. Here again the relative prices may be your guide.

The Chart

Comments on the vintage chart, region by region:

Bordeaux reds: The time-to-drink values are mostly for the Médoc and Graves where the large portion of the grapes used are Cabernets. In Saint Emilion and Pomerol the hardness of the Cabernet is tempered by the Merlot grape which allows wines of those regions to mature on the average 10 to 20 per cent faster.

Bordeaux whites: Mostly apply to Graves. It's up to one's personal taste how long to age better whites be they of Graves or elsewhere. With a few years in the bottle these wines may lose some of their acidity and acquire a certain amount of charm and character, which may be preferable in most cases. The times given are average.

Barsacs and Sauternes: Most sweet wines age well, with the sugar acting as a preservative. Twenty-year-old Sauternes from good years are not at all unusual. Also their best-to-drink peaks are longer and more gradual than those of other wines.

Red Burgundies: (from the Côte d'Or) These wines age noticeably faster than Bordeaux, and because of their style drink well long before they peak. Within the Côte d'Or district, the Côte de Nuits wines take longer to mature than those of the Côte de Beaune.

White Burgundies: See white Bordeaux. The best aging wines are from the Montrachet group, Corton-Charlemagne and the better Meursaults.

Beaujolais: These are of course drunk young. However a few first growth appellations such as Morgon may benefit from some bottle age.

Côtes du Rhône: The reds of the southern Côtes are now made generally in much lighter styles than they used to be. Most Côtes du Rhône blends may be consumed within two to four years of the vintage. Drink most Châteauneuf-du-Papes and Gigondas within three to six years. A few Châteauneufs, mostly estate bottled, are still made in the old, big, tannic style which, on the average, drink best within six to ten years of the vintage. The northern Côtes' mighty Hermitage needs at least ten years to show its muscles (the whites also age extremely well) and its cousin Côte Rôtie may take nearly as long to show its elegance. The big reds of Crozes-Hermitage and Saint-Joseph need six to eight years to reach their potential.

Rhine and Mosel: Most inexpensive (relatively speaking) German wines are meant to be quaffed while young and fresh. However, the wines of the "Qualitätswein mit Prädikat" rating such as Spätlesen, Auslesen, Beerenaulesen and Trockenbeerenauslesen all become richer and more concentrated with some bottle age. As a rule, the sweeter the wine the longer time it needs to reach its potential. A good Auslese from the great vintage of 1971 should still be at its peak now while a Trockenbeerenauslese from the same year may keep on improving for another ten years.

Piedmont: Northern Italy's Barolos, Barbarescos, and Gattinaras, made from the Nebbiolo grapes, usually need good aging. In an average year a well-made Barolo needs at least eight to twelve years to mellow its hardness. In a fine year it may take 15 to 20 years. Give the other Nebbiolo based wines 5 to 8 years on the average with the understanding that some of these wines, which of course include Barolos, sometimes seem to stay hard and tannic forever.

Tuscany: Chianti Classicos vary somewhat in style from house to house but on the average may be drunk within 4 to 6 years. The Riservas should be fine within 6 to 8. Great Brunello di Montalcino shouldn't be even tried before it is at least 10 years old.

California: Despite their relatively short modern history. the wines of Napa and Sonoma have proven their fine keeping potential. Yet, because of the style, most can be enjoyed well before their prolonged peak. On the average, however, one should resist pulling the cork from one of the fine Cabernets of the district for about 7 to 8 years. Most Pinot Noirs are noticeably faster as are the majority of other varietals. The whites should be ready within 1 to 4 years. The top Chardonnays and some Sauvignons should be kept longer. (See Bordeaux whites).

Finally though, if in doubt as to when the time is ripe to open one of your fine bottles of wine, remember that while it may be annoying to drink it before its time, it is sad to wait until its charms start fading away.

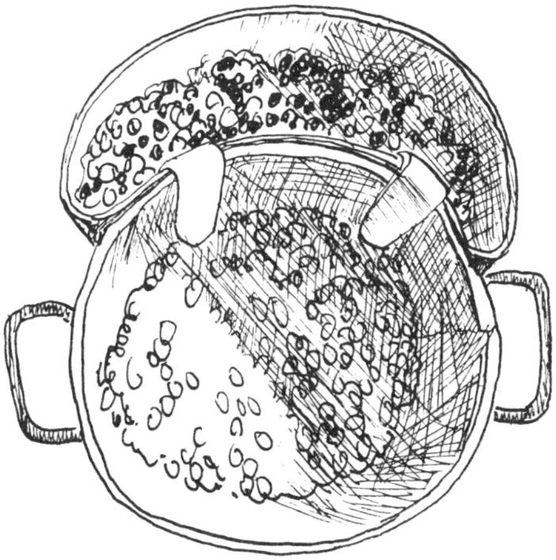

The extra container hanging on the side of the picking basket is to segregate the grapes happily "rotted" by botrytis cinerea.

This Claret of which we Dream!

by Kenneth Christie, M. W.

There are many occasions when definitive comments covering the keeping qualities of wines of every conceivable quality and maturity are discussed. Conclusions vary, not because of a reluctance to be decisive, but are dependent on how the wines have been stored.

There is a basic concept which must be understood concerning how wine matures. It is simply that wine gains maturity by experience of temperature rather than the passage of days, nights, months and years. It is therefore essential when discussing vintages to accept that there are over-many exceptions to general rules and these are too frequently the result of sloppy, uncaring attention at the hands of the vendor or buyers. The difficulties experienced in shipping wine are legion and there are many possibilities for wines to be damaged between their leaving the region of their bottling and arrival in the customer's cellar, or upon his table. There are indeed frequent tales of delays in shipment, where wines are caught in dock strikes or in transportation delays resulting in their passing the summer months lying in the sunshine. The wines then incubate, oxydize and begin their decline from quality to mediocrity. On the more positive side, providing that wines have been correctly stored, the progress to their eventual collapse is not dissimilar to that of their eventual consumers - the cradle, adolescence, and thereafter a sad but inevitable gradual decline!

Of all the wines of the world, few indeed have any pretence to quality, and of those not many derive any great benefit through being stored until mature. However, of those wines which evidently gain quality through gentle ageing the most celebrated is undoubtedly claret. Claret, described as "un gentilhomme par excellence, le vin d'une correction impeccable"; even considered by the Sun King, Louis XIV, as "un petit vin passable," is unquestionably the perfect wine. Granting, as we must, that the best wine is the wine that we like best, there is no denying the fact that the vineyards of Bordeaux produce wines of the highest quality in greater quantity and also more interesting variety than any of the other vineyards in France.

Generally claret is made of a selected blend of noble grapes, their hardness and austerity coming from the Cabernet Sauvignon, their charm and elegance from the Malbec and Verdot, and their generosity and fragrance from the Merlot. And so, when different proportions of these vine varieties are blended the end result differs, even within the same vintage or from the same cellar. But generally vintages have a character of their own, a special "personality" that the expert can identify and describe to the layman, who in turn, recognizes and commits to his or her memory.

There is little interest in the vintages of many years ago, for their merits or demerits have passed into history, and their wines have disappeared from the glass to oblivion. So let us consider the wines which we might still find today, from the oldest to the youngest, borrowing Maurice Healy's words "at its age is still drank graciously, with not more than a suspicion of fading."

1970

Throughout the whole Bordeaux region the vintage was plentiful and produced full rich wines with good colour and bouquet. Almost all the wines were well balanced and fruity. The uniformity of the quality through all the red wines was welcomed universally after two previous years of mediocre style. Most of these wines have been consumed, but those that remain have plenty of life, and the big wines should be sampled as they are beginning to show their tremendous quality.

1971

A mixed vintage, but the better wines have quite remarkable depth and staying power. With international demand increasing through the "financial boom," this vintage was even more expensive than its predecessor. The harvest was not universally good, but most wines have colour and depth. Most of the bourgeois growths have now been consumed but those that remain should be drunk without undue delay as they are beginning to lose their charm.

1972

This year was launched onto a ready market which appeared to be able to buy anything at any price, although a collapse was to come! Although the year lacked quality, prices continued to march upwards until October of 1973 when the first oil crisis produced a decline in the financial world and with it collapsing prices for claret. From that time the wines have been judged on their merit alone, and by any assessment the quality of 1972 was indifferent.

1973

The wines were nice and light. It was an easily appreciated year. A long hot summer was followed by rain before and during the harvesting of the grapes, producing low acidity levels and unbalanced wines. However those that remain have colour and charm, although they will not last long and are ready for drinking now, they represent good value where they can still be purchased. Strangely the price of the greatest wines, those of first growths and similarly well considered wines, has hardly changed since the opening of the market.

1974

This year produced uninteresting wines. Little was sold by the growers until 1976 when the North American markets took the stocks off the growers' hands - to the evident delight of the more traditional buyers and the French wine trade. The vintage is best left alone, no matter which label is offered.

1975

Really fine, a great vintage, which becomes daily more appreciated. All the wines are deep in colour, with an excellent balance of fruit and tannin. The better ones have a long and glorious future in the bottle, perhaps for 30 years. The complex nature of the '75s make them unattractive for early drinking as plenty of time is needed to soften their tannin. Prices have escalated steadily since the first offering but it is still possible to buy the better Cru Bourgeois which have become drinkable although their austerity is still evident. Providing that the wines are well cellared they will rank with the greatest of all claret vintages including the '29s, '45s and even the 1961s.

1976

Throughout the summer of this year the whole of Europe was blessed with long hot and dry days and wine lovers felt sure that they were to enjoy another great vintage. Counting chickens before they are hatched is rarely a fault of the wine farmer, but the rain of early September spoilt some of the wines. Those picked in the rain are light, fragrant and drinkable, others have much depth and tannin and will last for many years. Careful selection has rewarded those people that have taken the time to learn about the better years but wherever the 1976s can be found it is worthwhile taking a chance on this vintage.

1977

It is difficult to find good wines from this vintage for the prospects were spoilt by the frosts of March, a cold wet summer, and disease in the grapes that ruined the chances of many growers. Although the wines are not particularly good it is still strange that prices rank with the 1976s. Best advice would be to give this year a miss.

1978

The first sign of the great quality of the 1978s was the feverish buying from the very earliest offerings of this vintage. The Bordeaux trade, quietly but steadily, set about buying whichever wines were placed on the market and, although they seemed at the beginning to be expensive, the consensus is that 1978 will be the finest year of the decade. The wines made of the Cabernet Sauvignon are particularly fine and this has enhanced the qualities of the Médoc but not to the detriment of St. Emilion and Pomerol, whose wines are also very fine. In the Blaye and Bourg regions the petits châteaux are much sought after, as they give many of the qualities of the more expensive regions at an economic price level. Well stocked wine cellars should include a range of this vintage.

1979

Although the wines are not showing as well as the 1978s or 1976s they are generally better than the 1977s and will be early maturing, easy wines for every-day drinking. They are not wines for keeping too long but will give pleasure for their sturdiness and while not generous, they are sound and well balanced.

1980

Variable weather conditions resulted in a crop only marginally larger than the 1977. The red wines lack extract, have inconsistent acidity levels and show evidence of being made from unripe grapes. Rot was a problem for growers who could not afford antibotrytis sprays. St. Emilion has probably the best wines of the region.

In conclusion the red wines of Bordeaux are delightful for the variety of their vintages and are invariably worthy of conversation. The classification of Bordeaux in 1855 has not been forgotten but it is now largely redundant as great wines from other regions of Bordeaux have been added to those of the Médoc which, with the exception of Château Haut Brion, were the only wines included in the 1855 rankings. And so the advances in vine cultivation and winemaking have made it essential that personal tastings and experience should be brought into play in judging the wines of this remarkable area lying in the southwest of France. Claret was once considered to be the Englishman's wine, even from the time of Queen Mary Tudor. Today its prestige has rightly been spread around the globe and, for many, the increased cost of red bordeaux has resulted in claret being merely the wine of which we dream.

1981

A very good year which had been eagerly awaited by growers and merchants anxious to gain the financial benefit of the offer of a successful vintage at the 'en primeur' (newly fermented) stage.

The finished wines have been rather overlooked in the aftermath of the subsequent year, but a sure sign of their quality can be found at the châteaux, where the growers have (largely) delayed bottling until late in 1983 to allow the wines time to gain maximum benefit from maturation in their oakwood casks.

1982

Flowering in perfect conditions on vines; well ripened by the fine weather of the previous autumn. This lead to the setting of a massive crop, and new records of production. However, upon this promising situation was superimposed the excellence of the summer of 1982, hot and dry, with only sufficient August rain to swell the ripening grapes to their optimum maturity at harvest time.

The result of the natural factors, with the skill of the winemakers, will be a vintage of surpassing quality. So much has already been recorded about the '82s that there is little left to say, except that over some of the wines will be a question - "Will they have enough fixed acidity to ensure their long life?" When the wines are finally in bottle this small query will be answered, but it seems that the omens are wholly favourable.

GLOSSARY OF TASTING TERMS - THE BOUQUET

Acetic: a sharp smell of vinegar, usually rather pricking at the top of the nose.

Acidity: all wines contain acid; it is harsh and sour to the nose in bad years and refreshing in better vintages.

Apples: the fresh malic smell of 'Granny Smiths' which frequently marks out immature young wine.

Austere: hard and unyielding, difficult to smell, frequently the smell of fine wines before they mature.

Baked: a sugary smell produced by grapes which have been excessively ripened in very hot years, or in naturally very hot areas such as Sicily, Greece, (even) Southern California.

Blackcurrants: the typical perfume of the Cabernet Sauvignon, the classic vine of Bordeaux, now widely planted in many countries.

Bottle sickness: wines immediately after bottling demonstrate this rather vulgar smell which reminds one of hot plastic.

Bouquet [aroma]: the smell given off by wine; made up of volatile esters and aldehydes formed in the presence of fruit acids and alcohol.

Cedarwood: a smell which is traditionally attributed to the finest wines of Bordeaux, particularly Château Lynch Bages, a fifth growth from the village of Pauillac.

Clean [straightforward]: wines which are typically 'winey' without any unpleasant or unusual odour.

Cooked: sweet smell associated with wines which have been heavily sweetened with raw sugar before fermentation.

Corked: once experienced, never forgotten, yet for all the talk of 'corked' wines it is very rare. The smell is precisely that of 'dry-rot' in wood.

Corky: associated with 'corked', the wine has a slight smell of cork but may still be drinkable.

Dumb: very little bouquet but one which 'promises' to develop into a fine quality.

Flint-stone: an aroma characterized by the wines of the Upper Loire (Sancerre and Pouilly Fumé) and the drier Moselles. Rather cold austere clinical perfume.

Fragrant: an attractive flowery perfume, typical of the better Moselle wines.

Fruity: the ripe perfume of plums.

Geraniums: a strange and very unpleasant 'nose' originating from the excessive use of sorbic acid by the winemaker.

Grapey: the smell which recalls the lovely Muscatel grapes which are often a part of the Christmas table.

Green: immature wine has so much acidity that it frequently smells of young green sticks and vegetables. The same odour is a characteristic of very young wine.

Hydrogen sulphide [bad eggs]: usually associated with poor cellar treatment; or with the overuse of dry sulphur.

Maderisé: frequently found in wines which have grown old under ideal storage conditions. Often identified by a brown tinted colouring in white wines.

Malic [see apples]: the mouthwatering acid smell of cooking apples brought about by the inclusion of unripe grapes in the press.

Mouldy: an unpleasant odour associated with the rotten grapes found in wet vintage years. Can be caused by the use of poor or unclean casks.

Pepper: so frequently a word used in the description of fine Rhône wines. The perfume is that of fresh green peppers rather than ground pepper.

Piquant: a vigorous, fresh and sappy fragrance found in fine Moselle wines or those made from the Sauvignon grape of Bordeaux and Sancerre.

Pricked: the sharp smell of acetic acid which is caused by a build-up of volatile acidity. When tested, pricked wines have a distinctly prickly taste on the tongue.

Profound: a deep bouquet found in many fine wines at the time of their optimum maturity. While not being categorized as fragrant, this is nonetheless a wholly attractive bouquet.

Shut-in: a small hard smell which, nevertheless, tempts the taster to believe that with development the bouquet will develop and increase its power.

Sour: one of the odours of excessive acidity where the acid overwhelms the fragrance of the grape.

Stalks: the self-describing perfume of wine made from unripe grapes or where many of the stalks or pips have been included.

SO [sulphur dioxide]: the element of the winemaker which has been used since the wine was first stabilized. When overused the strong, pungent smell of sulphur overcomes all the other delicate perfumes of the wine. When over-sulphured wines grow to maturity there is usually a build up of the 'bad egg' smell.

Sweet: although many wines smell sweet this is usually caused by the use of grapes which have been effected by botrytis cinerea (noble rot), the phenomenal mould growth responsible for the great dessert wines of Sauternes and Germany.

Vanilla: strongly reminiscent of the real perfume of this flavouring spice. Usually found in mediocre white wines produced in poor regions.

Volatile: when wine is in good condition, volatile acidity is unnoticeable, however as wine deteriorates there is build-up of this sharp aroma which will eventually lead to the wine becoming unsound.

Wet wool: the damp smell in wine caused by the contact with poor or unsound casks.

Woody[ed]: self-descriptive bouquet caused by keeping the wine too long in contact with old wooden vats (as in Chianti), or overlong in new oakwood.

Yeast: the strong bready smell of yeast which may be found in wines that have been poorly handled. If live yeasts are found in wine they will surely give rise to a secondary fermentation.

GLOSSARY OF TASTING TERMS - THE PALATE

Acetic: vinegary taste associated with wines that have been left open or perhaps carelessly handled.

Acid: the natural and benevolent compounds found in fruit, which in wine give it a mouthwatering flavour and character. Acids in white wines, and tannin in red wines are the preserving agents which holds the wines in good condition.

Astringent: the harsh drying effect of excessive tannin, which in combination with acidity causes the mouth to dry out.

Balance: one of the words beloved of wine merchants, which describes the happy relationship between all the natural components of the wine.

Big: description of the full flavour of a wine high in alcohol and extract, with a concentrated flavour.

Bite: the sappy acidity of good (if young) wine.

Bitter: a particular flavour which points to the wine being affected by contamination with the heavy metals used in the winery (copper, bronze).

Body: the sensation of weight in the mouth coming from the alcohol and other physical constituents.

Breed: a difficult winetaster's word but one which sums up the finesse of wine, red or white, when it has superior balance.

Character: the distinctive flavour of wine which marks out its origin; for example, the rich cedarwood flavour of certain Pauillacs.

Cloying: rich, sickly sweetness which quickly bores the taster. Frequently found in cheap dessert wines but very rarely in the great wines of Sauternes and Barsac.

Coarse: a vulgar flavour indicating sloppy or indifferently made wines. Also characterizes many of the wines fermented at high temperatures.

Common: possibly sound but usually boring and coarse.

Delicate: the charming flavour which suggests lightness of alcohol but fragrance and quality.

Depth: a rich, compound and complex flavour.

Dull: a sound wine which gives and promises little.

Earthy: the characteristic 'gout de terroir' found in many strong red wines; derived from the particular soil in which the vines grow.

Elegant: a much used word which denotes good balance and superior quality.

Farewell: the long lingering aftertaste which reinforces the early impressions made upon contact with the palate.

Fat: usually describes a wine which during a full and careful fermentation has built up a high natural glycerine content.

Finesse: the combination of elegance and balance.

Finish: similar to farewell; the effect of the tannins and acidity in combination with alcohol after the wine has left the palate.

Foxy: the peculiar and characteristic flavour of wines made from the native North American varieties of vines. The flavour is rather similar to the taste of face powder or cosmetics.

Fresh: that sappy, zingy flavour of youthful acidity in white and (young) red wines.

Fruit: rarely is this a flavour of the grape; more it is an impression of fruit of all kinds and points to sound, ripe grapes being used to make the wine.

Full: a high volume of alcohol and concentration of natural grape extract.

Grapey: a flavour associated with the Muscat grape, although to a lesser extent now found in the German crossed vines such as Müller-Thurgau and Scheurebe.

Green: unripe, unready, tannic.

Grip: firmness on the palate - a good sign.

Hard: the excess of tannin or acidity which roughened the palate; originates in the stalks and skins.

Harsh: raw; as 'hard,' comes from the tannin and acidity.

Light: low in alcohol; either a good or bad sign depending upon the character of the wine being tasted.

Mellow: the delicious softness that comes with maturity when all the constistuents form an easy harmony.

Mould: the taste of rotten wood which indicates that bad grapes were used in the blend.

Mousy: a rather unpleasant sour, musty flavour.

Nutty: the fine, crisp flavour of fine, full white wines and sherries.

Ripe: the flavour of wine that has reached its optimum maturity when its balance is entirely harmonious.

Robust: full, yet well rounded; usually applied to strong wines of high alcohol.

Sappy: a strong vegetable taste (rather of spinach) used to describe fine young red wines.

Sharp: implies excessive acidity, possibly volatile.

Smooth: an easy soft wine; drinkable.

Soft: describes wine that has lost all its hard, harsh tannin and has become mellow in maturity.

Tannic: used to describe the essential grape and wine preservative tannin, which imparts a hard, furry flavour to the palate. As wine matures the tannin is deposited as sediment where it is contained with acids and compounds of colouring pigments.

Tart: frequently found in older wines of poorer vintage where the fruit has been deposited leaving merely an excess of tannin and acidity.

Thin: a self-descriptive term describing wines of mediocre quality.

Vigorous: the stage at which red wines are first bottled and change their style and character as they soften in the bottle.

Well balanced: all wines are made up of many compounds of acidity, proteins, minerals, colloids. This describes the happy blending of all these with the alcohol and residual sugar.